What Everybody Really Wants to Know About Money

What Everybody Really Wants to Know About Money

Frances Hutchinson

With a chapter by Alan Freeman

Foreword by Helena Norberg-Hodge

JON CARPENTER

Our books may be ordered from bookshops or (post free) from
Jon Carpenter Publishing, 2 The Spendlove Centre, Charlbury, England OX7 3PQ
Please send for our free catalogue
Credit card orders should be phoned or faxed to 01689 870437 or 01608 811969

Our US distributor is Paul and Company, PO Box 442, Concord, MA 01742
(phone 978 369 3049, fax 978 369 2385)

First published in 1998 by
Jon Carpenter Publishing
The Spendlove Centre, Charlbury, Oxfordshire OX7 3PQ
☎ 01608 811969

© Frances Hutchinson 1998

ISBN 1 897766 33 5

Printed in England by J. W. Arrowsmith Ltd., Bristol

This book is dedicated to my parents

Contents

Author's note

I wish to thank all the authors whose work is quoted and referred to in this book. It would be impossible to produce a work of this type without the legacy of themes and ideas from untold past generations of writers. In common with all those who ever wielded a pen, hacked away on a typewriter or rearranged the blips on a screen, I owe past authors an incalculable debt.

Warmest thanks to Lauraine Palmeri for permission to include her beautiful poem *Seahorse*. I am equally grateful to Alan Freeman, not only for the contribution of his chapter but also for the fund of ideas which have flowed into the material included in the Appendix.

My thanks are extended to all who painstakingly read through initial drafts of these chapters, including Jill and John Gant, Mary Mellor, Rachael Tibbett, Brian Burkitt, Michael Rowbotham, Richard Douthwaite, Keith Hutchinson and last, but by no means least, Jon Carpenter, my long-suffering publisher. Their dedicated attempts to knock the book into shape are much appreciated.

Ideas and advice on the contents were readily offered by Karen Spencer of the Commonweal Collection, Pauline Ford and Jean Gale. I am also grateful to my much-neglected family and friends, especially my husband, Keith, without whose support this book could not have been written.

Social credit

A historical note

Between 1918 and 1922 C. H. Douglas, an engineer by profession, and A. R. Orage, editor of the guild socialist weekly *The New Age*, developed an economics of guild socialism. Subsequently, the body of theory was popularised through the world-wide social credit movement.

The spectacular political success of the social credit movement in the prairie states of Canada during the 1930s led to circulation of many corrupted interpretations of the Douglas texts as a result of which some people have come to associate social credit with various forms of political extremism.

This book is not concerned with these more recent distortions, but with the original writings. It revives a valuable body of work first developed by Douglas and Orage, and replaces it firmly within the guild socialist tradition.

The poem *Seahorse* is in keeping with the guild socialist legacy, which allows space for the arts and sciences to flourish.

Seahorse

by Lauraine Palmeri

For Dr Amanda Vincent

Balanced on my curled prehensile, I am a musical
clef, a multiplication table of segments,
a spinal column of lyrical curvature patterning
singular notes in a roll-call of castanets
through my element the sea. I spell myself, count,
above all to my mate. We are greeting-partners
who brighten up on sight. First thing in the morning
we twirl and promenade, clinging to our holdfast,
pivoting like keys for tuning up each other
to a pitch of tropic colour. Proper mates we are:
when I am orange, she is in the pink. Ah,
how my chosen one undulates through the seagrass forest.
Come to me. Place your eggs in my cradle of wealth.
I shall bear us a brood to make the seas teem.

How they will all spill out, my skilled navigators,
hundreds in my own image dispersing to rise
to the surface of this shallow sea to gulp air
for the first time. Minuscule in the vastness
they will know from the start how to pump, swim, steer,
and for camouflage, change colour: defy
those enemy bands of snapper, skate and ray.
This pouch of mine is a carriage. I am guardian
of the future. In weeks my spiky babes, my miniatures
will all be ready to burst out. I feed them
from my own body. To make them strong
I suck through my snout larval fish and plankton,
these digested without stomach or teeth. Pregnancy
makes me hungry, wary of attack. My burden
is precious. I shall not lose it to a crab.

I am more valuable than silver. In the market
I hang on a piece of string, to be handled by the curious
and assessed for dubious use. Bleached and dried
we are big business. Our misfortune lies
in being known as faithful fish; — once mated
we do not stray, and this is rated amatory
prowess — it's for this we hang in the sun and die.
Shrivelled by the wind, our futures locked within
we await encapsulation, labelling and sale:
"Aphrodisiac, seahorse, male".
I am a pennant, my lost song trailing.

Dr. Amanda Vincent is assistant professor at McGill University in Canada, where she teaches aquatic conservation and political ecology. Dr. Vincent leads Project Seahorse, a global integrated programme for the management and conservation of seahorses, their relatives and their habitats. Seahorse populations are now threatened by over-exploitation for traditional medicines, tonic foods, aquarium fishes, and curiosities. China's economic growth is probably the single largest factor promoting greater consumption; increased demand encourages subsistence fishers to switch to catching seahorses as other marine resources collapse. Project Seahorse seeks to ensure the long-term survival of seahorses while recognising the needs of people who depend on them. It includes community-based marine management in villages of the central Philippines, small-scale seahorse aquaculture and trade monitoring in Vietnam, and research into seahorse biology, ecology, genetics and trade. The male seahorse carries the young.

Foreword

by Helena Norberg-Hodge

Globalisation is often portrayed as the natural result of economic 'efficiency' or as an inevitable evolutionary trend. As everything we hold dear seems threatened, we feel insecure in our working lives, in our neighbourhoods and streets, even in our own homes. Despite massive public awareness campaigns and educational efforts, the environment continues to deteriorate from year to year, communities and families fragment, ethnic conflict, poverty, crime and violence continue to grow, and democracy slips away. Economic globalisation is having a disastrous impact — socially, politically and environmentally. But globalisation is far from a natural process: it is occurring because governments are actively promoting it and subsidising the framework necessary to support it. What is needed now is a fundamental shift in direction towards economic localisation.

Many people find it difficult to imagine a shift towards a more local economy. 'Time has moved on,' one hears: 'We live in a globalised world.' Many such misconceptions can make the shift towards the local seem impractical or utopian. An emphasis on the local economy, for example, can easily be misconstrued as meaning total self-reliance on a village level, without any trade at all. But the most urgent issue today is not whether people have oranges in cold climates, but whether their wheat, their eggs, their milk — in short, their basic food needs — should travel thousands of miles when they could all be produced within a fifty-mile radius. The goal of localisation would not be to eliminate all trade, but to reduce unnecessary transport while encouraging changes that would strengthen and diversify economies at the community as well as national level.

Another stumbling block is the belief that people in the South need access to Northern markets in a globalised economy to shift them out of poverty, and that a greater degree of self-reliance in the North would therefore undermine the economies of the Third World. The truth of the matter is that a shift towards smaller-scale and more localised production would benefit both North *and* South — and facilitate meaningful work everywhere. The globalised economy requires the South to send a large portion of its natural resources to the North as raw materials; its best agricultural land must be devoted to growing food, fibres and even flowers for the North. Rather than further impoverishing the South, producing more ourselves would allow the South to keep more of its resources, labour and production for itself. Globalisation means pulling millions of people away from sure subsistence in a land-based economy into urban slums from which they have little hope of ever escaping.

The idea of localisation also runs counter to today's general belief that fast-paced urban areas are the locus of 'real' culture, while small, local communities are isolated backwaters, relics of a past when small-mindedness and prejudice were the norm. The past is assumed to have been brutish, a time when exploitation was fierce, intolerance rampant, violence commonplace — a situation that the modern world has largely risen above. These assumptions echo the elitist or racist belief that modernised people are superior — more highly evolved even — than their underdeveloped rural counterparts. Yet it is not surprising that these beliefs are so widespread. The whole process of industrialisation has meant a systematic removal of political and economic power from rural areas, and a concomitant loss of self-respect in rural populations. In small communities today people are often living on the periphery, while power — and even what we call 'culture' — is centralised somewhere else.

In order to see what communities are like when people retain real economic power at the local level, we would have to look back, in some cases hundreds of years, before the enclosures in England, for example, or before the colonial era in the South. The relatively isolated region of Ladakh, or 'Little Tibet', provides some clues about life in largely self-reliant communities. Unaffected by colonialism or, until recently, development, Ladakh's traditional community-based culture was suffused with vibrancy, joy, and a tolerance of others that was clearly connected with people's sense of self-esteem and control over their own lives. But in less than a generation, this culture was dramatically changed by development. Development effectively dismantled the local economy; it shifted decision-making power away from the household and village to bureaucracies in distant urban centres; it changed the education of the children away from a focus on local resources and needs, towards a lifestyle completely unrelated to Ladakh; and it implicitly informed them that urban life was glamorous, exciting and easy, and that the life of a farmer was backward and primitive. Because of these changes, there had been a loss of self-esteem, an increase in pettiness and small-minded gossip, and unprecedented levels of divisiveness and friction. If these trends continue, future impressions of village life in Ladakh may soon differ little from unfavourable Western stereotypes of small town life.

Often, we also imagine that 'there are too many people to go back to the land'. It is noteworthy that a similar scepticism does not accompany the notion of urbanising the world's population. It is considered 'utopian' to suggest a ruralisation of America's or Europe's population, while China's plan to move 440 million people off the land into cities in the next few decades hardly elicits surprise. This 'modernisation' of China's economy is part of the same process that has led to unmanageable urban explosion all over the South — from Bangkok and Mexico City to Bombay, Jakarta, and Lagos. In these cities, unemployment is rampant, millions are homeless or live in slums, and the social fabric is unravelling.

Even in the North, an unhealthy urbanisation continues. From the most affluent sections of Paris to the slums of Calcutta, urban populations depend on transport for their food, so that every pound of food consumed is accompanied by several pounds of petroleum consumption, as well as significant amounts of pollution and waste. Meanwhile, rural communities are being steadily dismantled, their populations pushed into spreading suburbanised megalopolises. In the United States, where only 2% still live on the land, farms are disappearing at the rate of 35,000 per year. But where are the people saying: 'We are too many to move to the city'?

It is precisely because there are so many people that it is essential to support knowledge systems and economic models that are based on an intimate understanding of diverse regions and their unique climates, soils and resources. For some years now the International Society for Ecology and Culture (ISEC) has provided study materials to enable concerned individuals to come together in their own communities for the purpose of studying alternatives to rampant globalisation. In this context, *What Everybody Really Wants to Know About Money* revives a half-forgotten debate on the potential for community control of money in order to divert resources towards local needs and away from the massive centralised system of production and distribution. I welcome this book as a valuable resource for all who seek to re-awaken a sense of conscious connection between our everyday lives and the community and place in which we live.

Helena Norberg-Hodge
April 1998

Introduction

DOES IT SEEM ODD to think of money as a socially acceptable addiction? ... But what else would you call a substance or activity that we reach for compulsively even though it doesn't bring fulfilment? What else would you call something that we are convinced we could not live without? Indeed, the very thought of not having it fills us with fear. What else would you call a need that is intense, chronic and seen as essential to our sense of wholeness? What else would you call something that goes beyond a rational concern, that fills our daydreams and our nightdreams as well? What else would you call something that becomes more important to us than our relationships with family and friends, the acquiring of which becomes an end in itself? What else would you call something that we hoard, building up unreasonably large supplies in order to feel secure? An addiction is a need that's gotten out of control, that's become a cancer, migrating into healthy tissue and eventually consuming its host.[1]

This book sets out to challenge the view that we have no alternative but to accept the inevitability of escalating social injustice and ecological degradation. It tackles the highly emotive question of the intimate relationship of money with all aspects of our lives, drawing upon examples from past and present movements for reform. The guild socialist and social credit movements, informed by the economics of Major C. H. Douglas and A. R. Orage, provide the theoretical framework for this book.

In *Your Money or Your Life* the authors describe the way we acquire money and debt in order to surround ourselves with the material trappings of status associated with our earning power: the house in a select area, the car, clothes are as necessary as the expense of the journey to work, convenience foods, dining out, shopping sprees and holidays to compensate for the stress of work. Surrounded by many things, we have too little time for the things we really want to do. Leisure is luxury, the only time when we can think for ourselves. However, where work and money are inextricably intertwined, even vocations may be crippled. As teachers, artists, preachers and carers working for money we find ourselves trapped in form-filling, meeting targets, taking care not to be controversial and raising funds to enable the work to continue. Addicted to getting and spending money, we have no time to take stock of our own role in sustaining the unsustainable money economy.

Money as the deciding factor

In decisions great and small, money becomes the deciding factor above all others. Four examples illustrate the point.

(1) *Money and health care*

In September 1997 journalist Martin Bright described the hospital care given to his 88-year-old grandmother. Although elderly and suffering from angina, diabetes, glaucoma, thyroid problems and weak lungs, she survived a stroke through the genius of the medical staff at the local accident and emergency department. However, there were no free beds in the whole hospital. For the rest of the day she lay on a trolley in a corridor waiting for a bed. Desperately thirsty, the following day she managed to ask for a cup of tea. This could not be given because of risks of infection associated with paralysis. Her family were informed that she would have to wait until Monday, Tuesday, or even Wednesday to see the speech therapist before a drink could be given. It was then Saturday morning. No doctor was available. The family were told it was perfectly normal for a patient not to see a doctor for 48 hours. 'Resources' were scarce, so scarce that a drip could not be given, sheets could not be changed, and the patient was left lying in urine and faeces until the family lodged an official complaint. What may happen to patients with less articulate families does not bear thinking about.

Shortage of money was, Bright concluded, at the root of the problem. However, 'no amount of news stories about bed shortages, low pay, poor morale, budget cuts, and the onward march of the quangocrats can prepare you for the sight of your own grandmother being left to die'.

(2) *Money and child care*

The tragic death of Matthew Eappen while in the care of 19-year-old Louise Woodward encapsulates the impact of money-dominated culture on family life in the 'developed' world. According to market forces it makes sense for the parents of a young child to earn high salaries, leaving the child for long hours in the care of an inexperienced, low-paid baby minder. Proper child care may cost money. However, children require more than first class minding. Babies need loving care, the bulk of which needs to be provided by one or two people with a strong emotional bond with the child. Carers working for money should not establish the same deep emotional attachment between child and carer. If they do, the parting can be deeply emotionally damaging for the child, especially for a baby. The money culture deceives parents into imagining that physical warmth and security can be bought at market prices, and that children need nothing more.

(3) *Money and armaments*

When President Suharto came to power in Indonesia through a coup in 1965, around a million of the country's citizens were massacred in a purge of all who openly opposed his regime. Ten years later Indonesia invaded the neighbouring country of East Timor. Despite United Nations calls for Indonesia to withdraw, one third of the population of Indonesia, around 200,000 people, have been killed by the Indonesian military or died of disease or starvation caused by resettlement policies. Ignoring pleas for justice in East Timor, Britain became Indonesia's largest weapons supplier, anxious to ingratiate itself with the Suharto regime as a means to secure access to Indonesia's vast reserves of oil, minerals, timber and its huge supply of cheap labour.

In 1992 British Aerospace (BAe) announced a new deal to supply 24 Hawk aircraft to Indonesia. Endorsed by the British government on the dubious grounds that it would provide employment for British industry, the deal was opposed by thousands of campaigners in Britain. Despite massive opposition, it became clear early in 1995 that the sale would proceed. Noting that delivery was scheduled in early 1996, a group of women met each weekend for nearly a year planning to stop the Hawks from leaving by disarming them in a Ploughshares action.[2]

Having succeeded in disarming a Hawk on 29 January 1996, the four women, Lotta Kronlid, Jo Wilson, Andrea Needham and Angie Zelter, publicised their action and were remanded in custody for six months, risking prison sentences of around ten years. Their surprise acquittal when the case came to court at the end of July indicated that the jury supported the view that their action was designed to prevent BAe from aiding and abetting genocide. Nevertheless, the sale was endorsed by the incoming Labour government. Despite the prayers and vigils of Ploughshares activists across the world, governments in the developed world appear powerless to resist the demands of international finance (see Chapter 7).

(4) *Money and farming*

In an article in *The Sunday Times* on 23 February 1997, John Humphreys described two farms on the edge of the Berkshire Downs, in southern England. He concluded that organic farming does make money when properly done. It enriches the soil, and the produce is in high demand. However, the use of chemicals on the land to kill weeds and insects entails less labour time, attracts far higher subsidies, and yields a far more substantial profit. Inevitably, chemicals run off the land, polluting water courses and destroying natural ecosystems. However, while the system of subsidies for particular crops like wheat and oilseed rape, organised through Brussels, allows some individual farmers to pick up cheques of £1 million without selling one grain of wheat, the move to traditional patterns of mixed farming remains an unprofitable proposition. Under the illusion that we are getting cheap food, we actually pay for our food three times over. 'The cash that goes to Sainsbury or Tesco is only part of it. We must add to that the money it costs to clean up the mess that intensive agriculture creates. BSE alone cost us £3.3 billion'. That money alone would buy a fair number of organic carrots. The bill rises by further billions as costs of capital equipment to remove pesticides and nitrates from drinking water are added. Costs to human health, the loss of topsoil to erosion and the impact of environmental degradation upon future generations cannot be calculated.

Intensive farming is profitable in money terms. However, added to the unknown effects on health of the chemical cocktail sprayed on fields and crops is the growing awareness that foods grown in this way are deficient in minerals and trace elements vital to healthy child development.

Money as the dominant value system

The four examples illustrate the consequences of allowing money to supplant all other values. Traditionally, care of people and care for the land has been under-pinned by non-monetary value systems. Economic 'progress' has created the illusion that translating every decision into market values is more rational and efficient than personal judgements based upon notions of right livelihood and personal responsibility to the local community. It becomes no more than a fact of life that money can create a relentless sea of cars, tyres, plastic toys, gut-corroding drinks in disposable cans and other signs of 'wealth'. Meanwhile there is 'no money' to provide for the sick and the elderly, and we have no time to spend with our children, our families and the people we respect and admire. In the following chapters we explore alternative views from the past which may enable us to create a socially just and ecologically viable future.

Previous attempts to understand the role of money

During the interwar years tens of thousands of people in many different countries studied guild socialist economics, often under the name of 'social credit'. Guild socialist economics became popular in many countries among small farmers, women, artists, the unemployed, the churches and people concerned with social justice and environmental protection. In the UK the movement rivalled the Labour Party in popularity. As a result, leading labour economists published *What Everybody Wants to Know About Money*[3] in an attempt to counteract the spread of social credit. The title of this present book revives discussion of the social credit proposals to convert money from master to servant of the community's wealth-creation process. The debate was silenced by the economic 'success' of World War II.

The social credit movement originated in a body of theory developed between 1918 and 1922 by Major C. H. Douglas in collaboration with A. R. Orage, a leading guild socialist. This almost forgotten body of theory formed a coherent alternative to both capitalism and labourism (Old Labour and communism). Subsequently the vastly popular social credit movement perpetuated particular themes. At times they ran true to the original body of theory, while at others they became corrupted and nonsensical. Unfortunately the very popularity of certain corrupted forms of social credit pedalled by high-profile eccentrics enable the early body of ideas to be rejected by the mainstream. This book seeks to set the record straight.

The body of theory known as 'Douglas social credit' and its subsequent history has been set on record recently.[4] Douglas demonstrated through his much maligned A+B theorem that decisions relating to the production and distribution of wealth, and hence to the welfare of all, were dependent upon an archaic system of accounting dating back to the pre-industrial era of single-stage production. According to orthodox theory, encapsulated in Say's Law, goods and services exchange in barter-like conditions where markets clear: no commodities are left unsold and there is no involuntary unemployment. Say implied that in barter, a seller must also be a buyer, and if a good is sold, someone must have bought it. It followed that there could be no underutilisation of resources on the free market because supply creates its own demand. Significantly, these economists regarded money as a commodity, one among many, but one which was useful for exchange.

In reality money (unlike barter) plays a determining role in defining the ownership and use of the common heritage of goods, resources, skills and knowledge accumulated by society as a whole over untold past generations. Financial viability determines choices even when needs go unmet and resources lie idle.

Social credit was rooted in the belief that skills belong to the community: hence all can be expected to offer their skills in service to benefit the whole community, whatever their talents and training. Today the concept that all might be expected to have regard to the public good may appear naive and old fashioned. Nevertheless, the competitive, devil-take-the-hindmost, free market competitive economy is utterly reliant upon a bedrock of just such service. If everybody demanded the highest money reward available for every service they offered to others, the economy would grind to an immediate halt. Social credit was an attempt to act upon recognition of this basic fact of economic life by bringing finance under community control. This book seeks to re-open a vital debate.

The problem of misleading information

The challenge is formidable. Through our educational systems and the mass media we are bombarded with a world view in which earning and spending money is a crucial part of everyday reality. Hence *any* challenge to this value-system can be dismissed as an aberration, its adherents being portrayed as cranks. This is no accidental or random state of affairs, as Sharon Beder shows. Large corporations dominate the mass media, promoting facts, ideas and political choices conducive to profit maximisation and discrediting those which are not. There is no mystery about the apparent evaporation of interest in the issues of decaying ecosystems, ozone depletion and global warming since the late 1980s. Vast sums of money have been made available by corporate interests to turn the public against the environmental lobby, rendering it 'superfluous, an anachronism'. Beder quotes the retailing analyst Victor Lebow: 'Our enormously productive economy ... demands that we make consumption our way of life, that we convert the buying and use of goods into rituals, that we seek spiritual satisfaction, our ego satisfaction, in consumption ... We need things, consumed, burned up, worn out, replaced, and discarded at an ever-increasing rate'.[5] Consumption has become the new religion, and money-making its sacred task.

As Beder explains, the average American is exposed to 3,000 advertising sermons every day. In America more money is spent on persuading people to consume than is spent on higher education or Medicare. Children are the prime target. Meanwhile, attempts to introduce environmental education into schools are attacked as political indoctrination. Thousands of corporately funded think-tanks and PR companies have been set up to swamp the public with misleading information contradicting the scientific consensus on the global environmental crisis. Hence the Cato Institute, funded by the American Farm Bureau Federation, the American Petroleum Institute, Coca-Cola, Exxon, the Ford Motor Company, Monsanto, Philip Morris and the Proctor and Gamble Fund, published a book containing, among others, the 'fact' that the impact of man-made chlorofluorocarbons (CFCs) on the ozone layer is a 'complex question' depending on 'murky evidence, tentative conclusions, conflicting interpretations, and changing predictions'. The book concludes that ozone depletion, like the other environmental problems it explores, is 'less a crisis than a nuisance'.[6]

The media routinely ignore the sources of misleading propaganda of this type, presenting it as independent opinion. The real problem is no longer the environmental crisis itself, but the massive corporate obstacle to the ability of the public to understand and hence take steps towards solving the problem. 'A new wave of environmentalism is now called for. One that will engage in the task of exposing corporate myths and methods of manipulation.'[7] As ever-increasing partnership between industry and higher education determines what is researched and taught in universities, the raising of public concern must be a monumental task.

The real picture

Currently, it is left to obscure individuals to research and present known facts to the public. In December 1997 The Corner House published *Climate and Equity: After Kyoto*, the third of their briefings. They document the evidence of present and future impacts of human activity upon the environment, including the devastating effects of abrupt swings in the climate and upheavals likely to result from rising levels of manufactured greenhouse gases, including carbon dioxide, methane and nitrous oxide. In 1995, 2000 of the world's leading scientists endorsed the findings of the Intergovernmental Panel on Climate Change (IPCC), the United Nations body set up to assess the causes and likely impacts of climate change. They concluded that unless action is taken, surface temperatures will rise by between 1.5 and 4.5 degrees centigrade by the end of the next century. Over the past two million years temperatures on earth have never been more than 2 degrees centigrade warmer than at present.

Within a century — hardly any time at all in the history of the earth — our descendants and those of other living creatures could face temperatures well outside their evolutionary experience. The implications for many species, including man, are potentially catastrophic ...

One of the central predictions of the climate scientists is that weather extremes — such as storms, hurricanes, floods, droughts and severe winters — will become more frequent, with significant implications for human livelihoods. The impacts will not be the same around the globe, however. Some regions (particularly drylands in the Third World) are predicted to dry out, causing severe land degradation; others, such as Britain, to become considerably colder because of changes in the Gulf Stream.[8]

The authors of this briefing provide details of the following impacts which can be predicted from available evidence: rising sea levels and the flooding of low-lying islands and many coastal areas; increased drought and flooding as hydrological cycles are disrupted; an increase in insect-borne diseases; severe land and water pollution as toxic chemicals now bound up in the soil or held in coastal landfills are released due to flooding; increased conflict as people are forced to move because their lands have become uninhabitable; major disruptions to food supplies, exacerbating hunger and malnutrition; the collapse of many ecosystems leading to sharp increases in the rate of species loss; and major infrastructure and other financial costs due to storms, flooding, drought-related wildfires and other climatic disruptions.

The incalculable costs likely to be caused by climate change are known by political leaders, who nevertheless remain powerless to take effective action. The briefing quotes the evidence of Sir Robert May, Chief Scientific Advisor to the British government, in a report prepared for Prime Minister Tony Blair in September 1997:

A major study has attempted to assess the economic value of the 'ecosystem services' delivered by natural ecological processes: soil formation, water supplies, nutrient cycling, waste processing, pollination and much else. The assessment, necessarily very rough, is around £10 to £34 trillion per year, with a best guess of around £21 trillion, most of it outside the market. This is roughly twice the conventional global GNP, at around £11 trillion per year. Large swathes of this £10-34 trillion are at risk from the possible environmental and ecological changes sketched by the IPCC.[9]

The authors of this report continue: 'Put simply, humanity — or, more accurately, that part of humanity responsible for increasing atmospheric levels of greenhouse gases — stands accused [by an Earth Action Briefing in September 1997] of "conducting a giant scientific experiment with the planet, and the consequences could be disastrous"'. National governments remain helpless in the face of the evidence because they do not have the money to bring about change. The authors of the briefing call urgently for a 'new politics based on cooperative efforts to protect climate through rebuilding and protecting local economies'.

Television programmes on species loss, oppressive regimes, global warming, shortages of medical care and Third World debt can raise an uneasy awareness of an interconnected web of problems which cannot be solved by making a money donation to one or two good causes. This book is designed for the concerned person in the home, shopping mall and workplace. We may not think of ourselves as economists, but nevertheless we are all engaged in getting and spending within the free market economy, making the decisions which enable it to function.

Towards a value-based political economy

In these chapters we examine the role of money and the sources of power in the modern economy, taking as a starting point a body of writings on 'alternative' economics popular in the inter-war years and studied by tens of thousands of ordinary people across the world. The themes, popularised by the social credit movement, are linked with present-day problems throughout the book.

The main theme of the book is the progressive dispossession of people of the means of providing for themselves within the local community. Loss of rights of access to knowledge and land, coupled with an absence of control over (and responsibility for) the outcome of one's own labour, have led to the predominance of a money-value system which is beyond community control. The end result flows from the systematic indoctrination of children and young people into the belief that working for money must take precedence over all other forms of social interaction. The institutions of global capitalism are founded upon the rejection of all traditional cultural forms which relate to specific communities and localities.

Neoliberal materialism, the philosophy underlying modern culture, accepts impersonal forces of 'progress' and 'change' as inevitable. The fundamental belief in nothing but objective facts creates a determinism which is at least as rigid as older religious forms. Although it has no formal catechism, it is taught very effectively to the young through educational establishments and the mass media. This blanket indoctrination into corporate values in the name of a nebulous 'freedom' is unlike earlier forms of political or religious teachings. It deprives protest groups — workers, road protesters, peace campaigners, small farmers, animal rights activists, anti-poverty and environmental activists and so on — of any clear focal point for their protests. The 'authorities' are nebulous, distant entities operating under the illusion of political and economic freedoms. This book therefore revives an earlier debate on alternatives to the tyranny of non-accountable financial and business structures which operate under the illusion of economic democracy.

Warning! You may find parts of this book disturbing

Many, many years ago, while walking through a remote village in Sierra Leone with some African friends, I became aware of a group of young children running away in terror at the sight of my white skin. Recognising the reaction as instinctive and irrational, I was sad, nevertheless because I would not wish to be the cause of any child's distress. Curiously, I had a similar sensation at the initial reactions of readers to certain passages in the draft version of these chapters. In view of these reactions, I include a few words of explanation.

Global corporate culture

In this book I have set out to revive the debate about a holistic body of political economic thought which was widely discussed by lay people and professionals, men and women, Christians and non-Christians in many countries of the world. Today, however, global corporate culture has so coloured our value-system mechanisms that politics, religion and gender relations are considered taboo subjects, to be introduced with great trepidation so as not to cause offence. It therefore becomes necessary to pave the way, so that the reader can pick his or her way through a potentially emotive minefield.

According to neo-liberal materialist doctrine, a book on the role of money in the economy should avoid sensitive value-laden matters or risk alienating the reader. This I have been told by sympathetic colleagues. Nevertheless, following the example of the early guild socialists and social crediters, and the writers upon whom they drew, I have taken that risk. The following chapters revive the work of writers who did *not* regard the body of thought known as orthodox economics as value-neutral in terms of politics, religion and gender relations.

Politics

When I lecture on guild socialism and social credit in academic circles I am given to understand that the issues I raise are sideline matters, of some historical interest but not to be taken seriously today. In universities throughout the UK and the USA, the study of political economy is being phased out of departments of economics, while research on utopian movements is confined to departments of sociology or literature, to be considered as aberrations from the normal or mainstream. Only cranks believe there could be serious alternatives to global capitalism: there is no place for such beliefs in university departments. Hence the career economist faces a stark choice between accepting the values of corporate culture at face value or abandoning his (it normally is 'his') career.[10]

This phenomenon is not new. Nobel Prize-winning economist Professor James Meade followed a distinguished career in economics after reading C. H. Douglas' early writings, being introduced to them by an elderly aunt who read *The New Age*. Meade adopted certain social credit concepts in so far as they accorded with orthodoxy, and his work reflects that influence.[11] However, as he explained to me in an interview before he died, he had to be careful to dissociate himself from social credit in order to pursue his career. Furthermore, in Meade's opinion, Keynes and other leading economists abstracted ideas from Douglas' theories without acknowledgement.[12] At issue here is the consideration that economics cannot be divorced from politics: it is not value-neutral. Rather, it forms an integral part of the value-system of global corporate capitalism.

Additionally, I am frequently informed that social crediters are fascists. Certainly it is possible to find social crediters who adhere to extremist politics, although they can as often be found on the far left as on the far right. The reason is not hard to find. The prevailing political practice is to accept economic ortho-doxy. Hence the politician, like the economist, must reject heresy in order to pursue a career. By definition, then, heretics tend to extremes. Furthermore, noting the strength of support for a sane and well-argued alternative to growth economics, some social crediters adopted a 'conspiracy theory' explanation of their failure to engage in serious debate with the mainstream. Anti-banker senti-ments of this type are readily translated into anti-semitism. However, this is no reason to drop all consideration of the original theories. To do so is on a par with equating Stalin's regime with socialism. The same line of reasoning implies that since Hitler was a vegetarian and held some 'green' views, all vege-tarians and environmentalists should be regarded with suspicion as proto-fascists.[13]

Christianity

A large proportion of social credit writers and supporters were committed Christians. I have followed in this tradition, quoting from Biblical and other Christian sources to reflect the ways in which alternatives to the money=values system are rooted in Western culture. This is not to indicate a lack of respect for Muslims, Hindus, Buddhists or humanitarian atheists. On the contrary, the concept of social justice unites Christians with those other belief systems. The sole value-system which takes substantial exception to Christian social teaching is that of Rational Economic Man (REM) and his neo-liberal free-market indi-vidualism. According to REM, religious beliefs are matters of individual conscience, to be confined to the private sphere.

Christianity encompasses values which enable the individual to set their own rights and responsibilities within the broader social context. In sharp contrast, neo-liberalism sets all relationships within the context of market mechanisms, where money is the sole indicator of value. Global capitalism demotes spiritual and ethical values to matters of private individual conscience, of no relevance to the public sphere of life, the so-called level playing field of the market economy. Only in the world of REM can a child be considered as merely another consumer good upon which the parents can choose to spend their money as an alternative to a car or other luxury commodities.[14]

By contrast, guild socialists and social crediters looked back to an era when economic relations were openly recognised as relationships between social beings. Within the Christian context, the old and the young, men and women, the very poor and the very rich, foreigners, religious minorities, leaders and rejects of society, the highly articulate and the non-articulate all have a place and deserve consideration as social beings. Christians can raise the issue of whether what's good for the economy is good for the health of the population. The rational economic agent cannot deal with issues which do not relate directly to the formal (i.e. money) economy.

Gender relations

In my search for the origins of the cash economy I have drawn upon the writings of the American economist Thorstein Veblen, whose work substantially influenced Douglas and the guild socialists. In his famous *Theory of the Leisure Class*, written over a hundred years ago, Veblen noted that what is good for the community is 'disserviceable to the individual'. All tasks traditionally undertaken by women, and certain essential tasks performed by men or women, including labouring, farming, pure invention (idle curiosity) and craftsmanship, carried low status and low economic rewards. Searching for the origins of the money economy, Veblen placed the source of the 'pecuniary fanaticism of the business chieftain' in the predatory exploits of barbarian warlords. As Veblen explains:

> Manual labour, industry, whatever has to do directly with the everyday work of getting a livelihood, is the exclusive occupation of the inferior class. This inferior class includes slaves and other dependents, and ordinarily also all women. If there are several grades of aristocracy, the women of high rank are commonly exempt from industrial [i.e. useful and productive] employment, or at least from the more vulgar kinds of manual labor. The men of the upper classes are not only exempt, but by prescriptive custom they are debarred from all industrial occupations. The range of employments open to them is rigidly defined... (T)hese employments are government, warfare, religious observances and sports. These four lines of activity govern the scheme of life for the upper classes, and for the highest rank — the kings and chieftains — these are the only kinds of activity that custom and the common sense of the community will allow... To the lower grades of the leisure class certain other employments are open, but they are employments that are subsidiary to one or another of these typical leisure-class occupations. Such are, for instance, the manufacture and care of arms and accoutrements and of war canoes, the dressing and handling of horses, dogs and hawks, the preparation of sacred apparatus, etc. The lower classes are excluded from these secondary honourable employments, except from such as are plainly of an industrial [productive] character...[15]

Veblen traces the origins of these customs to nomadic hunting tribes where 'the women are, by prescriptive custom, held to those employments out of which the industrial occupations proper' will eventually emerge. 'The men are exempt from these vulgar employments and are reserved for war, hunting, sports, and devout observances'.[16] With industrialisation this division of labour between the working class and the leisure class becomes more pronounced. Virtually the whole range of industrial (practical, socially useful) employments is an outgrowth of what is classed as 'woman's work' in pre-industrial society. Elite males engage in 'war, politics, sports, learning and the priestly office', with some developing the manufacture of armaments, sporting goods and luxury items which do not contribute to the common good.[17]

Veblen goes to considerable lengths to clarify this point. In pre-industrial society men's work doubtless made a considerable contribution to the welfare of the community as a whole. However, men have always drawn a distinction between 'man's work', which brings dignity and respect, and women's essential and necessary work. 'His work may conduce to the maintenance of the group, but it is felt that it does so through an excellence and an efficacy of a kind that cannot without derogation be compared with the uneventful diligence of the women'.[18]

Writing in late nineteenth-century America, Veblen drew a distinction between activities and motivations which were productive, useful, workmanlike and beneficial to the community, and those which were ostentatious, honorific, businesslike, pecuniary and predatory. He argued that business enterprise and the money economy are founded on the pursuit of status and power by elite males, who must be seen to waste time and resources on useless but prestigious pursuits. It follows that the formal (money) economy is predatory upon the cooperative work of men and women of low status, who undertake essential tasks within the community. This theory has vast implications for feminists and 'low status' men and women who seek emulative status within elite male hierarchies.

Veblen's main theme was the frustration of human ingenuity and invention by the conspicuous consumption of the power elite, who corrupt human ingenuity and the resources of the community in order to produce useless and wasteful items merely for pecuniary competitive advantage. Additionally, he described the development of emulative consumption, which offers the workers the illusion of status through consumption of a range of 'luxury' items: through advertising, workers are persuaded that if they buy certain goods they will be identified with the elite.

Social credit in context

The money economy developed in parallel with industrialisation and the spread of capitalism. In the pre-industrial world most people spent most of their lives working on the land, providing for themselves and their families directly from natural materials, local knowledge and the skills of their hands. Some people spent some part of their lives working for money as a supplement to their subsistence livelihoods. However, even those who worked 'full-time' for the rich received some payment in kind, e.g. as food and lodgings. All servants and slaves received orders from their masters. Meanwhile the peasants, even if their land was leased from a landowner, determined their own work patterns and lifestyles. As the money economy entered everyday life in an unprecedented way during industrialisation, traditional relationships were undermined.

As industrialisation advanced it became the focus of study by the newly-emerging 'social sciences'. Research into the wealth-creating process was undertaken under the heading of 'political economy'. Just as the domestic economy of the household could be studied, so could the political economy of the nation state became the focus for research and debate. Eventually, towards the end of the nineteenth century a new phenomenon emerged. Certain economists held that economic relations could be studied like a science. Economic actions undertaken by 'economic agents' (people) could be studied in isolation from the rest of social life (see Appendix). So a person seeking a successful career in economics had to assume as a starting point that people always sold their labour to the highest bidder and bought as consumers on the cheapest markets. Issues of ethics, social conscience, art and culture were excluded from the scientific study of economics. Hence the term 'political economy' was phased out of mainstream orthodox economic research. Economists were trained to see themselves as drawing upon pure scientific data in order to advise politicians and other social scientists.

Thinkers outside schools of economic orthodoxy retained the conviction that, far from being a neutral tool, economics was a body of pseudo-scientific thought useful to those with a particular world view. In the early decades of the twentieth century a group of writers reviewed economic relationships within capitalism, shedding new insights upon the relationship between worker and employer under the wage-slavery system that is taken for granted in industrial capitalism. Known as guild socialism, that body of thought flourished briefly in the UK, and was widely debated elsewhere.[19] Its initial weakness was its failure to develop a realistic theory of the role of money in the relationship between production (what it is decided should be made) and distribution (who has an income and so can buy the products).

This defect of guild socialism was remedied by the collaboration between Orage and Douglas. For reasons too complex to outline here, after the early 1920s guild socialism failed to develop as a body of political economic theory.[20] Although social credit became closely associated with Douglas' concepts of monetary reform, the body of theory as a whole reflects many of the themes which were first developed within the guild socialist movement.

Later (post-1950) perceptions of social credit have focused almost exclusively on monetary reform, in isolation from the wider social considerations encompassed within guild socialism. Ideally, the term 'guild socialism and social credit' should be used to describe the theories explored in this book. Since this is too cumbersome, I use which ever of the two terms seems most appropriate in the context. However, I would wish to dissociate myself from a great deal of the nonsense which has been written since the 1930s under the heading of 'social credit'.

According to Smith,[21] the 'quintessence of socialism is the absence of economic conflict'. Falling within that brand of socialism known as guild socialism, social credit can be defined as *social control over credit* (the creation and lending of money).

Outline of the book

Chapter 1 sets out the basic principles of social credit, reviewing the role of money in determining what is produced and who should have an income. The key social credit concepts of sufficiency, money and debt, the common cultural inheritance and the need for decentralisation of power are outlined.

The shortcomings of orthodox economic theory are explored in the Appendix. This is the only chapter which may prove a little difficult for the reader coming 'cold' to neoclassical terminology. In this event, it can be treated as reference material. However, since this critique of economic orthodoxy forms a key to the underlying propositions of this book, the 'economically literate' may prefer to turn to this section before tackling the other chapters.

Chapter 2 provides a short account of the forgotten history of the social credit movement. In conventional economics the basic building blocks of community life — knowledge, land and labour — can be bought and sold for money. Chapters 3 to 5 describe the history of the loss of community control over basic economic resources. In each of these chapters we examine the historical process through which hunting and warfare gave way to competition in trade, providing power and status for a minority elite, regardless of social justice and environmental sustainability. The role of money in the gradual erosion of community control over resources is related to the emergence of elite structures. Chapter 6 explores the history of money from a social credit perspective, while Chapter 7 (written by Alan Freeman) summarises the progressive enclosure of the intellectual and physical commons by global corporations and calls for united action against capitalism.

Chapter 8 takes a more detailed look at social credit economic concepts. Chapter 9 reviews the continued relevance of guild socialist economic theory, introducing a new 'Home Economics'. Chapter 10 concludes the main book.

Notes throughout the book provide sources for the facts and ideas discussed. Further contact addresses and information are included in the Resources at the end of the book.

NOTES

1   Dominguez, Joe and Robin, Vicki (1992) *Your Money or Your Life: Transforming Your Relationship with Money and Achieving Financial Independence.* Harmondsworth. Penguin. pp78-9.
2   The first Ploughshares action in the United States in 1980 was inspired by the Biblical injunction of Isaiah to 'beat swords into ploughshares'. Needham, Angela (1996) 'Hawks and Doves' *Squall* No.13. Summer. pp34-5.
3   Cole, G. D. H. (ed) (1933) *What Everybody Wants to Know About Money* London. Gollancz.
4   See Hutchinson, Frances and Burkitt, Brian (1997) *The Political Economy Of Social Credit and Guild Socialism* London and New York. Routledge.
5   Quoted in Beder, Sharon (1997) *Global Spin: The Corporate Assault on Environmentalism* Totnes. Green Books.
6   Quoted in Beder op. cit.

7 Quoted in Beder op. cit.
8 The Corner House (1997) *Climate and Equity: After Kyoto* Briefing No.3. Available from The Corner House, Box 3137, Sturminster Newton, Dorset DT10 1YJ, England.
9 Quoted in The Corner House, op. cit.
10 For more on this subject see Beder op. cit.
11 See, for example: Meade, James E. (1993) *Liberty, Equality and Efficiency: Apologia pro Agathotopia mea* London. Macmillan.
12 See King, John E. (1988) *Economic Exiles* London. Macmillan, for some limited discussion on this point.
13 For an example of an entire book written in this vein, see Bramwell, Anna (1989) *Ecology in the 20th Century* London. Yale University Press.
14 See Becker, Gary, (1976) *The Economic Approach to Human Behavior* Chicago. University of Chicago Press for a notable example of this type of economic research. For discussion of the issues raised, see Hamilton, Clive (1994) *The Mystic Economist* Fyshwick, Australia. Willow Park Press.
15 Veblen, Thorstein (1899) *The Theory of the Leisure Class* New York. Mentor Books (1953 edn). p22.
16 Ibid p23.
17 Ibid
18 Ibid
19 See Carpenter, Niles (1922) *Guild Socialism: An Historical and Critical Analysis* New York and London. D. Appleton.
20 See Hutchinson and Burkitt op. cit. and Carpenter op. cit. for a full exploration of guild socialist theory.
21 Smith, Henry (1962) *The Economics of Socialism Reconsidered*. London and New York. Oxford University Press. p158.

Chapter 1

Key principles of guild socialist economics

I WOULD COMMEND ... to you a most serious consideration of this issue, whether you wish the economic system to be made the vehicle for an unseen government over which you have no control, which you did not elect, and which you cannot remove so long as you accept its premises.

Douglas (1923)[1]

Guild socialist economics was studied outside universities in the local communities where people lived, worked and spent their 'free' time. This chapter introduces some of the central themes which together form the building blocks of a coherent body of economic thought.

The role of money in production and distribution

Money and work

If offered a secure income of, for example, £10,000 per year, very few people would reject it in favour of an offer of employment at the same pay. In other words, the demand for employment is, in reality, a demand for purchasing power in the form of money.

In the minds of the vast majority of people a continuous supply of money is inseparably linked with employment. Hence the first step in seeking to understand the money system is to examine the relationship between money and income. It is necessary to set aside ethical considerations (i.e. that money reward must flow from the moral obligation to work) in order to see the money system as a purely practical device for determining economic relationships. Production takes place when people cooperate: they do not have to be employed in order to cooperate in the productive process. Indeed, if all available labour was set to work with all available real capital (tools, machines, land) the result would be an output so colossal that only the organised destruction of global warfare could handle it. Over-production and unemployment are twin aspects of a financial system which has remained outside democratic scrutiny and control throughout the period of industrialisation.

Politicians have reacted to inflation and deflation by attempting to tinker with the existing financial system, seeking solutions to individual problems in a piecemeal fashion. On the one hand, inflation can give rise to uncontrollable price rises, speculation, centralisation of economic power, wage-slavery and over-production leading to economic and military warfare. On the other hand deflation lowers prices and standards of living, causing industrial stagnation, unemployment and bankruptcies. Traditionally, the provision of employment has been high on the political agenda. However, many forms of paid employment are no more than a means to an end: they give the employee money with which to buy a supply of goods and services. If the desire for goods and services could be met without resort to wasteful forms of production, a giant step would have been taken towards creating a socially just and environmentally sustainable economy.

The production of sufficiency

Could everybody be supplied with a sufficiency of goods and services without the need for all to be employed full-time in the productive processes? There is no doubt that this is the case. Using roughly one-tenth of available labour power, modern technology could supply an ample sufficiency for everybody. All that has been lacking to date has been the motivation for change. Whether in agriculture or industry, production is not a problem.[2] The real difficulty lies in the question of distribution.

Organised distribution

The allocation of an income can be compared to the allotment of seats in a theatre or coach, or of benefit in a dividend-bearing commercial venture. Hence if the problem is one of unsatisfactory distribution, it makes sense to pay close attention to the working of the 'ticket system'. The all-encompassing ticket system under which economic distribution occurs is called money. On the one hand we have a producing system with the capacity to provide goods, while on the other hand we have a body of customers requiring goods. Standing between and outside both is a money system, that is, a banking and financial system, with its own agenda. The objectives of the money system are entirely separate from the interests of the producers or the consumers.

The origins of money

In order to grasp the role of banking and finance in the economy, it is necessary to understand the extraordinary powers which are vested in the banking system and the financier. First, we consider legal tender. In the UK this consists of coins and treasury notes issued debt-free by the Bank of England on behalf of the government. Like all forms of money, this money only has value through the consent of the community of individuals who make up the nation, that is, through their willingness to accept the money in return for goods and services.

However, there is a great deal more money circulating in the country than there is legal tender. The latter, £25 billion, makes up a mere 3 per cent of the total money supply of £680 billion. Roughly 97 per cent of the money circulating in the financial system takes the form of bank deposits, overdrafts and discounted bills. For practical purposes, all this money is indistinguishable from legal tender. The ordinary individual draws no distinction between a ten-pound note in their purse and ten pounds in their current account with one of the banks. However, something curious must have happened to transform the total money supply of the £25 billion legal tender into £680 billion. No matter how often money changes hands in trade, it remains the same in total quantity. The increased money in circulation comes into being through the creation of new money by banks and financial institutions. The new money is equal in rank with legal tender as purchasing power. The process is neither mysterious nor complicated.[3]

Suppose a new bank is set up, with ten depositors each placing £100 in treasury notes in the bank. The bank's liabilities to the public are now £1,000. The ten depositors have business with each other. Rather than drawing out cash and handing it over personally, they find it more convenient to write cheques instructing the banker to adjust their accounts. The banker discovers that in practice considerably less than 10 per cent of his business is done in cash, the rest being merely book-keeping. Now image that Depositor No. 10, a manufacturer, receives a large order for his product. In order to carry out the production he needs more money than he can command, to pay out in wages, salaries and other expenses. He consults his banker, who agrees to allow him to withdraw from his account not merely his own £100 but also an overdraft of £100, making in all a total of £200, on condition that he repays, say, £102 in three months time. The overdraft is a credit to the account of Depositor No.10, who can now draw £200.

The banker's liabilities to the public are now £1,100. However, none of the original depositors have had their credits of £100 reduced by the transaction. Furthermore, they were not even consulted about the transformation. What has happened is that £100 of new money has been created at the stroke of a banker's pen. The key point at issue here is that *the banker has a completely free hand in the control of the situation*. Neither the consumers nor the other nine depositors have any say in the matter at all. The decision to create the extra money in the form of that particular loan is guided by the interests of the banker alone. All other parties to the transaction are powerless to influence events. If, collectively, the banks refuse to make a loan, both producers and consumers are helpless. A banker is in the unique position of being able to lend something without parting with anything, while making a profit on the transaction.

However, in the last resort the power of the banker rests on public consent.

The distribution of money

If we follow the story further, we discover that Depositor No.10 takes his overdraft and pays it out to his employees in the form of wages and salaries. In this way the new money is distributed as incomes to individuals. In the meantime, all the wages, salaries, and other expenses, together with the banker's interest charges, form the costs which determine the price the consumers must pay for the finished goods. When Depositor No. 10 repays the banker for the original loan, he uses £102 of the money he obtained from the public in exchange for his goods. There is now an extra £100-worth of goods in the world, but the newly-created money they represent is back in the bank. Unless another loan is made, that money is withdrawn from the system.

It is in the nature of economic activity that the manufacturer must look to the public in the form of the consumer for his demand. The only form of demand which can be recognised is demand backed by money ('effective demand'). However, money does not come from the consumer, who originates the demand. Every 'order' starts with the financier, who pursues his own interests by investing in a productive venture which he considers will prove to be financially profitable. Money enters the economic system in the form of an investment offered to a manufacturer, and only eventually percolates through the industrial system to the consumer. Just as the manufacturer receives money as a loan which has to be repaid to the bank, so also his employee receives a 'loan' (i.e. conditional access to money) in the form of wages. The employee's loan is repaid in the form of prices, which are determined over time as the production process is financed through the various stages from raw material to finished product. What is produced, how and where it is produced and who is paid to produce it (and hence entitled to become a consumer) is determined by the banking and financial system within which money originates.

Money comes into the system as debt created for profitable investment. When it returns to the bank it must be re-invested on the basis of profitability. However, what is useful and necessary for survival is not necessarily profitable. The point is best illustrated by an example often used by economics lecturers to demonstrate to their students the objective impartiality of the money system.

The diamond / water paradox

Economists hold that scarcity is the determining factor in profitability. They take as an example two commodities, diamonds and water. Water is essential for life, necessary for drinking and irrigation. Diamonds are not at all essential for life. Nevertheless, water is cheap in comparison with diamonds.

Economists argue that price is determined by marginal, not total, utility. 'Utility' means 'usefulness', the total want-satisfying power that a commodity possesses. Consumers are assumed to base their decisions on their desire to maximise 'utility'. Clearly the *total* utility of water outweighs that of diamonds. A person with no water at all will be prepared to pay a very high price for some in order to stay alive. However, in normal circumstances water is in plentiful supply. Hence people are only prepared to pay a low price for their last unit of water. This last unit is termed the 'marginal' unit. Economists argue that what happens 'on the margin' is what determines price. They are interested in the change in the total situation caused by a single-unit increase in inputs. Once we have enough water, its 'marginal utility' — the desire for another cupful — diminishes, becoming quite small relative to the total quantity consumed. By contrast, diamonds are relatively scarce. Hence the marginal utility of the last diamond is quite high.

At this point the perceptive student brings up the question of *ability* to pay. Why is it that some people can pay a very high price for diamonds while others lack the money to buy clean water and basic food? Economists skirt around the awkward point by arguing that a particular market situation is the same for all. Hence the price of water will be the same for all who buy it within that market. Similarly, in the market for diamonds, the price of a diamond will be the same for anybody who buys it. Every unit will sell for what the 'marginal' (the last and hence least useful or desirable) unit sells for. The paradox only appears to occur because people confuse total utility with marginal utility. Economists believe that what people are willing to pay for a particular commodity is determined by marginal utility, the usefulness to them of the last additional unit.

The premises upon which orthodox economic theory rests are examined in more detail in the Appendix. Here it is sufficient to note that at a cursory examination, the so-called diamond/water paradox does not 'hold water'. Diamonds are not scarce. Like any other commodity, they are in abundant supply relative to utility. Diamond-producing companies go to great lengths to restrict the supply of diamonds, relative to market demand, while using sophisticated marketing techniques in order to raise the 'marginal utility' of diamonds through advertising. As our perceptive student noted, it all depends upon ability to pay money. That, in turn, depends upon the ways in which money is fed into the system to stimulate 'profitable' production, for which incomes of various kinds are paid out. In the place of diamonds, it is possible to substitute legal and illegal drugs, armaments, cars and all manner of manufactured goods which are brought into production through the money system.

At the inception of the industrial market economy it could be taken for granted that basic necessities of food, water, fuel, shelter and clothing were available outside the money economy for the vast majority of people. In that case, the notion of markets operating according to marginal utility might plausibly have had some relevance. Denial of rights of access to natural resources, and the knowledge of how to use those resources, has, as we shall see, rendered economic theory a superfluous irrelevance.[4] The development of genetic engineering now enables life itself to be enclosed, manufactured as a product for sale within the money system.[5]

Where is the money to come from?

In short, people need to make and use goods and services. The earth can provide all we need, and there are many willing hands to train and technologies to develop according to need and circumstance. In the 'developed' world, however, commodities and the resources with which to make them can only be obtained through the agency of money. The money system is not a natural system. It is a wholly artificial construct created for specific purposes. Although the possession of money creates a valid claim to goods and services, the mechanisms which give money to certain people and not to others are poorly understood.

Money has to be created and fed into the system. The creation of money by private individuals involves the power to arrange the lives of others. For reasons outlined in Chapter 6, the process of money creation has, historically, been dominated by motivations of competition and private gain. By bringing the mechanisms of money creation under communal scrutiny and control, it would be possible to regulate production and distribution in the interests of the common good.

A socially equitable and ecologically sustainable economy could be achieved through adaptation of the present system. At present the banker creates additional purchasing power through the creation of overdrafts and credit instruments for his own purposes. Instead, newly created credit could be fed into the system as producers' credits, to encourage certain socially desirable forms of production. Alternatively, or in conjunction with this method, consumers' credits, or 'dividends', representing a claim to a share in the pre-existing communal wealth, could be introduced under careful monitoring. There is no reason to suppose that new methods of introducing money into the system — and withdrawing it, if appropriate — would be any less sound than the present system. The largest hurdle to be overcome is resistance to erosion of the link between employment and income distribution.

The purpose of this book is to raise questions as to the nature of the formal economy which has come to dominate all aspects of decision-making, not only economic but also political, cultural and spiritual.

The economics of guild socialism

The central element of the new economics was the need to distinguish, in an economic sense, between ownership and control. A person may own a farm, a factory, or even their own labour. However, ownership gives economic control only to the extent that the productive resource in question (land, labour or capital) is in 'demand', that is, if somebody has the money to pay for it. The farmer can take produce to market, but it will only sell if there is money to buy it. In other words, demand (the willingness and ability to pay money) is determined by price, which is in its turn determined by financial mechanisms which regulate the supply and availability of money. Control of the market does not lie with the legal owners of the physical means of production, or with the consumer, but with the creators of financial credit. The presence (or absence) of money determines the relationship of supply to demand through price. Many guild socialists concluded that the creation of credit (money) was a social affair which should be monitored and regulated by the community at large, devolved to the most local level practicable. Hence the use of the term social credit.[6]

In the interwar years social credit was the focus of popular media attention, with a profile on a par with that of Greenpeace today. Like modern environmentalists, social crediters deplored the degradation of the cultural and physical environment in the name of industrial 'progress'. However, social credit went further than mere protest at the waste of human and natural resources. It embraced a coherent body of economic theory with the potential to create an economics of sufficiency through a relatively minor adaptation of the institution of finance. Today Greenpeace attracts violent condemnation for its disruption of global capitalism. In the 1920s and 1930s social credit attracted vehement attack, verging on the irrational, from a wide range of economic and political 'experts'.

A critique of capitalism entirely lacking in validity could be ignored as a harmless diversion. Instead, social credit was lambasted from every direction. In a twelve-page appendix to his definitive text on money, which served a generation of neoclassical economists, Geoffrey Crowther expressed suspicion of social credit's appeal to the general public:

> Social Credit deals with the extremely difficult and technical subject of monetary theory, which one would not expect to have a wide popular appeal ... one is naturally suspicious of a theory that promises the 'abolition of poverty, the reduction of the likelihood of war to zero, rapidly diminishing crime, the beginning of economic freedom for the individual, and the introduction of the leisure State' — and all by means of simple bookkeeping.[7]

Although he examined social credit theory in detail, the only serious flaw Crowther could present was its popularity with the general public. Despite the disapproval of mainstream economists, throughout the interwar years countless publications, public meetings and radio programmes debated the pros and cons of social credit theory and its relevance to the lives of ordinary people. Curiously, today knowledge of social credit has faded from the public consciousness as if it had never existed.

Social credit proposals for monetary reform have been dismissed as a misguided attempt to create a strong economy in conventional terms. According to orthodox economists, the introduction of 'funny money' would merely prove inflationary. It would not rescue the country from depression or solve the problem of unemployment. If, indeed, social credit was no more than a question of 'simple bookkeeping', Crowther's peremptory rejection of its wider claims would be fully justified. However, on closer examination social credit turns out to be a constructive critique of the political economy of industrial capitalism. It emerged from within a broad tradition of opposition to the desecration of the countryside, with its attendant erosion of all cultural values save those dominated by money and based upon individual self-interest.

Major Clifford Hugh Douglas

In 1916 Major Clifford Hugh Douglas, then an unknown engineer turned accountant, lighted upon a curious observation. Sifting through the accounts of Farnborough Aircraft Factory with the aid of early tabulating machines, Douglas noted that the factory was generating costs at a much faster rate than it was distributing incomes. He examined over one hundred large businesses in the UK, finding the same observation held true. It followed that, at a particular point in time, only a part of the final product could be distributed through the incomes generated by its production. Furthermore, as technology changes and industrial processes lengthen, the ratio of overheads to current wages increases, indicating an escalating fall in the proportion of the final product capable of being distributed through income generated at that stage. Hence distribution of the remainder depends upon work in progress on future production, financed by loan credit, export credits, centralisation of industrial power and consumer borrowing. Production is debt financed. The result is an enormous waste of human effort and the earth's resources in order to maintain 'full employment'. Douglas concluded that the resultant necessity for economic growth led inevitably to economic and military warfare between nations, accompanied by environmental degradation. These observations provided the basis for Douglas' guild socialist economic theories.

Five key concepts

Monetary reform cannot of itself deliver a sustainable economic system. It is also necessary to understand the role of the non-money value system in sustaining economic relations among people and between communities and their local environments. The five key ideas emphasised by social credit thought are outlined here.

(1) *Sufficiency*

Politicians and social reformers have long laboured under the misapprehension that the main problem of civilisation is to maintain an ever-increasing flow of production in order to meet unlimited demands for goods and services. Diminishing production must, it is thought, reduce the opportunity for a more equitable distribution of the products which the formal economy alone can provide.

However, the abundance of nature combined with human ingenuity and invention can provide an ample sufficiency for all. The problem is not so much to increase production as to limit it to meeting the demand for sufficiency without having devastating effects upon the real economy (the natural environment and the people who rely upon it for their livelihoods).

The existing money system is incapable of handling inventions designed to create a pleasing sufficiency. By eliminating built-in obsolescence, superfluous packaging, transportation and waste, a sufficiency of high-quality local food, clothing and other essentials could be produced for local markets. But instead, the money system dictates that production must be based upon profitability. Advertising makes the simple and the homespun appear inferior and unattractive. As a result, children's demands for pop, burgers and fantastically-priced footwear cannot be denied by rational argument.

In a world where millions suffer from malnutrition, billions of dollars are spent on slimming aids and products to overcome the effects of over-indulgence. Cars choke the air in city centres, causing millions to seek medical aid for asthmatic and related disorders. Yet the spectre of reduced ability to consume is wielded as a clinching argument to discredit the would-be environmentalist. An ever-expanding economy offers the tantalising illusion that all will be well once all land, capital and labour are fully employed. In *The Growth Illusion* Richard Douthwaite offers a full and fascinating picture of the reality of poverty, ill-health, reductions in welfare and environmental degradation stemming from cancerous economic growth.

(2) *Money and debt*

'Where would our money come from if industry ceased to produce armaments, cars and cans of soft drinks with dubious contents?' you ask. 'A sustainable economy would not be economically viable. It is not what people *want*.' If the money system is taken as read, these arguments hold water. Money must be invested in productive enterprises so that incomes can be paid out in respect of work undertaken on profitable production. No matter whether it is wealth or waste that is being produced and consumed, producers and consumers must maintain a continuous stream of production and consumption so that debts can be repaid, and the process can start all over again. An understanding of the mechanisms of the debt-based money system is a vital pre-requisite for reform, but needs to be coupled with value-systems rooted in society and the natural environment.

(3) *Work and income*

There is no necessary link between work and income: employment in industries which yield a profit is not a logical or natural way to secure a livelihood. Professional economists may quote (with hearty approval) the saying that: 'If a job is worth doing, it is worth being paid to do it'. On the other hand, mothers, carers, artists and organic farmers are among the many who might hesitate to make their offers of service to others conditional upon recompense in terms of monetary reward. There is no earthly reason why a lone mother should place her young children in a creche in order to spend the major part of her day turning out landmines, fashion clothes or bubble-gum.

It is absurd to stipulate that in order to obtain an income every individual should seek employment regardless of demand for their services and no matter what their health, capacity for employment or better judgement might dictate. Nevertheless, the proposal that all should have a small basic unearned income as a right[8] is greeted by waves of shock and horror by many who are themselves bound in wage-slavery to the system. The familiar always appears attractive, the unfamiliar sinister. However, it is the intention in the rest of this book to encourage the reader to view apparently familiar concepts in a new light. The payment of a dividend in the form of a pension derived from investments establishes a principle which is capable of imaginative adaptation.

(4) *The common cultural inheritance*

In orthodox economics circles, seemingly endless debate has focused upon the question of the origin of value. Did the capitalists do a service to humanity by foregoing consumption in order to invest in the new technology which gave rise to the machine age? Or did the capitalists exploit the workers, seizing from them the surplus value which was theirs by right? How is value created? Is it through work? Through investment? Through exchange? It was necessary to determine who created value in order to determine how wealth should be distributed.

Social credit theory recognises none of these factors as making a significant contribution to wealth. The contribution of each individual, whether as worker, capitalist or financier, pales into minuscule insignificance when evaluated alongside the cultural legacy of the 'progress of the industrial arts', to use a phrase coined by Veblen[9] and often quoted by Douglas. Isolated individual endeavour can produce very little indeed. Production, whether material, intellectual or artistic, relies on the common cultural inheritance which forms the birthright of all citizens. Furthermore, cooperation in industry and other forms of collective activity gains an 'unearned increment of association'.

Therefore it is possible to imagine a country in which all inhabitants are regarded as shareholders in the birthright of the common property of real wealth, consisting of untapped and renewable natural resources and the cultural heritage of tools and processes. That is, each citizen has a claim to a share in the *potential* to produce, rather than being forced to participate in a system of production, distribution and exchange. The circulation of purchasing power can be made to reflect this situation, through payment of a 'dividend' on this inheritance. After an initial period of transition, wages could well be lower than the dividend, reflecting the relatively minor contribution of the individual to general welfare. It would be in each individual's interests to preserve and hand on the common inheritance: nothing would be gained by selfish appropriation of knowledge, for example, save social exclusion.

A 'social' or 'national' dividend would enable all citizens, including the sick, disabled and elderly, to participate in the economy on an equal footing. Freed from the harassment of an oppressive system, lone parents could make a rational choice as to the type of employment most appropriate to their circumstances. However, the change calls into question the very nature of productive work. Conventional economics sees a wage as a reward for unpleasant work. To use conventional terminology, labour is regarded as a 'disutility', something one does not want to do. In real life, many forms of work are intrinsically satisfying (see Chapter 5), while many forms of consumption are ephemeral. The acquisition and exercise of skills create satisfactions which cannot be measured by economists. An economy based upon the production, distribution and exchange of material artifacts and the services associated with their production is unsustainable over the long term. Its existence depends upon the unseen support of forms of non-monetised social cooperation, and on the natural environment's continuing ability to provide resources and absorb waste. As the common cultural inheritance is eroded, the formal economy ceases to function.

(5) *Towards the decentralisation of power*

In medieval times poverty arising from involuntary unemployment was rare. Craftsmen were independent, taking pride in their work whether of weaving, building, baking, brewing, carpentry or the many other crafts producing commodities for everyday use. The introduction of a profiteering money system enabled the financier to invest in machinery and profit from the work of others. With the advent of the limited liability company, policy formation was progressively separated from the worker, who became a mere wage-slave in an increasingly centralised system. Global conglomerates now dominate decision-making in the lives of their employees and consumers. Decisions as to what is made, where it is made, sold, packaged and distributed, are made in distant offices and conveyed to the consumer through the advertising media.

Small and medium-sized enterprises (SMEs), who still make up the vast majority (99%) of individual firms, are caught up in supply-chain pressures and remain powerless to determine outcomes. However, combined with the power of local consumers and employees, the potential for change rests in the cooperation of SMEs with voluntary groups seeking to create viable local economies.[10] Economic democracy involves curtailment of the power of a few to expropriate the common cultural inheritance of the community upon which all, ultimately, depend for the means of subsistence.

Conclusion

The Douglas critique of the capitalist economy remains as fresh and relevant today as when it formed the basis of a popular movement supported by tens of thousands in many countries across the world during the 1920s and 1930s.[11] Support for social credit ideas can be gauged from the wide range of books, pamphlets, articles, periodicals and study groups which abounded in those decades. Opposition to the Douglas theories was focused mainly in the economics profession itself, and those seeking to use orthodox economic theories in their quest for political power and authority. We therefore turn in the next chapter to a review of neoclassical theory for a resume of neoclassical theory, with a view to understanding the reasons for the exclusion of social credit from the formal system of academic thought.

NOTES

1 Douglas, Clifford H. (1923) *The Breakdown of the Employment System* The Manchester Economic Research Association.

2 See, for example, Mellanby, Kenneth (1975) *Can Britain Feed Itself?* London. Merlin Press.

3 For more detail see Rowbotham, Michael (1998) *The Grip of Death* Charlbury. Jon Carpenter.

4 See, for example, Goering, Peter, Norberg-Hodge, Helena and Page, John (1993) *From the Ground Up: Rethinking Industrial Agriculture* London and New Jersey. Zed Books and International Society for Ecology and Culture.

5 See, for example, Shiva, Vandana (1996) 'The Losers' Perspective' *in* Migues Bauman, Janet Bell, Florianne Koechlin and Michel Pimbert (eds) *The Life Industry: Biodiversity, People and Profits* London. Intermediate Technology Publications.

6 For more detail see Carpenter, Niles (1922) *Guild Socialism: An Historical and Critical Analysis* New York and London. D. Appleton. Also Hutchinson, Frances, and Burkitt, Brian (1997) *The Political Economy of Social Credit and Guild Socialism* London and New York. Routledge.

7 Crowther, Geoffrey (1940) *An Outline of Money* London and New York. Thomas Nelson. (1946 edn. p432.)

8 In the form, for example, of the 'national dividend' proposed by Douglas.

9 Veblen, Thorstein (1921) *The Engineers and the Price System* New York. Burlinghame (1965 edn).

10 See Douthwaite, Richard (1996) *Short Circuit: Strengthening Local Economies for Security in an Unstable World* Totnes. Green Books.

11 For more historical detail see Chapter 2.

Chapter 2

The social credit movement

A FEW CHURCHMEN and yet fewer of their lay supporters are aware of the necessity for the revaluation of life in terms of the organic because of its indivisibility from religion. But are the Churches as a whole opposed to industrialism, to the disappearance of craftsmanship, husbandry and responsible property? They are united on visiting their displeasure upon divorced persons but is there in any Church a passionate resolve to reunite the severed halves of man's being, the natural and the religious, each withering apart from the other? H. J. Massingham (1943)[1]

Forgotten voices from the past

Concern at the domination of money values over private and public decision making rarely features within the Western educational system based on technical training and dominated by corporate interests. We must therefore turn to the past for a glimpse of what might have been, and what might yet, perhaps, come to the forefront in public life. In 1935 popular novelist Storm Jameson observed the human need to lead a creative life:

An adult and civilised intelligence is one which seeks to know the truth and to discriminate between values. Civilisation itself is a tradition, which we are putting in danger by our blind worship of the machine. We let it throw human beings onto the scrap heap, invade quarters of life where it can only bungle jobs that need the living hand or mind, and — perhaps — we shall let it blow us and our cities to pieces and choke us with poison gas.

Beauty grows from the earth upwards, it does not descend to the people from a few angelic beings far removed from common life. When the mass of the people have no leisure, when the vital seed is killed in them by making machine serfs of them, when their best hope is that the work will never fail and their worst fear that of not being required to do the same stultifying task every day for fifty years, it will die from below ... In the end the only important business a human being has on earth is to create. If he is cheated of it, by the social circumstances of his life, he goes bad; in time the society which contains him and his million fellows goes bad, too, and smells as foul as its slums.[2]

Also writing in the 1930s T. S. Eliot noted the emergence of belief in 'nothing but the values arising in a mechanised, urbanised way of life; it would be as well for us to face the permanent conditions upon which God allows us to live upon this planet'.[3] In 1943, during World War II, H. J. Massingham wrote of the vital human need for direct involvement with the natural world. Soil exhaustion and other symptoms of the earth's malaise were caused by 'the entire inorganic mode of life practised by modern populations'.

This mode is civilization's defiance of the Doctrine of Creation and because that Doctrine is the truth of the universe it is crumbling in catastrophe. It is the revolt whose messengers are malnutrition, under-consumption, animal and plant disease, human frustration, unemployment except for the purposes of destruction, neurosis, world strife, disintegration and an unreality, the worst symptoms of all, that persistently puts last things first and first things last, industrialism before agriculture, technics before life, acquisition before function, chemistry before nature and the State before God.[4]

The prophetic writings of Massingham and many others are omitted from the formal education as irrelevant to modern concerns. Hence today, as in the 1940s, students are led to believe that:

chemistry is the dictator of the organism; cash of cropping; measurement of life; finance of the farm. Food comes not from the fields but from the factory; and thought is denatured as well as food. Houses are pre-fabricated and owe nothing to rock, soil or timber. Our native earth was once our home; then it became our recreation; now it is a business like any other industry, not a livelihood. Distance has become a value in itself by the obsolescence of the home-sense. The horizon rules our affairs, not the threshold and internationalism is the new word for neighbourliness. The concrete, the realistic and the empirical are replaced by the abstract and the schematic, while the natural stuff of life is regarded as machinery to be ruled and regulated by machinery. Nature's family — father, mother, child — is merged into the atomic mass and the replacement of regional by centralized forces logically follows.[5]

Historical setting

Neither social credit nor guild socialism sprang up out of nowhere as the brainchild of a single individual. On the contrary, these movements were grounded in a body of theory which has existed in parallel to the mainstream ever since the inception of the industrial revolution. Opposed to global capitalism's world view, they are normally considered unsuitable matter for teaching in schools and universities of Western 'civilisation', except as examples of aberration. If an alternative is to be created, these theories and movements require considerably more detailed study than can be devoted to them in this present work.

Marx's legacy

Like capitalism, socialism in its many forms arose within industrialised countries. As nineteenth century England became the workshop of the world, urban industrial settlements grew, allowing capitalists to thrive at the expense of the broad mass of people who lived in unprecedented squalor. Luddites, chartists and early trade unionists fought to secure political and economic justice. However, it was that most notable theorist of the nineteenth century Karl Marx who established a world view which has coalesced into virtual tablets of stone. Although ostensibly attacking capitalism, Marx regarded industrial development as the height of progress from pre-industrial squalor, one step on the way to the worker state. While capitalists and 'labourists' may dispute the division of the cake between them, they have shared the opinion that without capitalism there would have been little increase in productivity and hence of wealth.

The twin pillars of the political economy of capitalism endorsed by Marx were progress and competition. In Marx's view, civilisation was prefaced by a state of rural anarchy where bright ideas for technological advance were swamped by the dreary battle to wrest a living from the land. Progress started when some men enslaved others, turning them into work-horses to construct the civilised surroundings of the city state. Feudalism was an advance on slavery, with the technical advances continuing to be made at the price of oppression by the feudal overlords. Finally, capitalism represented the ultimate of progress from primitive communism to technical mastery of the material world. The workers, however, remained locked in oppression. In due course they would succeed in their struggle, overthrowing the capitalists to create the worker state where all would cooperate for the common good.

Competition is the central tenet of Marxism. As slaves, serfs or workers the oppressed struggle for a share of the material bounty which their oppressors force them to produce. In the final stage workers and capitalists exist in an oppressive but symbiotic relationship as the greedy capitalists use their exclusive ownership of the means of production to wrest more produce from the workers. Finally, the technological progress achieved by the successive waves of dialectical materialism[6] will be sufficient to provide an abundance for all, so that 'from each according to his abilities, to each according to his need' will become the sole guiding principle of social life. As the evil of capitalism is overthrown, questions of organisation and motivation will become an irrelevance.

Throughout the twentieth century the twin elements of the inevitability of progress and the necessity for competition have been dazzling in their appeal to capitalists and socialists alike. It has become commonplace to accept that in the latest stages of progress capitalism has created a society in which all are better-off in material terms. Equally firm is the conviction that the cultural and spiritual life of the community are 'subjective' issues, therefore having no bearing on economic reality. From this viewpoint, it remains an 'objective' fact, for which statistics can be produced in evidence, that there are more cars, better communications, health, education and welfare, more food on the supermarket shelves, more people going on more holidays and so on. The quantity of material goods has swelled in volume, and that *must* be a 'good thing': only the perverse would label such progress a 'bad thing'.

Capitalism is viewed by most people as a natural and normal aspect of human evolution. It is not the product of any single mind or group of individuals imposing their views on others, or preventing others from 'doing their own thing'. It is argued that capitalism just happens naturally: it can therefore be studied objectively. Socialism, on the other hand, is thought up by impractical people for selfish or misguided ends. Furthermore, Marx's gloomy predictions have proved unfounded, showing communism to be both unworkable and unnecessary. Through the motivation of competition between capitalists and workers, scarce resources can be harnessed to supply the wants of all. As capitalism progresses, individuals can compete for a better share of the proceeds, protected by the right to vote and every legal safeguard of democracy. Capitalism is a human and efficient way to raise living standards for all, and there is no earthly reason for it to end. However, throughout the twentieth century many visionaries have voiced doubts about the value of material progress and the role of competition in working towards the common good.

Socialism

At the turn of the century socialism, like neoclassical economic theory, was in its infancy. Then, socialism comprised two elements: trade unions and middle-class intellectuals, of whom Marx was the most influential. In those far-off days trade unions were yet to become a form of centralised power. They had more in common with friendly societies, offering mutual aid to their local members, not only in terms of wage bargaining but also in the form of sickness and housing benefits for urban industrial workers in their own localities.

While Marx preached the inevitability of revolution to an international audience, trade unionists came together as and when the law allowed. They sought to alleviate the conditions of hardship and dire poverty under which families were forced to exist when they had nothing but their labour to sell as a means to gain subsistence. In the United Kingdom trade unionists sought political representation in order to protect wages and conditions of work and to provide municipal services to combat unhealthy conditions in the overcrowded industrial towns and cities.

Syndicalism

In France and the United States, however, trade union activity took the form of syndicalism, the pursuit of worker control of industry by local direct action in order to achieve a form of industrial organisation based upon self-governing workshops. Syndicalists regarded the ballot box as an irrelevance, so they did not seek to cooperate with political parties. Conventional socialists and Marxists were suspected of seeking to use trade unions to defend worker interests *within* capitalism. Syndicalists, who sought an end to the capitalist state through local action, made a distinctive contribution to the development of guild socialism.

Middle class intellectuals

Many joined the quest for alternatives to the harsh, degrading conditions of life and work endured by the urban poor. In addition to the trade unionism and syndicalism of the working classes, middle class intellectuals had an input to the development of socialist thought. The Fabian Society, founded in 1884, sought peaceful political progress towards socialism through electoral politics. Sidney Webb, a leading Fabian, was highly instrumental in shaping the policy of the early Labour Party. To him the 'inevitability of gradualness' replaced Marx's inevitability of revolution. However, Marx was a powerful background influence upon Fabians, as upon all socialists. Fabians sought the transfer to the state of all means of production so that the surplus earned could benefit society as a whole. In the immediate short term the Fabian Society acted as a research and policy formation centre, documenting the plight of the urban poor in order to seek redress.

The emergence of the Labour Party based upon a single class, the wage-earner, was bitterly resented by many socialists. It could only perpetuate capitalist-labour relations (wage-slavery) and hence capitalism itself. Fabian 'gas and water' socialism, supplying infrastructures to towns and municipalities, held little appeal for many who considered themselves as socialists.

Where capitalism protects the freedom of the individual to exploit the earth and fellow humans, socialism seeks freedom from exploitation so that an individual's talents can flourish in association with others in surroundings which are healthy and pleasing for all. The most glamorous form of socialism was described by Orage as 'stained glass "News from Nowhere"', in reference to William Morris' utopian novel of that name.

William Morris

Jeremy Seabrook's description of William Morris as a 'revolutionary craftsman' is most germane to these discussions, since Morris' legacy to guild socialism cannot be overstated. The writings of G. D. H. Cole, William Penty, S. G. Hobson, A. R. Orage, Maurice Reckitt and other leading guild socialists make frequent reference to their debt to Morris' work. For most of the twentieth century, however, Morris' vision of a green socialism has been shunted off into a utopian sideline. His very commercial success in producing arts and crafts of the highest quality and design under pleasing work conditions was held against him by the more practical brand of socialist. Above all, the air of sensual decadence surrounding his life and work, and his wealthy background itself, alienated him from the affections of Methodist labour socialists and the respectable workers of the protestant ethic.

Nevertheless, his *News from Nowhere* was a powerful attack upon industrial ugliness and the degradation of working class intellect and eye. Morris was a revolutionary, having read Marx and being an early member of the Social Democratic Federation, the first Marxist organisation in the United Kingdom. He deplored as degrading the pursuit of 'swinish luxury' by the rich and its emulation by the poor. Seabrook quotes Morris' description of pre-utopian capitalism, in which the 'iron rule of the world market' enslaved people into the toil of producing a never-ending series of 'sham or artificial necessaries'. Production of these useless items became as essential to the maintenance of everyday life as the necessaries that supported real life. 'By all this they burdened themselves with a prodigious mass of work merely for the sake of keeping their wretched system going'.[7]

'What a contrast this blistering denunciation is', concludes Seabrook in 1996, 'with the pronouncements of the leaders of the G-7, who urge "new products undreamed of", "the creating and conquest of new markets", "expanding free trade", and economic growth for its own sake disarticulated from human need. The people in Morris' dream had "cast away riches and found wealth". He writes of humanity "wrecked and wasted in one way or another, by penury or luxury"'.[8]

Political pluralism

Unlike the Labour Party, guild socialists questioned the reality of democratic freedom within a unitary state. They could not foresee a situation where legislation endorsing a capitalist property regime might be reversed by popular vote. According to Hilaire Belloc the unitary or 'servile' state was incapable of transformation into something closer to Morris' vision. Welfare provision of pensions, compulsory education and so forth could do nothing to enhance individual freedom to work for and within the community on terms decided by the individual citizen him or herself at the point of action. Attacks upon welfare provisions conditional upon wage-slave employment made little sense when many families faced the stark choice between employment, if available, Poor Law charity or starvation. However, as the guild socialists anticipated, the all-powerful unitary state may grant or rescind rights and freedoms at the whim of a centralised and virtually unaccountable bureaucracy.

The concept of a unitary state — of one sole authority endorsing the legality of property regimes, financial institutions and all inter-personal contractual relations — has, like capitalism, become accepted as a natural state of affairs. Pluralist political theory, however, rejects the notion that the state is necessarily the sole source of power and focus of authority. In medieval society church and monarchy were co-equal rulers, each holding authority over its own sphere, while the craft guilds and feudal landlord were governed by similar bonds of obligation to and from the citizen. In the late twentieth century centres of alternative political allegiance exist in the form of local authorities, trade unions, and industrial and commercial associations. However, the unitary state lays itself open to control by the most powerful of these 'centres', notably multinational business and financial corporations.

The guild system

Guild socialists followed John Ruskin in recognising in the nineteenth-century trade unions a continuation of some of the functions of the medieval guilds. Like the guilds, trade unions offered regulation of pay and working conditions together with support for members in sickness and adversity. By uniting masters and 'producers' (workers) on an industry-wide basis trade unions could develop into guilds capable of transforming work on lines in keeping with the vision of William Morris and the arts and crafts movement.

William Penty, a leading guild socialist, rejected Marx's notion that progress of any kind was achieved by class conflict. Undoubtedly there were periods of conflict, and it was true that material factors predominate in the decline of a civilisation. However, to view history as a permanent state of class warfare was ridiculous. In Penty's view, only a complete misinterpretation of history could describe social relations in the medieval period as rooted in class tyranny. Such misinterpretation gave rise to blind faith in industrial development. Notions of 'progress' from feudal bondage to freedom and from poverty to well-being were ill-founded. Rather, the masses had exchanged security for insecurity and status for wage-slavery. Industrialisation occurred through a process of social disintegration.

Penty viewed the small workshop based upon hand production primarily for the local market as the most appropriate alternative to a productive system motivated by greed and exploitation, resulting in mass production. Higher wages and improved working conditions for the working class would not end the evils of industrialism. S. G. Hobson expanded Penty's themes in *The National Guilds*. The commodification of labour was regarded as the greatest evil of capitalism, and one incapable of solution by state control over wages, security of employment, improved working conditions or unemployment and welfare benefits. By accepting wages the workers sold their common inheritance, their right to the industrial fabric of the economy.

Like other guild socialists, Hobson distinguished between wages which buy labour time, and payment for service. Professional people, including the armed forces, are not expected to produce a profit for an employer, and are payed when in training, in hospital or on standby. By contrast, the industrial employer is not concerned with the worker as a human being possessing functions, aims and aspirations beyond the employment situation.

Hobson envisaged a system of National Guilds in which the watchword 'service' replaced 'profit'. Within the guilds all workers, including the unskilled, clerical, manual and managers worked together on a cooperative basis. The guild vision provided the framework for all citizens to participate, with power being devolved to the local community. It was a pioneering attempt to reject the notion that wealth is created within the manufacturing sector of industry and that power over decision making should be centralised outside local communities. The guild idea extended from traditional industries like textiles, mining, fishing and building to agriculture and civil and domestic service. Law, medicine, education, priests, artists, craftsmen, journalists, authors and other professions were viewed as guilds in embryo. The guild system could be further extended to include 'housekeeping women', inventors, pure scientists engaged upon original research and all whose work for the well-being of the community could never be evaluated like a commodity and sold for a wage.[9]

Hobson rejected the traditional separation of economic actors into producers and consumers with antagonistic competing interests. For guild socialists all citizens were both producers and consumers, having mutually inclusive interests which required an institutional basis within the local community for their proper harmonisation. Although the precise proposals put forward by Hobson and other guild socialists, most notably the socialist economist G. D. H. Cole, would require adaptation for the twenty-first century, the theoretical framework retains considerable relevance. Guild socialism reached beyond competition and confrontational class politics to embrace arts, crafts, culture, a sense of sufficiency and a concern for the environment. However, as Orage explained:

> ... the whole idea of National Guilds, as formulated by Mr. S. G. Hobson and myself, and elaborated by Messrs. Cole, Reckitt and others, was wanting in some vital part ... (T)he trouble was always of the same nature — the relation of the whole scheme to the existing, or any prospective system of money.[10]

The guilds could not operate within the existing system of debt-finance. However, it was impossible for Orage and other guild socialists to combine the work of socialist economic theorists with guild socialist ideas on production, distribution and exchange.

Hence Douglas' simple observation of accounting at Farnborough fitted neatly into place as the missing element necessary for the full development of the political economy of guild socialism. Between 1918 and 1922 Douglas and Orage, editor of the influential guild socialist weekly, *The New Age*, worked together on an economics of sufficiency in which finance could be turned from master to slave.

Additionally, Douglas and other guild socialist writers drew from the works of Thorstein Veblen (see Introduction). Here we consider the historical events surrounding the original reception of social credit in the 1920s and 1930s. These events have been fully documented in *The Political Economy of Social Credit and Guild Socialism*, and are therefore only briefly outlined here.

The social credit movement

Douglas and Orage

Based upon the original writings of the Douglas/Orage collaboration, the world-wide social credit movement took on a life of its own outside the frame-work of formal state politics and the academic institutions which served that structure. Although all aspects of social credit theory were widely debated, the proposal for a national dividend was most easily comprehended. Consequently the 'National Dividend for All' became a popular demand in the depression years.

From the outset, neither Douglas nor Orage had any intention of founding a campaign or political movement dedicated to reform. Orage had an intense dislike of meetings and committees of all kinds, preferring to present ideas through the printed word and expecting people to weigh the arguments for themselves. Although Douglas turned out to be something of an orator he, too, thought the presentation of a well argued case would be sufficient in itself. In his view political institutions and their leaders were amenable to reason and common sense. Until 1922 both men imagined that the trade unions and the Labour Party would see the force of their arguments against the exploitation through wage-slavery of the mass of the population by debt-financed capitalism. A few years later Orage noted with some bitterness that trade unionists in the UK appeared to have no ambitions to manage their own industries on guild socialist lines. Workers were content to leave trade union officials and the Labour Party to lead the fight for better pay and conditions within the existing system.

'To clinch a matter that needed no clinching', wrote Orage from the United States in 1926:

> ...the parliamentary Labor party was by this time making good in its own eyes and in the eyes of the ambitious trade-union leaders. As habitually with them until recently, the English governing classes know how to stage a defeat and make a triumph out of it. No sooner had the Labor party actu-ally forced its way into Parliament than all the old stagers began at once to prepare it for their better digestion. Public honours were poured upon them. Absurd and really insulting compliments were addressed to them. Privately and personally they were treated with the condescending courtesy meted out to ex-butlers who have come into a moderate fortune. Above all, and artfullest stroke, their wives were patronised and begged by dowagers, in the name of their common class, to dissuade their husbands from ruining the old country.[11]

Many other socialists viewed the entry of the trade unions and the Labour Party into national politics with similar misgivings. Orage and Douglas made some headway in their attempt to interest trade unionists in the newly-developed social credit ideas. In Scotland discussion of the Draft Mining Scheme (see below) and proposals for a national dividend gave rise to demands for the Labour Party to give 'the scheme' serious consideration.

The Labour Party and social credit

The Fabians and the Labour Party were, perhaps understandably, reluctant to abandon their newly-adopted Constitution, resplendent with its Clause IV commitment to the gradual nationalisation of the means of production, in favour of a reform of finance which they did not understand. Indeed, even at this early stage in its history, the Labour Party was determined to conform with political and economic orthodoxy. Leading Fabians Sidney and Beatrice Webb used a legacy to found the London School of Economics so that potential socialists could receive a thorough grounding in economic orthodoxy. They also founded the *New Statesman* to counter guild socialism as propounded in Orage's influential weekly, *The New Age*.

The Labour Party and the trade unions, under the guidance of Sidney and Beatrice Webb, Cole, R. H. Tawney and many other members of the bourgeois intelligentsia, fought to make themselves respectable. To do so it was necessary to conform to the principles of a democratically unified state and economic orthodoxy. Cole, with his deep sympathies with William Morris, was remembered as *the* leading light in guild socialism long after other guild socialists were forgotten. Nevertheless, he could not envisage a world in which the master/worker relationship ceased to exist and the carrot and stick of the wage packet became redundant. His proposed municipal guild socialism based upon a complexity of elected committees was a generous spirited but unworkable attempt at reform of the status quo. It fell far short of a fundamental examination of the gap between economic and financial orthodoxy proposed in the Douglas texts.

The hastily convened 'Labour Party Committee of Inquiry into the Douglas-NEW AGE Scheme' decided on superficial examination that social credit was out of sympathy with Labour thought. Published in 1922 *The Labour Party and Social Credit: a Report on the Proposals of Major Douglas and the 'New Age'* listed Labour's leading economists among its authors, but the report had a surprisingly small circulation. Even at the height of the controversy between the Labour Party and the social credit movement in the 1930s it was never revised or reprinted.

The Labour Party's firm rejection of the new guild socialist economics, already being termed 'social credit', marked the end of its development as theory. The Labour Party embraced orthodox neoclassical general free market equilibrium theory in its quest to administer the capitalist state with justice and equity. Although the close collaboration between Douglas and Orage now ceased, this was not the end of the story. Orage settled for some years in the USA. He continued to publicise 'Douglas Social Credit' both in the USA and on his return to England a few years before his death in 1935. Meanwhile Douglas found himself to be the focal point for interest aroused by his original articles and books published through *The New Age*. Encouraged by the attention, he continued to write, publicising and elaborating upon the body of ideas which were increasingly attributed to him alone.

The early spread of social credit

Social credit was promoted by ordinary people, the unemployed, small farmers, women, clergy and leading figures in the arts. The range and extent of debate throughout the inter-war years can only be estimated from the vast numbers of social credit publications and the extent of orthodoxy's reaction to them.

Although many supporters of social credit wrote innumerable books, pamphlets and articles on the subject, Douglas remained the pivotal figure in the debate. He was called upon to explain his theories to select committees and at public meetings in universities, town halls, trade union gatherings, churches and on the radio. His travels included visits to Tokyo, Oslo and the USA. In 1933-4 a world tour took him once again to Canada, the USA, Australia and New Zealand, where he addressed meetings and broadcast on the radio to a popular audience. On 25 January 1934 Douglas addressed an audience of 12,000 in Sydney Stadium, five thousand being turned away. His address was relayed to an estimated radio audience of one million, factories being shut down to provide sufficient power for the event. His coast-to-coast broadcast in America was estimated to have reached ninety million, and he received an equally enthusiastic welcome in Canada. In each location his invitations to speak were organised by a network of study groups, often church-based, membership of which dated back to the early 1920s. Throughout the dominions disillusionment with the Bank of England was particularly strong, and active social credit supporters were estimated to be in their tens of thousands. However, the very success of his world tours was difficult for Douglas to handle.

Douglas' problem was that his work could be understood on two levels. His attacks upon wage slavery, consumerism and over-production together with his proposals for a national dividend could be, and were, readily disseminated by supporters across the globe. However, the Douglas proposals for financial reform and the 'just price' were based upon his critique of general equilibrium theory in the form of his 'A+B Theorem'. The nature and significance of this critique remained obscure to all but a handful of supporters. Attempts to engage in meaningful debate with economists and even political proponents of social credit on this aspect of social credit resulted in mutual frustration.

At best, he appeared to be peddling a glossy version of underconsumptionism by advocating the introduction of 'funny money' which could only be inflationary. In his frustration, Douglas became increasingly reticent about the 'technical' details of his 'plan'. Puzzled by the apparent failure of intelligent people to grasp the obvious, despite his best efforts at explanation, Douglas and his coterie of close supporters retreated into conspiracy-theory corral, blaming financial institutions for the ills of the world.

Nevertheless, from the early 1920s until the outbreak of World War II Douglas was a household name and his writings on social credit had reached a global audience. In 1921 his first two books, *Economic Democracy* and *Credit-Power and Democracy*, were used as textbooks by the economics department at Sydney University. In 1923 Douglas' work was sufficiently well known for him to be called to give evidence to the Canadian House of Commons Committee on Banking and Commerce, alongside Irving Fisher, Sir Frederick Taylor-Williams of the Bank of Montreal and Henry Ford. In 1931 he gave evidence before the House of Commons Macmillan Committee on Finance and Industry, responding to questions from Keynes. However, Douglas' major audience was outside orthodoxy, among trade unionists, the unemployed, churches and small farmers. Many women were drawn to study and campaign for this intriguing alternative to the free market individualism which ignored the existence of women as economic actors.

The churches and social credit

The social credit movement had no formal membership or constitution. Rather it consisted of networks of informal discussion groups, with publishers supplying a host of publications and periodicals and leading figures in the arts and the churches lending it support. Of these latter G. K. Chesterton, T. S. Eliot and Ezra Pound have had, perhaps, the highest profile.

Maurice Reckitt, a leading guild socialist and contributor to the *Church Socialist*, quoted the Reverend Widdrington's explanation of the need for Christian support for both social credit and the Labour Movement. Widdrington attacked wage labour as no better than slavery. His condemnation of the established church's support for an unjust system offers a fair reflection of the left-wing character of much Christian support for social credit.

> Either the Church must accept the challenge of the social problem or it must abdicate. It has been too long the Church Quiescent here on earth, content to serve as the scavenger of the capitalist system. If it refuses the challenge it may survive as a pietistic sect, providing devotional opportunities for a small and dwindling section of the community, a residuary solace for the world's defeated, administering religion as an anaesthetic to help men to endure the hateful operations of life, an ambulance picking up the wounded, entered on the Charities Register, an institution among institutions. But it will have ceased to be the organ of the Kingdom, building up the world out of itself: it will have abandoned its mission and become apostate.[12]

Widdrington stressed that the Church 'must criticise from its own standpoint.' In order to show its belief in the living faith it must make it 'the touchstone by which it tests all theories'. The Church had come to tolerate a fundamentally unjust economic system, criticising from the sidelines while drawing its financial resources from the same source. Widdrington captures the mood of many

Christians working and writing on guild socialism, social credit and a range of movements concerned with the separation of human society from the land by which it is nourished.

Women and social credit

John Hargrave, leader of the popular Greenshirts, explained the relevance of social credit for women in economic life:

By giving every woman a birthright income — i.e., the National Dividend based on the productive capacity of the community — it will ensure economic independence and freedom, for it will release her from being:-

1. Tied to the home when she wishes to live her own life.

2. Treated as a drudge, or as an inferior — i.e., the 'chattel' status.

3. Driven to marry for the sake of economic security.

4. Bound to some man who ill-treats her, or is in some other way unsuitable as a person to live with.

5. Driven into work-wage slavery in competition with men in order to keep alive.[13]

What about equal pay for equal work for women? Hargrave considered this would result:

1. Because a Social Credit Government will naturally stand for fair play for all citizens without distinction;

2. because employers will no longer need 'cheap labour'; and

3. because each individual woman will be able to say, 'If I do this job as well as a man could do it, I shall want the same pay as a man.' And if the employer says, 'No,' she will be able to say: 'Very well, I refuse the job. After all, I can live on my National Dividend.'[14]

A substantial number of women wrote pamphlets and articles and campaigned for social credit, including Storm Jameson, the popular novelist.

The Alberta Experiment

The events in the Canadian Province of Alberta in the 1930s illustrate the issues surrounding the quest to incorporate Christian values within practical politics. In 1935 a Social Credit Government was elected to power in the Province, gaining fifty-six out of the sixty-three seats in the Provincial Legislature. The new Social Credit Party being only a few months old, not one member had ever stood for, or been elected to, public office before. Its leader, William Aberhart, was the principal of a large state school in Calgary, and was known throughout the Province as the dean of the Prophetic Bible Institution. His skill as an orator and ability to use the radio as a communication medium contributed to his success. Drawn into politics through his awareness of grinding poverty, he had witnessed the despair of the families of students leaving his school to face unemployment. His Christianity and the suicide of one of his best students drove him to examine the causes of the poverty and injustice facing Alberta, a province rich in land, machines and people.

Aberhart entered politics at the mature age of 54, following his reading of a version of social credit theory as presented by Maurice Colbourne in *The Meaning of Social Credit*. When Aberhart came to power many members of the outgoing United Farmers' Government were keen social crediters. In 1923 Douglas had presented evidence to the Select Standing Committee of the Canadian House of Commons in Ottawa in 1923. Speaking largely without notes, he offered a prestigious body of experts a remarkably coherent account of the basic theories of social credit. His evidence filled over eighty pages of closely-typed text, giving rise to numerous publications and the formation of social credit study groups throughout Canada.

Interest was especially strong in the western farming provinces, where an urban financial system was wreaking havoc on the countryside. Largely from Eastern European farming stock, the population of Alberta could in theory have sustained itself comfortably on the fertile land. However, the land was mort-gaged to the financial system, and distant creditors were legally entitled to 'the crop that never fails', i.e. the interest on the debt. Taxation further exacerbated the situation. In the depression years the failure to maintain a high price for grain led to mortgage repossessions, causing a move from the land and a steep rise in the urban unemployed.

Social credit was studied in depth throughout the western provinces of Canada. However, a degree of caution was exercised within existing political parties. Although the United Farmers' Association had initiated social credit study groups, the members of which subsequently turned to Aberhart, the leaders were not prepared to endorse social credit as a central election issue. This refusal brought Aberhart into politics.

As subsequent events demonstrated, Aberhart had at first only a superficial understanding of social credit theory, believing that financial reform was a simple matter of adjustment without wider political implications. The total lack of polit-ical experience of Aberhart and his entire cabinet, coupled with the threat of financial bankruptcy of the province following the mismanagement of the previous administration, presented further difficulties. Aberhart had already simplified Douglas' theories in an attempt to apply social credit to conditions in Alberta, with disastrous results. 'What he did not understand', wrote L. D. Byrne some years later, 'was that Social Credit is not a plan or scheme of monetary reform, but the "policy of a philosophy" of which the financial proposals are but one means to an end'.[15] Douglas and many of his supporters were uneasy from the outset, fearing that this ill-prepared attempt to introduce social credit through the ballot box would, by its failure, prove damaging to the movement as a whole. Their reservations were all too well founded.

Despite a clear mandate from the electorate, reinforced at subsequent elections, the introduction of social credit reform of finance was blocked by the Federal Government. The experience led Aberhart and Douglas to some degree of mutual understanding. Byrne, an exceptionally able social credit theorist, joined Aberhart as his official advisor in 1937. They became firm friends, working towards the goal of introducing social credit. On the outbreak of war they supported the war effort and were preparing for post-war reconstruction when Aberhart died in 1943. His successor, Ernest Manning, was ostensibly committed to social credit but led the party towards conventional finance and the far right, confirming the worst fears of early social crediters that the episode would be counter-productive. Oil revenues brought prosperity in line with orthodox finance, leaving social credit to become known as a rallying point for right-wing monetary cranks, often with fascist associations. Ever since, their political activities masquerading under the name of social credit have served to discredit the original work of Douglas and Orage.

Social credit publications

Nevertheless, interest in social credit has continued to surface. One economist considered that 'the Douglas theory is more sophisticated than he is given credit for', but had to admit that 'no writer in economics has made his thought so opaque to the reader'.[16] Mehta, the author of these words, followed a very long line of attempts to re-interpret Douglas economics through books, articles, pamphlets and study groups throughout the UK, Western Europe, the USA, Canada, South Africa, Australia and New Zealand. Debates about the accuracy and authenticity of these interpretations did little to enhance the clarity of the body of thought known as social credit. In the UK, as elsewhere, study groups met on a weekly basis to come to grips with the new economics. Throughout the UK the focal point for many groups was provided by local trade union supporters of guild socialism.

Douglas' publications

Douglas' first book, *Economic Democracy* (1919), originally serialised in the *New Age*, remains the most coherent statement of the philosophy of social credit. It was followed by *Credit-Power and Democracy* (1920), *The Control and Distribution of Production* (1922), *Social Credit* (1924) and *The Monopoly of Credit* (1931). In addition, Douglas published a wealth of papers, pamphlets and articles.

Popular interpretations of Douglas start as early as 1921 with Hilderic Cousens' *A New Policy for Labour: an essay on the Relevance of Credit Control* and W. A. Young's pamphlet entitled *Dividends for All: Being and Explanation of the Douglas Scheme*. Many opponents turned to Young's short but misleading pamphlet rather than plough through Douglas' original work, adding nothing to the quality of the debate. The volume of texts seeking to illuminate Douglas' original writings far exceeds the combined writings on Gesell, Soddy and other heterodox economists.

From the outset, social credit was at variance with orthodox economic theory. It rejects the notion of the freewheeling economic agent pursuing *his* own self-interest and claiming *his* just reward. Social credit recognises that the creation of wealth, however defined, is a communal activity which cannot be conducted in isolation from, and without reference to, the rest of the community. This central plank of social credit, encapsulated in the case for a national dividend payable to all citizens on the strength of the common cultural heritage, was relatively comprehensible. The focus of debate upon how exactly the national dividend could be introduced, leading to the more 'technical' question of the relationship between finance and the processes of production and distribution, was heated and obscure. Throughout the two decades of its popularity, the debate centred around the question of motivation in wealth creation as it relates to interest, profits and the necessity to work for a wage. Although Douglas was engaged in frequent debate by leading economists, the process led to little clarification of his theories, still less to further development of the economics of guild socialism.

Douglas' proposals for the reform of the financial system were often interpreted by opponents and proponents alike as solutions to the problems of depression and unemployment, a means to revive the economy and achieve material prosperity. Hence for much of its history, a misinterpretation of social credit was the subject of intense debate. Douglas' attempts to explain his non-equilibrium economics within the climate of neoclassical orthodoxy remained obscure and puzzling. Social credit economics hit the same problem as Marx's: values are assumed to be determined in the 'sphere of production' while prices are created in some parallel but unconnected 'sphere of exchange'. Neoclassical theory is as incapable of handling Douglas' economics as it is Marx's.

The 'Credit Scheme' or 'Draft Mining Scheme', first designed to be read by members of the Miners Federation of Great Britain in 1920, provides an intriguing introduction to possible locally controlled mechanisms for introducing money to the system of production of goods and distribution of incomes.

The Douglas (Credit) Draft Mining Scheme

What follows is a paraphrase of the Draft Mining Scheme, taken from the Appendix to *Credit-Power and Democracy*.[17] It also appeared in pamphlet form, and was widely circulated throughout the UK, Canada, the USA, Australia and New Zealand. The Credit Scheme could be applied to any local 'industry' providing employment in diverse fields of farming, transport, education, retailing, arts, medicine, building and so forth. It follows the guild socialist reformist approach, whereby all who work in an 'industry' as producers cooperate with local consumers to gain control over their work and the distribution of its product. By this mechanism the community reclaims control over its resources, through a gradual dispossession of the profiteers.

The practical proposals were designed to apply to the mining industry of that time (1920). It was envisaged that employers and trade unions would work together at local level to create an industry which would meet the needs of the community and provide good work for its producers (all the workers, including the managers) while freeing producers and consumers from dependence upon decisions governed by the greed of private profiteers.

The Scheme entails:

1 The vesting of control over industrial credit, and hence over industrial policy, in the community.
2 The regulation of price so as to secure distribution of purchasing power in accordance with prices.
3 The establishment of as wide a degree of worker-as-producer control over administration of each 'industry' as is consistent with the common good.
4 The distribution of the communal product by the mechanism of a social dividend rather than primarily through hourly or productivity-related forms of pay.

The communalisation of credit could be achieved through new forms of direct action. In place of industrial disruption and strikes, the workers-as-producers in each industry can cooperate to take financial control of their own labour. This proposal rests upon the notion that labour-power forms an essential element in real credit. By virtue of its control over the labour-power in its industry, organised labour can issue financial credit just as the capitalist issues credit by virtue of ownership of plant and machinery.

The distinction between real and financial credit is crucial to an understanding of the proposals. As Douglas and Orage explained: 'Real Credit is concerned with the probability of the delivery of goods in their various forms; Financial Credit is concerned with the probability of the delivery of Money in its various forms'. Real credit is not measured according to the actual supply of commodities, but by their *potential* supply. For example, a machine represents real credit according to the measurable extent of its ability to produce and deliver goods in demand. Similarly, the real credit of an industrial plant, an organisation of personnel, even a whole nation, can be calculated.[18]

Real credit depends upon two factors, on the existence of the ability to produce and a need to be satisfied. Either is useless without the other. The consumer is a vital element in the production of real credit, as is the community at large. In terms of economics, a nation is an association of people engaged in the production of real credit. Hence the state can be regarded as the custodian of the real credit of the community, representing the interests of producer and consumer equally. The authors conclude that real credit is social or communal in origin and therefore belongs *neither* to the producer nor to the consumer, but to their *common* element, the community.

The following brief summary of the key ideas in the scheme may appear unduly technical on first reading. If so, you are advised to move on to Chapter 3.

Introduction to the Credit Scheme

The beauty of the Credit Scheme is its close similarity to existing practice, since its introduction would not involve major political or conceptual upheaval. However, the use of familiar terms and concepts in a slightly adapted framework creates some problems of understanding.

For example, under the present financial system the price of a product is *not* determined by haggling in shops at the point of sale. Rather, the producing firm decides the price *before* production is embarked upon. This is done by taking 'cost values' into account. These are not actual costs, in the sense of costs already incurred in the past, but costs predicted to be incurred, based on present prices. In the same way, the Scheme as a whole is based upon types of calculation which were (and are currently) occurring every day in the accounting departments of firms and in financial institutions. The Credit Scheme is a suggested mechanism for bringing such calculations into the open and subjecting them to community scrutiny and control.

A key element in the Scheme is the elimination of the debt-based financial system and its replacement by a credit-based system. Hence at national level the National Debt Account would be transformed into the National Credit Account. However, this brief introduction is not intended as a detailed blueprint for immediate implementation. The main focus of the argument is upon local control over production and income distribution, through the creation of locally controlled financial mechanisms. The full implications of these reforms in terms of national and international finance are beyond the scope of this work.

Stage 1

Stage 1 indicates the mechanism whereby the Scheme would convert the real credit of Industry A into financial credit through the creation of a (local) producers' bank.

1 (i)   In order to ensure maximum efficiency of operations, Industry A will be autonomously administered within the geographical area of a local authority (city or other sub-national unit of local government).

1 (ii)   Within each local area, worker/producers of Industry A will form a branch of a producers' bank. The bank will be legally recognised by the national government as an integral part of Industry A. The industry produces wealth, and the bank represents the financial aspects of the real credit created by the industry. The bank must be affiliated to the National Clearing House.

1 (iii) The shareholders of the bank shall consist of all persons engaged in Industry A, whose accounts are kept at the bank. Each shareholder is entitled to one vote at a shareholders' meeting.

1 (iv)   The bank as such will pay no dividend, although in time it will come to form part of the new banking system, paying out a national dividend to all citizens.

1 (v)   The owners of capital already invested in the property and plant of Industry A shall be entitled to a fixed return of, for example, 6 per cent. Together with all newly created capital, capital already invested will continue to carry all the privileges of capital administration, apart from price-fixing. Depreciation will be set against appreciation.

1 (vi)   The boards of directors in each area shall make all payments of wages and salaries direct to the producers' bank in bulk.

1 (vii)   In the case of a reduction in cost of working (for example through introduction of new technology) one half of such reduction shall be calculated within in the National Credit Account (which replaces the National Debt Account), one quarter shall be credited to the owners of capital in Industry A, and one quarter to the producers' bank.

1 (viii) From the outset, following the setting up of the producers' bank, all subsequent capital expenditure shall be financed jointly by the capital owners of Industry A and the producers' bank, in the ratio which total dividends bear to total wages and salaries. The benefits of such financing done by the producers' bank will accrue to depositors.

To summarise, Clause 1 (vi) is of central significance. The first step of the proposal is for all current wages and salaries in the local branch of the industry to be paid through the producers' bank. In this way the bank comes to represent in financial terms (financial credit) the labour power (real credit) of the industry. By issuing currency based upon the labour power of the industry, the producers' bank would gradually buy into control of Industry A. Worker-producers would control the bank, and through that the industry. As new money ceases to be created by absentee investors, the power of external capital owners is gradually reduced as their percentage share of ownership falls over time.

Furthermore, employees leaving the industry would retain their voting power in the producers' bank, serving to create local industry-community links, a vital aspect of the Scheme. As producers' banks developed they would come to represent the community at large, rather than merely those employed in the various industries to which the banks were attached. As new processes and technologies were introduced, displaced worker-producers would retain their economic rights. As time progressed, the majority of shareholders in an industry would be retired workers or heirs of former workers. In this way share ownership would be spread throughout local communities, enabling producers' banks to replace payment for specific productivity by payments of dividends on communal work.

However, *Stage 1 could not be effectively introduced under the present system of finance, in which prices are determined by financial considerations and bear no necessary relationship to the real needs and wishes of the people for sufficiency rooted in security.* Dividends and other payments (financial credit) would need to be carefully calculated on the basis of the productive capacity of the community (real credit). Hence the necessity for Stage 2 of the Scheme, the fixing of prices.

Stage 2

The Scheme offers a range of mechanisms for circulating purchasing power in the economy. Each mechanism is equally valid, and can be used in conjunction with others as appropriate. Purchasing power can be paid to the industries concerned, to be distributed as dividends to their shareholders, or as payments to other industries and converted by them into dividends. That is, the community would issue financial credit to the producing industry as fast as it turned out goods, deducting only that part of costs recovered by the industry through prices charged for final sale of goods. The essential principle is that, however it comes into circulation, purchasing power should always correlate with real credit. Hence the necessity to set price below cost, while making up the difference to the industry through the National Credit Account.

2 (i)   The government shall require from the owners of Industry A quarterly (half-yearly or annual) statement of the cost of production including all dividends.

2 (ii)   On the basis of this ascertained cost the government shall regulate the price of the product of Industry A at a percentage of ascertained cost.

2 (iii)   This price (of the product of Industry A sold directly to the consumer) shall bear the same ratio to cost as the total national consumption of commodities does to the total national production of credit. Cost relates to price as production relates to consumption:

$$\text{Price per unit} = \text{cost per unit} \times \frac{\text{cost value of total consumption}}{\text{money value of total production}}$$

Total national consumption includes capital depreciation and exports. Note that actual goods are only *part* of total production. The real credit of the community consists of the capacity to make more goods. This capacity takes the form of capital goods and improved processes. Total national production consists of consumer goods actually produced, capital goods as they appreciate, and imports. The Credit Scheme avoids the necessity for the constant consumption of the real credit of society in the form of creation and consumption of consumer goods, by providing an alternative way to keep money in circulation.

2 (iv)   That fraction of the product used by industry shall be debited to the users at cost plus an agreed percentage.

2 (v)   Export prices should be fixed from day to day in relation to the world market and the general interest of the community. In many cases the local community may prove to be the best location for consumption of the product.

2 (vi)   The government shall reimburse the owners of Industry A with the difference between their total cost incurred and their total price received, by means of treasury notes, such notes being debited to the National Credit Account.

Comment on the Douglas Credit Scheme

Through these mechanisms, the relation of goods to money would remain constant. Prices in general could not rise, while unnecessary production and consumption of commodities would not be essential to the maintenance of the financial system. The economy would be placed on a sound financial basis in which markets could operate according to the rules of supply and demand. Note that the Credit Scheme would use price to draw out of circulation the equivalent of the total depreciation of communal wealth. The fractional multiplier used to fix prices in this way charges to the consumption of any final good a portion of the cost value of total consumption in the community, much as a business enterprise allocates overheads to its various departments.

The power of fixing price is an important element in business policy. Only by bringing this power under local communal control can the community effectively govern its economic life. As citizens and consumers, the public would exercise their authority over economic activity through their vote in three main channels: its price fixing agencies, the National Credit Account and local producers' banks.

The final stage of the Scheme involves the steady withdrawal from active industry on the part of pre-existing shareholders of the banks. In this way, shareholders would consist mainly of economically passive recipients of the social dividend as proprietors of the industrial plant of the community. As the community was placed in effective control of its economic resources wage-slavery would become redundant. The community would be free to develop socially sound and environmentally sustainable interactive mechanisms, rendering redundant the question, 'Yes, but where is the money to come from?'

The standard objections to Douglas' thesis were contradictory. According to some, the cost-income gap was an illusion. They argued that Douglas had failed to realise that all costs represented sums paid out as incomes in previous periods; thus they ignored the time factor, the essence of his analysis. Others objected that Douglas merely stated the obvious, that the monetary and economic system must inevitably operate in this way to stimulate new production and maintain employment; thus they ignored Douglas' proposition that the objective of production should be to meet a sufficiency of consumer wants, and that employment or profit should not be ends in themselves. These technical aspects of social credit theory provide a viable basis for a coherent alternative to economic orthodoxy based upon general free market equilibrium.[19] However, monetary theories only give rise to popular movements when they are embedded within a wider social philosophy.

Conclusion

This chapter has provided a brief introduction to the key social credit debate of the 1920s and 1930s. In this lost history ordinary men and women studied and campaigned for an economic system based upon values of social justice and environmental sustainability. Like supporters of the present-day environmental movement, social crediters from all types of background came together in opposition to an unjust and environmentally damaging economic system. If remembered at all, social credit is classified as a far right movement concerned with monetary reform. However, as this chapter illustrates, the perception that economic affairs are part and parcel of social relations was once accepted as a commonplace fact of life by ordinary people as they sought the means to go about their everyday lives.

NOTES

1 Massingham, H. J. (1943) *The Tree of Life* London. Chapman Hall. pp195-6.

2 Jameson, Storm (1935) *The Soul of Man in the Age of Leisure* London. Stanley Nott.

3 Quoted in Massingham op. cit. p190.

4 Massingham op. cit. p190.

5 Massingham op. cit. p14.

6 See Glossary.

7 Seabrook, Jeremy (1996) 'Revolutionary Craftsman' *Red Pepper* September. pp28-9.

8 Seabrook op. cit.

9 Hobson, S. G. (1914) *National Guilds: An Inquiry into the Wage System and the Way Out* London. Bell. (1920) *National Guilds and the State* London. Bell.

10 Orage, A. R. (1926) 'An Editor's Progress' *The Commonweal* 1926 February. p402.

11 Orage op. cit. p376.

12 Quoted in Reckitt, Maurice B. (1941) *As it Happened: An Autobiography* London. Dent. p251.

13 Hargrave, John (1945) *Social Credit Clearly Explained: 101 Questions Answered* London. SCP Publishing. p52.

14 Quoted in Hutchinson, Frances 'A Heretical View of Economic Growth and Income Distribution' *in* Edith Kuiper and Yolande Sap (eds) *Out of the Margin: Feminist Perspectives on Economics* London and New York. Routledge. p28.

15 L. D. Byrne's introduction to Douglas, C. H. (1937) *The Alberta Experiment* Western Australia. Veritas. (1984 edn.) p(xviii).

16 Mehta, G. (1983) 'The Douglas Theory: A New Interpretation' *Indian Journal of Economics* 64. pp121-9.

17 Douglas, Clifford H. (1920) *Credit-Power and Democracy* London Cecil Palmer. pp152-212.

18 Douglas op. cit. pp157-8.

19 See the Appendix. Also see Rowbotham, Michael (1998) *The Grip of Death: A Study of Modern Money, Debt Slavery and Destructive Economics* Charlbury. Jon Carpenter for an extensive investigation of finance from a Douglas perspective.

Chapter 3

Customs and commons

IT WAS A SPRING without voices. On the mornings that had once throbbed with the dawn chorus of robins, catbirds, doves, jays, wrens, and scores of other bird voices there was now no sound; only silence lay over the fields and woods and marsh...

No witchcraft, no enemy action had silenced the rebirth of new life in this stricken world. The people had done it themselves.

Rachel Carson *Silent Spring* (1962)

In their critique of orthodox economics, guild socialists and social crediters stressed the essential human right of access to the resources necessary for survival. They identified the key resource as the 'common cultural inheritance' of knowledge about technology, processes, facts and skills. Unlike land, labour and capital (machines), this essential economic resource does not feature in economic theory. Hence the problems raised by the privatisation of access to knowledge would appear to lie outside the economic sphere. However, the control of access to education and information continues the process of enclosure. As public space and public access to information are restricted and brought under the control of the money economy, a fundamental of human rights becomes the private property of global capitalism. This chapter examines the progressive disempowerment of ordinary people as they act as economic agents within an information vacuum.

The values of global capitalism

Silent Spring catalogued the dangers of pollution by pesticides, herbicides and the many chemicals in the food chains and the bodies of the peoples of the world. It has been translated into virtually every language except Russian and Chinese, its author hailed by *The New York Times* as 'one of the most influential women of all time'. However, since the publication of *Silent Spring* in 1962 the destruction of the human habitat on a world scale has continued apace.

Species of plants and animals disappear, people leave the land, cities choke with cars and children are no longer free to explore the hedgerows of the countryside, yet global capitalism asserts that policy is informed by what the people *want.* Its spokesmen claim that there is no evidence to support the theory that policy formation should be guided by respect for the natural world, still less according to the subjective wishes of members of local communities. People all over the world *demand* McDonald's, Coca Cola, shopping malls, the drugs culture, Third World Debt and structural adjustment. Nobody has any right to impose their subjective views on the free market. While the churches and community groups are free to offer guidance to their members, the will of the free market is sacrosanct. Globally, the only value-system recognised and enforced in law is the 'free' market of the money economy. All other value systems are classed as 'subjective' private concerns which must not be allowed to interfere with the free workings of the money economy.

Money values dominate all aspects of policy-making under global capitalism. Decisions on the use of land and other natural resources, on methods of child care, care in the community, education and care of the environment are based upon the availability of money. Belief in money value is cultivated through educational systems founded upon the eradication of common sense. Traditional practices regulating social relations and the use of land are dismissed as unscientific ignorance, anachronistic reminders of an age governed by ignorance, superstition and poverty. Hence, the individual's right to spend their own money as they please is regarded as sacrosanct. Whether earned, inherited or given, money confers rights which over-ride all other rights. In this chapter and those that follow we cast a critical eye over the elements essential to produce a sustainable political economy.

Knowledge as common property

In educational textbooks human history relates the long years of preparation for the coming of Rational Economic Man (REM). By implication, his ancestral mother, Irrational Uneconomic Woman (IUW), wandered through a swamp of primeval ignorance. She never knew where her next meal was coming from, lived in a state of primitive promiscuity and bore vast numbers of children, few of whom survived. Closer examination of archaeological evidence in conjunction with studies of recently surviving gatherer/hunter societies presents an alternative view. From the evidence, it emerges that until the industrial revolution free men and women, as individuals, were vastly more knowledgeable than their modern descendants. Every person had free access to their common cultural inheritance of knowledge about the earth and the skills necessary for everyday survival. By contrast, individuals today have scarcely any knowledge of where their food comes from, who grew it, and under what conditions it was produced.

Some insights from traditional economies

While civilisations have come and gone throughout the millennia of human existence, traditional society have survived to the present day. Although each traditional society has its own pattern of rules and roles to suit its history and its geographical location, certain common features can be detected.

Structured traditional societies

In a traditional society competition is restricted. Since gender is an institutional category women form a large and powerful group, able to ensure that other groups and individuals do not infringe their interests, and those of generations to come. Operating within a rational universe, morality and reason match each other. There is a place and a role for each person, enabling them to integrate with the group. Leaders or 'principals' also have their allotted place and duties. The role of the king or chief is often supported by the 'queen mother', a role assigned to a senior, rather than a junior and inexperienced, woman. The priest can speak out and challenge the chief or king. The 'cross-cutting' of principal roles strengthens the integration of the society. It is echoed, for example, in the ability of the Pope (Church) to challenge the Emperor (State) in the middle ages. However, in traditional societies those holding principal roles are figureheads, not leaders, and no single interest dominates the rest. The principal positions of king and queen are duplicated in every level of society, including the village and the household, and there is scope for reversal of roles in carnival. Although this type of society is often rather loosely termed 'hierarchical' this is misleading. *The social role of king or chief does not embody the power to act against the will of the people.*[1]

Some examples

Our conventional Western education leads us to expect that the structured social framework of an indigenous society would encompass unsophisticated technology, high levels of ignorance, lack of personal freedoms and a low quality of life. As the writings of Chinua Achebe, Wole Soyinka and many others demonstrate, however, pre-colonial African society did not necessarily match this pattern. Although the chief allocated land to families and marked the passage of agricultural seasons, determining the time to plant and the time to harvest, his actions followed custom and were dictated by pragmatism and justice. As leading public servant, the chief benefited in good times but paid the ultimate price of death in times of adversity.

In this way land, knowledge and customs were held in common for the benefit of all members of an overtly cooperative society. Writing in *New Statesman and Society* in 1990, Chinua Achebe dissociated himself from the well-meaning but 'blasphemous' label of 'the man who invented African literature'. As he explained, he did so because of 'an artistic taboo among my people the Igbo of Nigeria, a prohibition — on pain of being finished off rather quickly by the gods — from laying proprietary hands on even the smallest item in that communal enterprise in creativity'. For Achebe, this illustrates his pre-colonial inheritance of art as 'the creative potential in all of us and of the need to exercise this latent energy again and again in artistic expression and communal, cooperative enterprises'.[2]

In *Africa Counts* Claudia Zaslavsky provides a fascinating account of number and pattern, indicating that learned knowledge does not have to be written in books to be valued by, and of value to, the community. She describes the significance of observation and reproduction of patterns, numerical and geometric in African cultures, particularly where societies have been non-literate until recently.

The Bushman in the Kalahari Desert walks miles to dig up a watery root whose location he had noted several months previously — and with no man-made markers to guide him! Cattle-herding folk have in their vocabularies dozens of words to describe their livestock on the basis of hide markings and dozens more to differentiate cattle by the shape of the horns. Each pattern in weaving, in wood carving, in cloth dying, has a special meaning... The scholars of Muslim West Africa associated astrology and numerology with arrays of numbers called magic squares.[3]

Seeking further understanding of the claims to superiority of the democratically free 'developed' world over indigenous tradition, we examine three beliefs, contrasting the evidence from both types of society. One word of caution. As the authors of the studies quoted are only too well aware, there is perceived to be a danger in adopting *ad hoc* arguments and drawing glib generalisations. Nevertheless, the greater danger remains in a preservation of the Western practice of fragmentation of knowledge within and between subject areas. Where specialists can only speak as individuals, power, as we shall see, ceases to rest with the people. The following examples of indigenous knowledge-systems have been selected from the wide and varied range of studies of indigenous peoples across the world, and are by no means exceptional.

(1) *Peasant farming*

Conventional teaching, reinforced by the information super-highway, claims that science and technology have brought the mass of the people out of rural ignorance and poverty, where life can only be nasty, brutish and short: it can only be a matter of time before all people benefit from the abundance created by scientific advance. Informed by this belief, Paul Richards (1985) embarked upon a study of the relationship between environmental science and the prospects for increased food production in West Africa. In the early 1980s he worked with a group of agriculture students in a West African university on a study of local small-scale farmers. The object of the study was to examine three 'typical' farms, providing a scientific assessment of the management of the farm with a view to suggesting technical improvements. 'The work was well done, and the report makes fascinating reading. I think many of the students were genuinely surprised to find out how much farmers already knew about the ecological processes at work in their farms'. The students were able to translate this knowledge into textbook scientific terms. They also sought advice from the farmers on problems occurring on the college farm.[4]

As Richards explains, because West African farmers 'tended to ride with rather than over-ride natural diversity it was assumed that their techniques were especially "ancient" and "primitive"'. Failure to invent the wheel and the plough were also seen as pure disadvantage. However, the studies revealed that farmers made the best use of natural conditions and capitalised on local diversity, rather than working to create uniformity and labour-intensive controls. In Western agriculture intercropping, the planting of different crops in the same field during the same season, is virtually unknown. The planting dates, maturity period and harvest dates are varied to give food in the 'hungry period' before the harvest, to reduce storage losses and eliminate labour bottlenecks. Richards lists four basic advantages of the systems of intercropping studied. Yields are better and more reliable, as the system guards against poor yields from a specific crop. The labour input profile is smoother. The control of pests, weeds and diseases is improved, since all crops are weeded in one operation and minor crops keep the weeds down. Finally, subsistence is ensured through use of a wide range of foods and crop varieties saved and cultivated for specific advantages, including lateness or earliness in season, ability to store well, resistance to drought and suitability to different soils.

In the three villages studied students noted one hundred different methods of intercropping. Significantly, these 'small farmers' were subsistence peasant farmers supplying foods for themselves and their families as well as the market. Their skills and knowledge were the product of the work of past generations, constantly updated as ordinary people went about their daily lives. Supplies were supplemented by 'wild' foods and medicinal herbs, including fruits from the forest to which all had access.

By contrast, the ordinary 'person in the street' in a developed nation does not know where or how their food has been grown, still less the qualities of the particular varieties, the times and seasons of their growth and the conditions for their storage. Four-fifths of foodstuffs are processed in some way before they reach the consumer, the eye deceived by artificial ripening and colourings. The monocultural intensive farming techniques practised by the few on behalf of the many are dependent upon the advice and supplies of experts in pharmaceutical firms for chemical means to remove blights, diseases and weeds. Loss of soil fertility is 'remedied' by chemical fertilisers which do nothing to improve the body of that most vital resource.

In spite of the wealth of information technology, ignorance about the land, the climate, the soils, local wildlife and vegetation has grown rather than abated since pre-industrial times. Knowledge of local wild foods is virtually non-existent. Children who can recite the names of dozens of branded products cannot name or identify common examples of their local flora and fauna. Skilled in the use of textbooks and computers, children learn of the ignorance of pre-industrial peasants and indigenous peoples across the world. For them, technology can supply all the answers. The problem remains, what is the question, who frames it and for what motives?

(2) *Family planning*

Another common misconception is that women in peasant cultures have no control over their bodies. It is assumed that in the absence of modern medicine and contraceptive knowledge they are condemned to bear a child every year, most of which do not survive infancy, succumbing to disease and malnutrition. In this event, women across the world have drawn nothing but benefit from the spread of Western civilisation and its roads, clean water supplies and medical services.

Anthropologist Richard Lee is no feminist. Nevertheless, his study of the !Kung San of the Kalahari offers revealing insights into the existence of 'stone age' reproductive technologies. He observed that a nomadic gathering and hunting society could support itself with relatively little physical effort, using knowledge of the local flora and fauna and the skills built up over generations. Food sources are known and tapped according to season, with resources of less favoured foods being noted as reserve in case of seasonal failure of the favourites. Collection is systematic, bearing no resemblance to random foraging, and providing all with an ample sufficiency for no more than two or three hours of work per day. This should come as no surprise. Humans are credited with higher intelligence than animals, and are known to eat an exceptionally wide range of foodstuffs. While animals locate themselves near to, and move between, their favoured food sources it would be incredible if humans decided to throw all caution to the wind by foraging far and wide on the off-chance of coming across something edible.

The nomadic !Kung may walk many miles in a day to collect a particular food-stuff and bring it back to share in the camp. It would be impossible for women, who undertake most of the gathering, to set off with one child in the womb, another at the breast and another on the back. If no form of family planning were practised, the casualty rates of children and mothers would be catastrophic in terms of physical and emotional stress. Generation after generation of maternal ancestors would have had to be incredibly stupid, and the survivors amazingly lucky, were this to have been the case. As Lee notes, it was possible for the !Kung to achieve wide birth spacing and low family size without resort to wide use of the less-favoured physically and emotionally draining birth control methods of abortion or infanticide. Methods of control, including the use of herbs and long breast feeding during which sexual abstinence is practised, can be found in a wide variety of studies. Indeed, the contraceptive pill was developed from indigenous knowledge of the herbal properties of plants in the Amazonian rain forest.

Among the nomadic !Kung San a child would not be weaned until thirty-six months and would be carried by the mother to the age of four. Lee[5] shows how Western civilisation impacted upon the culture. As some !Kung San settled to farming, birth spacing reduced, the birth rate increased and with it the incidence of emotional stress and physical disease. Richards[6] gives a further example of problems caused by 'development' being erroneously attributed to indigenous ignorance. He cites a study in the 1970s which revealed that the spread of tsetse flies and sleeping sickness in the early colonial period 'was a direct consequence of disruptions brought about by colonial conquest'. Contrary to contemporary preconceptions, the problems were not due to 'outmoded' and 'wasteful' cultivation practices of African farmers, most of whom are women.

Women in African villages have been subjected to further well-intentioned but misdirected introductions to the 'advantages' of civilisation. The introduction of piped water direct to houses in many villages was met with little enthusiasm. Turning on a tap might save the 'work' of carrying water. However, frequent trips to the stream were vital for social contact and communication. Electronic communications and the cash economy offer illusory 'progress'.

Isolated, women become far more powerless and ignorant than their prehistoric mothers. Their ancestors knew exactly how much strain a new baby would put upon the community in general and themselves as individuals in terms of demands on labour/time and strain on the local environment. Furthermore, no property rights denied them access to the common pool of inherited knowledge upon which they could base their individual and collective decisions.

(3) *Hierarchies and structures*

In pre-colonial Africa land was common property. Chiefs of tribes following settled farming practices would allocate the use of land according to need. This gave rise to the colonial misapprehension that the chief or 'king' had status and power similar to that of a medieval baron. However, this was not the case. In peasant communities across the world there is little evidence of 'civilised' despotic power-over land use based upon a top-down hierarchy of authority. Nevertheless, the belief in the superiority of democratic 'freedom' over despotic chieftains is compounded by the removal of indigenous checks and balances during the colonial period, leaving many indigenous cultures impoverished and inoperable.

Public space and private enclosure

It is often argued that Western culture operates on a level playing field based upon equality and freedom. However, no society can operate on the basis of isolated individuals operating at random. Whatever the theory, structures and integration are essential to all forms of human interaction. Western civil service bureaucracies and commercial and financial institutions are hierarchical structures in which centralised power operates on a top-down basis. Recruits are selected on the basis of their conformity to the requirements of the organisation. Those who do not conform to the world view of their superiors will not advance up the ladder of promotion. Those who reach the top of the promotional ladder gain powers of control and influence both within the organisation and in its external dealings. *In practice, power in the 'developed' world does not originate in the will and wisdom of the people, nor is it subject to democratic controls.*

In their study of the World Bank, Susan George and Fabrizio Sabelli provide a detailed examination of the internal culture of this exceptionally powerful supra-national, non-democratic institution. They compare the Bank to the Church in its power to affect the lives of ordinary people.

It took the Church several hundred years to convert only a part of humanity to Christianity — large areas of the globe have always remained beyond its reach. It took the Bank little more than a decade to impose structural adjustment worldwide, or very nearly. In the single year 1987 it was able to reorganise itself from top to bottom the better to serve this recent but all-pervading doctrine... The Bank is without contest the premier policy institution deciding how the South and the East are to be organised.[7]

Throughout the book, George and Sabelli speak of 'beliefs, faith, doctrine, prophecy, and fundamentalism'. Their use of words like 'ancestors' and 'initiation' demonstrate that this modern institutional phenomenon is in many ways no different from other human institutions. However, its vast power to develop global market capitalism carries with it the scope to obliterate common rights of access to land and to the means of subsistence conferred by the common cultural heritage of skills and knowledge. The New World Order of economic freedom 'has been installed in little over a decade without firing a shot. The only troops deployed have been the battalions of uniformed economists'.[8]

Human beings do not live like a collection of Robinson Crusoes on a desert island, each pursuing their own self-interest as social isolates. Whenever human beings come together they formulate a set of ground rules within an institutional framework, training new members to conform to those rules. The family and the World Bank are human institutions. However, the latter, like other global institutions, now wields vast and unaccountable power over the life choices of families across the globe. According to orthodox economic theory, institutional power structures do not exist: REM operates in a social vacuum, making every decision on the basis of market forces alone. It is therefore necessary to review the course of economic history from a different angle, a task undertaken in the following chapters. First, however, we take a closer look at the question of access to information, a crucial aspect of being a member of a human society.

The privatisation of the common cultural inheritance

A community without control over access to at least some of its land and the cultural knowledge vital to making that land productive ceases to be a living community. It becomes subject to the cultural power of global institutions. Significantly, some of the most powerful global institutions like the World Bank are dominated by the Anglo-American world view which regards gardens as a place for flowers and an opportunity for commercial exploitation. Furthermore, as shops and markets are turned into supermarkets and shopping malls, the right to congregate in the streets to sell wares and exchange information is curtailed.

Public institutions and even churches demand a money payment from people seeking to congregate in public space. It is the privatisation of the commons in all its forms, including seeds, life forms and knowledge itself, which is turning people into slaves dependent upon the whim of democratically unaccountable global institutions.

We have already mentioned the introduction of piped water to the houses of an African village as an example of modern technology having the potential to eliminate an established form of social contact. Similarly, denial of access to a plot of land as 'allotment' or 'garden' on which families can grow food creates complete dependence upon an unsustainable money system. For most peoples across the world, access to land upon which to grow food is vital, not merely to save money in the cash economy but also to gain access to public space and common knowledge. In Biblical times, even as slaves leaving the Egyptian civilisation the Jews took with them the herds of cattle they had continued to tend during their exile. Slum dwellers of urban India dream of a return to the land. Speaking of his parents, Shravan Maishe, a young father, explains why he sends money to his parents who have returned to their native place in Karnataka:

> This is what they always wanted. To cultivate their land in peace. When we were children they could not survive at home. People want to go back home if they have the land. No-one who had the choice would prefer to stay in the city if they were guaranteed a living from the land.[9]

Within Europe, both East and West, the tradition of growing a substantial proportion of food in shared garden areas or on family smallholdings has persisted throughout the industrial revolution. Across the world, knowledge of how to grow food appropriate to local soils and climates survives, but is coming under unprecedented attack as formal educational institutions imprint the values of global capitalism upon young minds.

The Brave New World of REM

Denied access to a body of common knowledge, people are easily assured that technology will take care of everything, so long as traditional obstructions to the free flow of global culture are removed. 'Pessimism about the future doesn't seem to be warranted', Bill Gates assures his readers in *The Road Ahead*. As Zac Goldsmith observes:

> Within a certain context he is absolutely right. For, as long as we remain religiously blind to the past and as long as we are trained to misinterpret each head of the Hydra as something separate, isolated and unconnected to the whole, then each symptom of the larger problem presents itself as a market opportunity. 'Biotechnology promises astounding breakthroughs that will greatly improve the human condition', (Gates) writes with confidence. Thus ocean pollution becomes an excuse for genetically engineered pollution-

eating bacteria, and each new victim of environmental contamination becomes a contributor to the booming cancer industry, and justification for the spending of further millions to isolate the 'cancer gene'.[10]

As the cocktail effects of exposure to agrochemicals, polychlorinated biphenyls (PCBs) and the like produce varied effects upon the reproductive fertility of animals and humans, the commercial opportunities appear endless.

REM's faith in the free market's ability to provide for all human needs is equally unbounded. In 1983 the Institute of Ecotechnics embarked upon an eleven-year experimental attempt to recreate the seven basic biomes of the earth. Funded by a Texas billionaire, a three-acre site in the Arizona desert was enclosed in a tightly sealed superstructure. Seven basic 'biomes' of 'Biosphere 1', the earth, were recreated in the man-made world, named 'Biosphere 2'. The seven were: marsh, savannah, tropical rainforest, desert, a 25-foot deep 'ocean and coral reef', intensive agriculture and human habitation. Only those species thought to be useful to humans were included in the man-made world: 'pests' and 'weeds' were omitted. Predictably, the attempt by four men and four women to survive for two years within this 'brave new world' failed miserably.[11] Nevertheless, as the international space programme demonstrates, the belief that people can do without the natural world, sustaining themselves by market forces alone, is powerfully persistent.

The market as institution

According to orthodox theory the economy is divinely ordered: clockwork markets operate like the movements of the planets. Economic trends cannot and should not be affected by mere mortals acting according to sets of preconceived subjective judgments. Theoretically there are no grounds for checks upon the individual's satisfaction of personal desires, save the physical availability of scarce resources.

Sociologists draw a distinction between 'negative freedom' in which individuals achieve freedom from control, interference and exploitation, and 'positive freedom' in which individuals control their lives through sharing public responsibilities. Positive freedom is often viewed with some suspicion as tending towards forms of oppression. Negative freedom allows individuals to create their private spheres in which to express and follow their own codes of practice: it also offers the freedom to starve, and to leave others to starve. Hence even the most ardent individualist allows the necessity for legislation to determine what may, or may not, be done in the public sphere.

At this crucial point, theory and logic part company. According to economic theory, political and financial institutions have no role to play because it is assumed they do not, or should not, exist. As E. P. Thompson explained:

It should not be necessary to argue that the model of a natural and self-adjusting economy, working providentially for the best good of all, is as much a superstition as the notions which upheld the paternalist [pre-industrial] model — although, curiously, it is a superstition which some economic historians have been the last to abandon.[12]

Economic theory is a belief system. Like many apparently outdated superstitions, economic notions are more realistically to be recognised as customs. Although they may convey meanings, customs are not mere searches for meanings. They 'are clearly connected to and rooted in, the material and social realities of life and work… Customs may provide a context in which people may do things it may be more difficult to do directly … they may keep the need for collective action, collective adjustment of interests, and collective expression of feelings and emotions' within the social group.[13]

Rejection of a body of custom in favour of the negative freedom of the market creates global market forces legitimated by international legislation. Where custom may provide the freedom of self-control, the free market gives free reign to disorderly desires. As Jeremy Seabrook observes, it appears to offer freedom from all traditional restraints leading to the 'satisfaction of limitless desire':

> For it is axiomatic in Western economics that human desire is infinite: and it is this which feeds the dogmas of perpetual growth and expansion of industrial society. Consumerism is the belief-system that 'rationalizes' this unreason. Its iconography now penetrates the whole world through the global media. The ideology shows human life … as endless fun, entertainment, escape, money, sex; and perpetual distraction from the pain and pleasure of being fully human.[14]

The rising tide of global expectations follows the redefinition of human needs and satisfactions in market material terms. Across the world Western transnationals offer emulative glimpses of the materialist paradise in the brand names of Sony, Mercedes, Adidas, Nike, Courreges, Cucci and Elizabeth Arden while the poor scrabble in the mounting dumps of waste. As the human species throws all the globe's resources onto the market in this way it threatens its own survival. A political economy founded upon the assumption that economic man can have a permanent place on the planet is not sustainable. Although it will never be possible to return to pre-capitalist 'human nature … a reminder of its alternative needs, expectations and codes may renew our sense of our nature's range of possibilities'.[15] A review of the operation of past and present human systems offers some insights.

Property rights and public policy

The money economy operates through denial of fundamental traditional rights of access to common property in the form of land and knowledge. It is here that the misapprehension of progress from primitive superstitious belief systems to enlightened rational self-interest is most misleading. Daniel Bromley has defined property as a benefit stream and a property right as a claim to a benefit stream which the state has agreed to protect. Bromley identifies four institutional types of resource management regimes: (1) state property regimes, (2) private property regimes, (3) common property regimes, and (4) non-property regimes of open access.

In a famous essay Garrett Hardin argued that in the absence of private owner-ship and control, common land would be over-grazed and destroyed by individuals pursuing their own self-interest. It was therefore necessary for private enclosure of the commons. Bromley argues that Hardin's 'tragedy of the commons' describes non-property regimes where open access is not controlled by tradition and custom. Equally, national governments and large private institutions are incapable of managing large amounts of natural resources.

> I suggest that the real and lasting 'tragedy of the commons' is the gradual breakdown of institutional arrangements in the newly independent nations of the tropics. First rapacious kings and princes, then alien colonial and imperial administrators, and finally often-inept national governments have all conspired to subvert or to destroy resource management schemes at local level... Any property system — whether private, common or state — is an authority system. In the absence of consistent and coherent institutional arrangements resource use is reduced to first come, first served.[16]

However, it is not only control of access to natural resources which is at issue. The rise of global institutions has brought with it the ability of private and unac-countable bodies to stake claims to the products of human invention and ingenuity through patents claiming the exclusive right to control agricultural and medical knowledge and even life forms themselves.[17] Access to common cultural knowledge is now regulated through the money economy. A telephone call, the purchase of a book, an educational course or access to an art gallery or museum cost money. If property is a 'benefit stream' and a property right a 'claim to a benefit stream', the enclosure of the common cultural heritage of knowledge itself has fundamental implications.

'Progress' and dis-information

It is possible to put two interpretations upon history: that we have progressed, or that so-called 'progress' is illusory. Human society may have evolved from primitive pre-industrial forms of society where life was nasty, brutish, short and riddled with superstitions. In the new developed world excellent communications and clean food and water are available to all for a minimum requirement to work for the cash economy. Alternatively, longer hours of work, increased ignorance and reduced autonomy may be the lot of the average person in the street. Compared with pre-industrial times, the ordinary person is less capable of deciding matters of fundamental importance to themselves and their families.

For example, in the UK during the 1980s and 1990s it became apparent that a deadly disease was being transferred from cattle to humans. At first it was assumed that bovine spongiform encephalopathy (BSE), the so-called 'Mad Cow Disease', could not cross the species barrier from cattle to humans. When it became apparent that a new strain of Creutzfeldt-Jacob Disease (CJD) could be traced to consumption of beef, the matter was investigated further. It was found that the disease had occurred in cattle following the use of processed sheep carcasses as a winter feed. As every farmer knows, cattle are vegetarian. What the farmers did not know, and discovered to their horror, was the content of the pellets they were buying to feed their cattle. There was no indication on the sacks as to the composition of the pellets, merely a brand name. Farmers and customers alike had no means of judging the products they were buying. As livelihoods in the meat trade and among butchers and farmers were affected, attempts to reassure the public by fair means or foul predominated over rational discussion. Money values remained dominant.

As an isolated incident, the BSE story might have little more than curiosity value. However, new developments in biotechnology and genetic engineering present serious cause for concern, especially in relation to the deliberate transfer of genetic material between plants, animals and humans. Equally, suggestions of possible links between the use of organophosphates and increases in the incidence of neurodegenerative diseases such as Parkinson's Disease, Alzheimer's Disease and multiple sclerosis are dismissed as pure speculation.[18]

Conclusion

Blind belief in the ability of market forces to produce solutions to each and every problem caused by the clash of interests thrown up by competition inevitably leads to policy-making which is irrational and uninformed. Across the world conservation and social cohesion, essential to the functioning of society, are tenuously surviving in spite of, and not because of, global capitalism. The relative claims of wage slavery and the peasant economy will be explored in the following chapters, alongside guild socialist notions of service to the community and the common cultural inheritance.

At this point it is necessary to observe that leaders of the global 'robber baron' economy (i.e. bankers and financiers) are not necessarily evil in intent. They have merely succeeded in a selection process based upon a particular world view. Preoccupied with their own version of daily reality, they have neither the skills nor the knowledge to act for the common good.

The following chapters explore the history of land, labour and money, the three vital means of production of a so-called 'developed'[19] economy. Threaded through this analysis is the consciousness that without access to the common cultural heritage of the 'intellectual commons', claims to the benefit streams of land and labour become ephemeral. The role of the institutions of finance in deciding matters of access to and power over the common inheritance of physical and intellectual property is explored so that we can consider ways in which money can be brought under communal control.

NOTES

1 This section is derived from the work of Mary Douglas. See, for example, Douglas, Mary (1992) *Risk and Blame: Essays in Cultural Theory* London and New York. Routledge (1994 edn).

2 Achebe, Chinua (1990) in *New Statesman and Society*, 9 Feb. See also Achebe, Chinua (1964) *Arrow of God* London, Ibadan, Nairobi, Lusaka. Heinemann (1977 edn).

3 Zaslavsky, Claudia (1973) *Africa Counts: Number and Pattern in African Culture* Connecticut. Lawrence Hill (1979 edn). p8.

4 Richards, Paul (1985) *Indigenous Agricultural Revolution: Ecology and Food Production in West Africa* London. Hutchinson. p9

5 Lee, Richard (1979) *The !Kung San. Men, Women and Work in a Foraging Society* Cambridge University Press.

6 Richards, op. cit. p11.

7 George, Susan and Sabelli, Fabrizio (1994) *Faith and Credit: The World Bank's Secular Empire* Penguin. p133.

8 George and Sabelli, op. cit. p66.

9 Maishe, Shravan (1997) 'City of Dreams' *New Internationalist* 290. May.

10 Goldsmith, Zac (1997) 'Virtual Future' *The Ecologist* Vol.27, No.4. July/August. pp162-3.

11 Luke, T. W. (1995) 'Reproducing Planet Earth?' *The Ecologist* 21 (4) pp157-62.

12 Thompson, Edward P. (1991) *Customs in Common* London. The Merlin Press. p203.

13 Gerald M. Sider, quoted in Thompson, op. cit. p14.

14 Seabrook, Jeremy (1997) 'A Curious Mysticism' *New Internationalist* 295. October. pp12-14.

15 Thompson, op. cit. p15.

16 Bromley, Daniel W. (1991) *Environment and Economy: Property Rights and Public Policy* Oxford, England, and Cambridge, USA. Blackwell.

17 See Baumann, Miges, *et al* (eds) (1996) *The Life Industry: Biodiversity, People and Profits* London. Intermediate Technology Publications.

18 Purdy, David (1992) 'Mad Cows and Warble Flies: A Link between BSE and Organophosphates?' *The Ecologist* Vol.22. No.2. March/April. pp52-57.

19 Vandana Shiva uses the term 'mal-developed' to describe the economies of the North.

Chapter 4

Land

ILL FARES THE LAND, to hast'ning ills a prey,
Where wealth accumulates, and men decay;
Princes or lords may flourish, or may fade;
A breath can make them, and a breath has made;
But a bold peasantry, their country's pride,
When once destroyed, can never be supplied.
A time there was, ere England's griefs began,
When every rood of ground maintained its man;
For him light labour spread her wholesome store,
Just gave what life required, but gave no more;
His best companions innocence and health,
And his best riches ignorance of wealth.

Oliver Goldsmith (1730-1774)

If economic theory is to be believed, land will soon become redundant. Sustained economic growth will enable technologies to render human economies independent of natural soils, microbes, animals, plants, forests, ecosystems and a stable climate. Hence a Yale University economist could claim in 1990 that a hotter climate would mainly affect 'those sectors [of the economy] that interact with unmanaged ecosystems such as agriculture, forestry and coastal activities'. Meanwhile, the 'carefully controlled environment' of shopping malls and office blocks would scarcely notice the change in weather patterns. 'The main factor to notice', William Nordhaus observed, 'is that the climate has little economic impact upon advanced industrial societies'.[1] As David Orr shows, it is possible for economists to argue that 'decline in agriculture and forestry would be of little consequence because they are only 3% of the US economy'. Arguing that the economy can still grow when these 'industries' are eliminated is 'equivalent to believing that since the heart is only 1% to 2% of bodyweight it can be removed or damaged without consequences for one's health'.[2]

To discover the reasons for the colossal misunderstanding of the relationship between the economy and the land, it is necessary to set aside some preconceptions about economic progress. This chapter explores the ways in which humans have cooperated to provide for themselves from the land, and sets ancient beliefs about the relationship between people and the land within the modern context.

Territorial equilibrium

For almost 100,000 years human beings have lived by hunting and gathering. During the past 3000-8000 years some humans in a few parts of the world developed urban civilisations, supported by a hinterland. As civilisations came and went, the majority of people lived out their lives in a sustainable equilibrium upon the land. As European civilisation entered its colonial period 'primitive' indigenous peoples practising 'stone age' economics were found in Africa and elsewhere. Regarded as less than human, these peoples were taken into slavery, transported across the oceans or forced to work in mines and plantations. More recent reviews of the lifestyle of 'stone age' economies indicate a high degree of sophistication in the relationship between the people and their land. The 'lazy' native had achieved an enviable lifestyle.

Richard Wilkinson[3] questions the very notion of progress. In his view, 'primitive societies appear less poor than we imagine, and advanced ones less rich'. Human beings appear to have moved from a low-work, high-labour-productivity style of life as hunter gatherers towards a high-work culture with diminishing rewards to labour, involving more activity and less leisure. Humans have found themselves forced to adapt technologies in order to compensate for an upset in equilibrium. Hence environmental degradation is combined with a rise in population caused by the breakdown of natural and conscious checking mechanisms. The resultant disequilibrium necessitates technological and social adaptation to the changed situation.

Like other species of animals, humans require defined territories for the provision of their needs. Starvation occurs only in periods of transition. Most animal populations remain in stable equilibrium with their food supplies. Wilkinson cites a well-known experiment with the nesting sites of blue tits. In a given area more nesting boxes were provided. As a result, more pairs bred successfully early in the season. However, the numbers of birds raised were reduced and second hatchings were less successful, with fewer eggs laid and more eggs broken. As a result, the bird population remained in stable equilibrium with its territory and hence food supply. Successful predators do not wipe out their food supplies, but maintain a stable relationship with them. Birds with ill-defined feeding areas such as sea birds have fixed nesting sites. Failure to secure a place prevents a bird from breeding, although it is not excluded from the colony. Some of these colonies are very old, with names dating back a thousand years, such as Lundy, the Isle of Puffins. Breeding territories for seals and turtles are similarly defined.

Wilkinson argues that the conception of 'primitive' societies scratching a living from the soil has arisen as a result of disruptions caused by Western cultural invasion. Perpetual hardship, large families and malnutrition are not normal features of animal populations. Humans are credited with greater intelligence than most animal species. As the work of this writer and many others shows, human groups were perfectly capable of maintaining a stable relationship with their food sources by limiting their populations within defined territories. Indigenous natives were 'lazy' because they had worked out a satisfactory lifestyle, gathering, hunting, occasionally herding and often 'cultivating' patches of favoured foodstuffs so that they could be found in abundance in following years. Free from oppression, the 'disutility' of labour was low and rewards high so long as population remained in stable relationship with the land.

Land in the Bible[4]

The concept of private ownership of land is foreign to many cultures outside the 'developed' countries.[5] Moreover, even within the Judeo-Christian culture from which global capitalism emerged, land was deemed to be held in trust for future generations. In exploring the relationship between humankind and the land we take up the story with the origins of Judeo-Christian culture and the Biblical story of Genesis. Two very different types of land tenure systems can be discerned.

The Israelites were nomadic pastoralists, moving their herds of cattle across the plains of Canaan, buying grain from settled farmers to complement their diet of animal products. In addition, they collected 'choice fruits of the land', such as 'balm … honey, gum, resin, pistachio nuts and almonds', using animal skins and wood to create tents as shelter (Genesis 43:11). At this time tribes in the area were in competition over rights to cultivate the land, to rear cattle and to collect the wild produce of the land. In time of famine the Israelites were forced to leave the land of Canaan to seek food in the fertile plains of Egypt.

One of their number, Joseph, had gone ahead to secure a position of authority in the court of the Egyptian Pharaoh. Pharaoh's dream, interpreted by Joseph, foretold seven years of plenty followed by seven years of famine. During the seven years of plenty Joseph went 'through all the land of Egypt' gathering up food from the fields around each city and storing it against the famine years to come. During the years of famine he sold the stored grain back to the people. 'Joseph collected up all the money to be found in the land of Egypt and in the land of Canaan, in exchange for the grain that they bought: and Joseph brought the money into Pharaoh's house'. One year, when all the money was spent, Joseph gave the people food in exchange for their livestock, taking 'the horses, the flocks, the herds and the donkeys'. Finally, as the famine came to an end, the people sold themselves and their land in return for food and seed. The land became Pharaoh's, and all the people except the priests became 'slaves' or, more accurately, serfs, allowed to farm their land on a twenty per cent rental to Pharaoh (Genesis 47). The centralised system of land tenure was a novelty, contrasting with the common access which was a feature of tribal traditions in the surrounding lands. In this way a top-down hierarchy dominated by the Pharaoh or King was created.

Pharaoh had power over the land and its people, issuing proclamations and decrees which all must obey. Themselves enslaved by later Pharaohs, the Children of Israel were led by their God to flee from their oppression. Taking with them their flocks and herds, the Israelites followed their prophet Moses across the Wasteland to the Promised Land. In the course of their wanderings they received the Ten Commandments, telling them how to live according to God's law in an egalitarian community.

Unlike when living under the Pharaohs, each individual in the community had a duty to follow the Commandments and to live in accordance with God's word as revealed by the prophets. No earthly authority of a king or temporal ruler came between the people and their land. When the people hankered after the material lifestyle they had enjoyed in slavery in Egypt, creating a graven image and desiring an earthly leader, they were punished by God. For forty years they were left to wander in the Wasteland before being allowed to reach the Promised Land.

When the Hebrews finally settled in the Promised Land, it was under a covenant between God and His people. The Covenant was an agreement with communities, not with individuals. As a people, the Israelites were urged to listen to the prophets and create a caring and sharing community. The land is owned by God, and the people were given laws by which they should abide. In Leviticus 26 God speaks to His people as a community, not to their leaders. The *people* are to obey God's statutes and keep His commandments. If they do so, they will have rain in due season, and the fields and trees will yield their harvest. The people will be strong and live in security and peace. If not, sickness will fall on the people and the land will be laid waste. 'I will break your proud glory, and I will make your sky like iron and your earth like copper. Your strength shall be spent to no purpose; your land shall not yield its produce, and the trees of the land shall not yield their fruit' (Leviticus 26:19-20). The cities will be laid waste, and the land will be uninhabitable. The land will 'enjoy its sabbath years', becoming wasteland for ever more (Leviticus 26:34).

The plan outlined by Moses was for the Hebrews to settle in the Promised Land. Every family was to have a fair share of the land so that they could support themselves. Families would maintain their members, none being left destitute and none achieving vast wealth. They would be ruled by law and custom rather than by kings, with judges settling disputes impartially. The God of the Israelites loved justice and hated oppression. His laws would bring prosperity to all, not just a favoured few, in a land flowing with milk and honey. This contrasted with their previous state of slavery in Egypt, and with the practices of the surrounding tribes who followed the dictates of earthly kings. The just God demanded justice as well as worship.

Frequently, the people ignored the words of God's prophets, desiring powerful kings like the neighbouring tribes. However, the kings introduced to Israel were judged on their loyalty to God and their ability to protect against the worship of false gods and materialism. The success of these earthly rulers in this respect was not spectacular. Kings had a habit of exploiting the land while causing division between the people, bringing ruin to the land and exile to the people. The Old Testament tells the story of God's patient renewal of His covenant with the people.

Jotham's fable

One day the trees went out
to anoint a king to rule them.
They said to the olive tree, 'Be our king!'
The olive tree replied,
'Must I forgo my oil
which gives honour to gods and men
to stand and sway over the trees?'

Then the trees said to the fig tree,
'You come and be our king!'

The fig tree replied,
'Must I forgo my sweetness,
forgo my excellent fruit,
to go and sway over the trees?'

Then the trees said to the vine,
'You come and be our king!'

The vine replied,
'Must I forgo my wine
which cheers gods and men,
to go and sway over the trees?'

Then the trees said to the thorn bush,
'You come and be our king!'

And the thorn bush replied to the trees,
'If you are anointing me in good faith to be your king,
come and shelter in my shade.
But if not, fire will come out of the thorn bush
and devour the cedars of Lebanon.'

(Judges 9:8-15)

Jotham's fable illustrates the dangers of giving power to earthly kings. Unwisely, the people select the thorn or bramble, a threat and menace to crops, their choice condoned by the more dignified olive, fig and vine. In this way the people are deceived, becoming subjects of a cruel and vicious despot. The Old Testament provides much excellent proof that the quest for earthly power is rarely compatible with justice for all and respect for God's laws on caring for the land.

Stewardship of the land

Throughout the Old Testament (the word 'testament' means covenant or agreement) the people are told that prosperity comes to the land through obedience to the Lord. Within the New Testament the underlying philosophy is in keeping with peasant cultures throughout the world. Peasants who farm the land do not speak in terms of conquest or control. Rather, they have a natural humility which stems from direct experience of nature.

Mosaic law as set out in Leviticus 25 determines the relationship between the people and the land. The land belongs to God, not to individuals or earthly rulers. Just as people should rest on the sabbath, every seventh year the land should lie fallow in order for it to recover its fertility. However, when seven times seven brings round the fiftieth year, a jubilee is declared when all land in the Promised Land reverts to the family to which it was originally allocated. Property lies in the use of the land, not in ownership. If a family falls on hard times they may sell the use of their land. However, the price should fall as the jubilee approaches 'for it is a certain number of harvests that are being sold to you'. Explaining God's word, Moses declared: 'The land shall not be sold in perpetuity, for the land is mine; with me you are but aliens or tenants. Throughout the land that you hold, you shall provide for the redemption of the land' (Leviticus 25:1-28). Right living on the land includes being neighbourly, just, kind to one another, generous to strangers, honest in trading. 'The land is described as an inheritance: the community exists in time, it includes the dead and the unborn. But the only thing we can do for the unborn is to pass on to them the land, which requires the practice of good husbandry'.[6]

The covenant regime introduced under Mosaic law is comparable with commons regimes where individuals are answerable to the local community for their right use of the land. Under such regimes abuse of the land brings exclusion or punishment to the individual. In Biblical times widespread abuse resulted in God's anger bringing blight on the land and calamity on the people.

Land tenure systems

1 Commons regimes

Hunters and gatherers, nomadic pastoralists and shifting cultivators develop highly complex customs governing access to the resources of the land by the members of their communities. Food from the land, the sea and the forest is shared among the community, none going hungry while there is any food to be shared. Where land is farmed, plots are allocated according to the size and needs of each family, often on an annual basis. Fruit trees may not be monopolised, even where they fall inside a family plot. Food, fuel and building resources from the wild remain an essential element in the economy, even where farm lands are permanently settled.

2 Military hierarchies

Throughout history some land has fallen under the sway of military rulers for a period of time. In Old Testament times the Pharaohs ruled Egypt. Elsewhere kings or emperors held sway over the lands where people lived. Jesus was born into a peasant community on the outskirts of the Roman Empire. Those living within the lands governed by Rome paid tributes and taxes similar to the 'rents' charged by the Pharaohs. Peasants continued to farm the land according to ancient customs. However, the demand for food to feed vast armies of soldiers, and to supply the urban populations, necessitated the setting up of *latifundae* or slave estates. Here the relationship between human beings and the land changed out of all recognition. Forced to work under pain of death or starvation, slaves cease to be accountable for their actions.

3 Medieval hierarchy

Here the king holds the land by divine right, apportioning land to his nobles on the basis of a set of rights and obligations. Peasants on the land appear power-less. However, the land remains productive where oppression is minimal. Wars and famine are closely related.

4 Individualism

Where traditional patterns of rights and obligations are broken down, the land is worked by slaves or landless labourers. To the 'owners' of alienated land, profit replaces sustainability as the dominant policy consideration.

The peasant and the slave

In *The English Countryman* H. J. Massingham goes to considerable lengths to distinguish between slaves and landless labourers on the one hand and peasants belonging to a traditional farm-village society on the other. The key distinction concerns access to land. Peasants are free people with rights of access to their land. The term covers many forms of small farmers who, as tenants, sharecrop-pers, labourers or crofters, lived on the land in an agricultural community. Even when part of their produce is taken in the form of tithes or other dues, peasants work for themselves, giving them a vested interest in the productivity of the land. The English peasant culture of the traditional village system, with its three fields, common pasture, waste and woodland, was self-sufficient, representing a cultural form of egalitarian cooperation where all had rights and duties. Peasant culture is older than 'civilised' mass production based on the slave labour of the *latifundia*. It did not evolve from slavery, but survived in spite of widespread disruption of traditional patterns of land tenure. The sense of responsibility for what you do and how you do it, vital to the relationship between people and the land, is lost in the slave and the landless labourer, however well-educated. Massingham goes to great lengths to correct the historical inaccuracy which assumes that peasant culture evolved out of slavery. The crucial point is the continuity of traditional forms of land conservation.

Enclosure in Britain

In economic theory 'land' and 'labour' are anonymous concepts outside place and time. In real life land is a particular place on the earth, known and loved by people. There is a past to respect, a present in which to respect it and a tradition to be handed on to future generations.

Nowhere in the world has this basic fact of life been so completely forgotten as in the 'sceptred isle' which spawned the industrial revolution. Nowhere in the world has the need to protect the land from desecration been so powerfully expressed as in 'England's green and pleasant land'.

Private profit was the motive for enclosure of land in the British Isles. Peasants with rights over the land respected traditions designed to guard against its exploitation. Therefore they were an inconvenience to be removed by 'improving' landlords. The systematic removal of peasants from their land, with the backing of the law, is powerfully recounted by J. Prebble in *The Highland Clearances*, by William Cobbett and by many others. Although temporary enclosure of common land occurred from time to time in global history, the systematic denial of common rights of access to land was a fundamental precondition for the development of an industrialised market economy.

Enclosure brought about a profound change in the social order. Land was redefined as 'property', becoming a commodity which could be traded on the market. As the market system was rapidly expanded, the majority of people, denied access to the land, became wage labourers trading their labour as a commodity. Furthermore, enclosure introduced the notion of profitable 'improvement' leading to acceptance of 'development' and 'economic growth' as desirable outcomes. The first legal act enforcing enclosure, the Statute of Merton in 1235, referred to the need to improve the land in order to extract a greater rent. From that time onwards, accelerating between the fifteenth and the nineteenth centuries, the land of the British Isles was taken from the people and enclosed as private or state-owned property.

In pre-industrial Britain traditional forms of land access shared common features with peasant land tenure patterns throughout the world. Throughout the Middle Ages the farm-village system centred upon open fields in the form of communally managed strips of arable land. The unfenced arable land could be worked cooperatively, with flexibility in size of holdings and levels of contributions according to the changes in family size over the years. Although some villagers were obliged to work on the local lord's land for certain fixed periods, for most of the time they were free to work their own plots. After harvest, villagers pastured animals on the stubble. They practised rotation and allowed the land to lie fallow in certain years to regain fertility. In 1086 the *Domesday Book* recorded that over half the arable land belonged to the villagers.

In addition to rights to farm arable land, villagers had established rights of access to defined areas of common and wasteland, all of which were managed communally. Rights included the pasture of animals under certain conditions, collection of berries, nuts, animals and other wild foods, fuel and herbs. In the interests of good husbandry, an elective body determined fines for over-stocking, failure to cut thistles, neglect of repair to gates, ditches, drainage and turning stock on the stubble before the church bell rang. There was a network of bye-laws

> for tethering stock on the 'sikes' or unploughed roughage of the arable fields, for the limited use of bulls and rams among the stock, for opening the aftermath of the Lammas meadows. Yet these rules were not formulae nor forms to fill up nor impositions applied from the top downwards, but adaptable, informal, flexible, spontaneous and annually born of the common need. When the Duke of Portland's keepers were fined for taking anthills off the common as peasant food, it is clear that they [the rules] were operated without fear or favour, and that if they were voluntary at source, they were also firm in execution.[7]

The ambitious landlord wishing to breed specialised sheep for personal profit faced a problem. He could not function within this system. However, the Black Death resulted in a substantial fall in population, freeing some lands for use as improved pasture for individual profit. For a while it was possible for two systems to co-exist. In time, however, the booming wool export market led to ambitious landowners taking over the land in order to turn it over to sheep. Thousands of peasants were evicted from their lands. Others were forced off the land through the enclosure of their common and waste lands, which formed a vital part of their sustainable economy. Enclosure was a legal process. In theory, the peasants had rights: in practice the courts were biased against the poor. The traditional rhyme neatly sums up the situation:

> They hang the man and flog the woman
> That steal the goose from off the common,
> But let the greater villain loose
> That steals the common from the goose.

By the sixteenth century the thousands of landless poor begging from door to door were seen as a law and order problem. The Elizabethan Poor Laws were an attempt to deal with the situation. Although temporarily checked under the Tudors, the process of enclosure was speeded up as the English revolution of 1647-1660 brought to power the class of landowners that benefited from enclosure. By 1876 the *New Domesday Book* calculated that about 2,250 people owned half the agricultural land of England and Wales, 0.6 per cent owning 98.5 per cent of it.[8]

In short, the appalling rural poverty which pre-dated the industrial revolution was a direct result of the early stages of Western civilisation's quest to prioritise the exploitation of the land and its riches for private profit. Subsequent introduction of so-called 'improved' farming techniques by Turnip Townsend *et al* brought a cheap and plentiful supply of food to feed the urban industrial proletariat now forced to seek employment in profitable export industries in order to survive. But at what cost? It is no accident that local capitalists discouraged the reservation of plots of land as allotments where workers could grow food for their families. The capitalist system functions most 'efficiently' when it exercises complete control over land and labour.

By and large, economic historians have embraced the myth of progress from rural insecurity, ignorance and poverty to the wealth and welfare of the modern industrial state supported by its monocultural agriculture. Writers expressing degrees of reservation at the separation of the people from the land have been dismissed as reactionary utopians ignorant of the true facts and determined to cause trouble. As social theorists attempt to come to grips with the causes of drug-related crime and other forms of urban industrial malaise, William Cobbett's work appears to be well focused and precise. The following passage, for example, demonstrates his holistic view of the relationship between the people and the land:

> Those who are so eager for new inclosure seem to argue as if the wasteland in its present state produced nothing at all. But is this the fact? Can anyone point out a single inch of it which does not produce something and the produce of which is made use of? It goes to the feeding of sheep, of cows, of cattle of all descriptions, and ... it helps to rear in health and vigour, numerous families of the children of the labourers, which children, were it not for these wastes, must be crammed into the stinking suburbs of towns amidst filth of all sorts, and congregating together in the practice of every species of idleness and vice.[9]

Interest in the nineteenth-century work of William Cobbett was revived by H. J. Massingham around the time of World War II.

The wisdom of the fields

As World War II ended Massingham called for support in the 'the greatest of all wars, the war of values' which lay ahead. He quoted Chesterton:

> I saw great Cobbett riding,
> The Horseman of the shires;
> And his face was red with judgement
> And a light of Luddite fires.
> A trailing meteor on the Downs he rides above the rotting towns,
> The Horseman of Apocalypse, the Rider of the Shires.

'When Cobbett thought of nature', wrote Massingham, 'he was thinking of the fields he knew, Little Foxhanger, the Seven Acres, Haw Croft, Priest Croft, Barley Close, Grunt Drove Meadow, plots of land that demanded individual treatment and had been named by his own people who for centuries had a responsible stake in them'.[10] Cobbett constantly attacked the financial system which encouraged the pursuit of wealth not for any specific purpose but merely as an end in itself. Cobbett sought to maintain the fabric of things, by which society and the land held together. Social disintegration flowed from the removal of traditional religious and ethical checks upon economic expansion.

In opposing the disintegration of cottage crafts and the migration of rural workers to the towns, 'Cobbett stood like a barrier reef against a whole sea of change'. Agriculture was being brought to ruin by finance. When money was used to breed money it diverted resources from nurturing the land. Cobbett was well aware that as prices rose during the long years of the French wars, the land and agriculture had become 'objects of speculation'. The result was disruption in the 'whole agricultural equilibrium'.[11]

Farmers were living on borrowed money, and small farms were being absorbed into larger ones.

Cobbett did realise, as few enough modern farmers do, the inveterate hostility of finance and industrialism to agriculture. So, though not understanding the detailed workings of currency, he was sound in his demand for a steady one... He prophesied that this financial 'THING' would destroy the stable agriculture of a thousand years and in the fullness of time it did destroy it... [He] foresaw that the debt system would become a millstone round the neck of the nation, and so it has become. He dreaded that, as taxation increased to feed an insatiable Debt, so security in and responsibility for property would result in loss of property for the many and much too much of it for the few. History has justified him.[12]

The British form of land ownership by the few contrasts starkly with the meshes of power internal to commons regimes, where people do not so much own the land as see themselves 'owned by' the land and water resources of which they are stewards.

Debt lays waste the land

Soil erosion appears to have been a major contributor to the decline and fall of the great empires of the past. The sites where they once stood are now desert. Massingham was one of the many to forecast the fall of Western civilisation for the same reason, with the vital distinction that for the first time soil exhaustion threatens the very survival of the human species as exploitative Western patterns of land ownership spread across the globe. Writing over five decades ago, Massingham quoted figures showing that in the United States alone 'monoculture, overstocking, over-cropping, cashing-in on fertility, artificials replacing defect of humus, excess mechanisation, loss of rotation, large-scale production, a number of cereal crops in succession, without giving the land a rest and replacing what is taken out of it' had caused the loss of 253 million acres of cultivated land. Similar depletion was then (1941) taking place in Scotland, India, Wales and Victoria due to the export of meat and dairy products.[13] In a passage holding as true today as in 1943, Massingham describes the effects of the replacement of the natural law of Christianity and of the peasant with the 'Hobbesian mechanism' on a global scale:

Debt was a harder taskmaster than drought, waste than the utmost rigours of nature. The national greed for raw materials which expanded the greed of the combine, which expanded the greed of individual 'enterprise' have, in North America alone exhausted more than a quarter of a million acres of fertile soil, more than a quarter of the iron deposits, more than three quarters of the timber ... Every year the peoples of Europe and the United States pour down into the seas and rivers nearly 20 million tons of nitrogen, potassium and phosphorus for every million of their populations, and every cargo of beef or milk products, every shipload of bones left the exporting country the poorer in the fruitfulness of its soil. The depletion of the Scottish hills drove the peasant-crofter from his starved or sterile home. Australia, Canada, South Africa, Uganda, Kenya, Tanganyika, Nigeria, the Ukraine, the Argentine and other countries have seen their land slipping from under the feet of their peoples.[14]

Massingham quoted Steinbeck's *The Grapes of Wrath*, Whyte's *The Rape of the Earth* and many other contemporary expressions of concern at the exhaustion of the earth's soils. Only a few countries like Denmark allowed 'little property owners' to till the soil in harmony with nature. There the soils hold fast, 'the wheel of life circles from decay to renewal and the sickness of soil, plant, and animal ... was kept at bay'.[15]

Agrarian populism

In his introduction to *Indigenous Agricultural Revolution* Richards presents the case for a 'people's science' based upon a 'decentralised, participatory R & D [Research and Development] system which seeks to support, rather than replace, local initiative'.[16] He cites the work of Chayanov, an agricultural economist seeking to defend peasant economic interests and cultural values in the early days of Russian communism. After the revolution populist intellectuals rejected Marxist notions of evolutionary change, seeking improvement in existing peasant institutions and systems of production rather than transition to socialism through capitalist agriculture. Following detailed study of peasant farming systems, Chayanov noted their emphasis on the durability of the peasantry as a social grouping, and the 'non-capitalist rationality' of many peasant decision-making processes. Such ideas ran counter to the Leninist belief that a class of capitalist farmers would emerge to exploit the mass of landless labourers. The pro-peasant development programme worked out by Chayanov and his colleagues was rejected as 'capitalist'. Traditional peasant farming systems were swept aside by collectivisation and industrial methods of agricultural production in Soviet Russia.[17]

In the USA populism emerged as a political force in the late nineteenth century, organised by small and medium-sized farmers in opposition to urban-based financial speculators. In the cotton belt and prairie wheat lands many family farmers with excellent commercial and technical expertise were threatened by poor prices and high credit charges. Similarly, opposition to colonial exploitation led to populist pro-rural, pro-peasant development strategies in other parts of the world, notably Africa. Small-scale farmers are characterised by the capacity to make adaptive changes with the potential to maintain a sustainable relationship between society and the land.

Conclusion

The economic theory which informs Western policy makers in their allocation of land use offers little guidance in the quest to preserve the fertility of this vital resource.

You have looked for much, and, lo, it came to little; and when you brought it home I blew it away. Why? says the Lord of Hosts. Because my house lies in ruins while all of you hurry off to your own houses. Therefore the heavens above you have withheld the dew and the earth has withheld its produce. And I have called for a drought on the land and the hills, on the grain, the new wine, the oil, on what the soil produces, on human beings and animals, and on all their labours.

(Haggai 1:9-11)

This Old Testament text remains as fresh and relevant as when it was first written well over 2000 years ago. The economy of the 'developed' world takes the earth for granted at its peril. Despite its apparent sophistication, it remains in a timeless dependence upon a few inches of topsoil.

NOTES

1   Quoted in Orr, David (1994) *Earth in Mind: On Education, Environment, and the Human Prospect.* Washington DC. Island Press.

2   Orr, op. cit pp80-83.

3   Wilkinson, Richard D. (1973) *Poverty and Progress* London. Methuen.

4   A historical examination of the origins of farming is beyond the scope of this book. See, for example, Bender, Barbara (1975) *Farming in Prehistory: From hunter-gatherer to food producer* London. John Baker. Note also that the Bible is here cited primarily as a historical record rather than as a religious text.

5   See, for example, Hamilton, Clive (1994) *The Mystic Economist* Fyshwick, Australia. Willow Park Press. (Distributed in the UK by Jon Carpenter.)

6   Berry, Wendell (1981) *Gift of Good Land* North Point Press.

7   Massingham, H. J. (1942) *The English Countryman: A Study of the English Tradition* London. Batsford. pp4-5.

8   *The Ecologist*(1992) 'Whose Common Future?' Vol.22. No.4. July/August. pp132-3.

9   William Cobbett 1813, quoted in *The Ecologist.* op. cit. p133. See also Cobbett, William, (1835) *Rural Rides* London. J. M. Dent & Sons (1948 edn).

10   Massingham (1942) op. cit. p17.

11   Massingham (1942) op. cit. p18.

12 Massingham (1942) op. cit. pp18-19.
13 Massingham, H. J. (1941) *Remembrance: An Autobiography* London. Batsford. p128.
14 Massingham, H. J. (1943) *The Tree of Life* London. Chapman and Hall. p147.
15 Massingham (1943) op. cit. p149.
16 Richards, Paul (1985) *Indigenous Agricultural Revolution: Ecology and Food Production in Africa* London. Hutchinson. p15.
17 Richards, op. cit. p15.

Chapter 5

Labour

No man shall have any more land than he can labour himself, or have others to labour with him in love.

Gerrard Winstanley (1649)

The industrial revolution flowed from the theft of the land from the labourer. The process converted people into a commodity to be hired and fired according to the requirements of distant economic agents operating on the basis of the economic 'laws' outlined in the Appendix. The present chapter explores the historical development of human activity from 'good work' to hired labour.

Work and leisure in the Kalahari

Throughout the major part of human history work was indistinguishable from leisure. Autonomous work, i.e. work which we can control for ourselves, is intrinsically satisfying. Many weighty tomes written by learned men have served to obscure this most basic fact of life. Obsessed with recording the struggles through which the few sought power over the many in warfare and in trade, historical and social studies have forgotten that for most of the time people derive satisfaction from their daily lives. Hence anthropological studies of so-called primitive or indigenous peoples classify activities according to Western thought. The following examples indicate the limitations of this approach to an understanding of what it is to be human.[1]

In the 1960s and 1970s studies like those of Richard Lee's of the !Kung San of the Kalahari brought refreshing new light upon the lifestyles of gatherer/hunters. In contradiction to previous assumptions, longevity compared well with the percentage of elderly in industrial populations. Indeed, the elderly, even when blind or crippled, were respected for their special knowledge and skills, participating in decision making and ritual curing. Furthermore, young people were not expected to provide food until they were married, at around twenty years of age. Hence about forty per cent of the population supported the surprisingly large percentage of the population who were 'unproductive' and contributed relatively little to the food supplies. 'This allocation of work to young and middle-aged adults allows for a relatively carefree childhood and adolescence and a relatively unstrenuous old age'.[1]

Lee studied the amount of time devoted to the quest for food, the most important single activity in the life of gatherer/hunters. Although the number of people
in a camp varied as visitors came and went, it was possible to count the number
of adults engaged in gathering, hunting, staying 'at home' or visiting. It was also
possible to calculate 'the number of man-days [sic] of work as a percentage of
total number of man-days of consumption'. In order to make comparisons with
a Western lifestyle, Lee calculated the work activities of the people on the basis
of a seven-day 'work-week'. On average, the adults worked two and a half days
per week, perhaps twelve to nineteen hours a week, getting food, despite the
harshness of their environment.

Since the !Kung do not collect and store a surplus of foods, they have no times
of exceptionally heavy work, such as planting and harvesting, and no periods of
unemployment. Typically, each woman gathers sufficient food on one day to feed
her family for three days. The rest of her time is spent 'resting' in camp. In
company with the other women she may embroider, visit other camps, or enter-
tain visitors. On a typical day at home, one to three hours of her time are taken
up with 'kitchen routines, such as cooking, nut cracking, collecting firewood, and
fetching water'. The steady rhythm of work and leisure is maintained throughout
the year.[2]

Despite the apparent inhospitability of the landscape, what emerges from Lee's
study is a picture of a hassle-free lifestyle. Even in this study, however, words like
'unemployment' are used to contrast 'work' and 'leisure'. By inference, 'productive employment' is unpleasing. This is highly misleading. Fetching water,
minding children, selecting foods and other necessities from the wild are intrinsically satisfying activities, a part of the pattern of life conducted as a social
activity, not in isolation for individual gain within a power structure which operates on a 'carrot and stick' principle. Individuals participate fully according to
their age, skills and talents. In a clearly structured society, all stand to gain satisfaction from their mastery of the inherited body of knowledge. Responsibility for
daily tasks is not delegated to unknown power figures beyond the control of the
individual.

Man the hunter

I have been advised that the following section is too stridently feminist and
ought to be omitted. I apologise. It is not meant that way. Curiously, my feminist
friends do not approve either, as they dislike seeing women portrayed as the
natural providers. I am simply using factual material which is widely available.
These examples are selected from a considerable range of studies drawn from
indigenous societies. Whatever the activity, if it is done by men it is considered
prestigious, whereas if it is done by women it carries little public prestige outside
women's social groupings. I refer the reader to the passages on Thorstein Veblen
in the Introduction.

Illuminating though studies by Lee and others may be, they remain premised upon the misleading assumption that male activities are central to human survival. Hence they devote particular attention to hunting as the precursor to 'productive' economic activity and trade.

In the 'hunting made us human' tradition, Bailey[3] observed the Efe of Central Africa, one of the last remaining gatherer/hunter societies. Already influenced by social, economic and ecological pressures from beyond their borders, Efe women work on neighbouring farmlands to supplement their collecting activities. Meanwhile, the men continue to hunt, fashioning arrows tipped with poison, only one in eight of which will ever find its target. The men favour the less productive group hunts which enable each man to bring at least some meat home to be divided according to custom and shared with their wives and children. It looks suspiciously as if the men had a strong desire to bring back some food some of the time in order to share in the everyday food supply provided by the women. As in other gatherer/hunter societies, Efe women, children and men were predominantly dependent for survival upon the bounty of nature as harvested by women. Efe men exhibited no particular desire to ensure that 'their' women and children did not go hungry. Bailey offers no explanation of the men's reasons for taking back to camp such little meat as was acquired in order for it to be shared. The men might as soon have made a fire in the forest and eaten it all themselves.

Indeed, in an incident described at length by Bailey, the men spent the day obtaining a hive full of honey from the top of a tree. Making no attempt whatsoever to share their haul with the women and children, they gorged themselves until their normally flat stomachs were round and distended. Each ate a pound and a half of honey and larvae in the space of thirty minutes, emitting large burps. Having eaten the honey, the men returned to camp with bloated stomachs, informing their wives that they had worked hard, but there was little in the hive. Although Bailey notes that on such evenings the wives made little attempt to cook for the hunters, he does not pause to indicate how the wives and the children manage to avoid starvation. The men spent over a tenth of their waking hours foraging for honey: honey was rarely brought back to the camp.

While historical man-the-hunter was 'bringing home the bacon' in this way, historical woman was engaged in 'non-productive' child care and the development of the motor, emotional, artistic, social and political skills essential to human survival. There is no reason to suppose that throughout prehistory people existed in a state of mind-boggling ignorance while awaiting the appearance of civilised Man. The happy-go-lucky, boys-will-be-boys approach to hunting would not appear to be a sound basis for the origins of human knowledge and learning.

Hunting as a luxury activity

Most forms of animal life survive by locating themselves in close proximity to their food supplies. Humans can live in most habitats, and eat a wide variety of foods. As human groups moved into new territories, inedible foods were rejected and new foods and medicines identified. Individuals in indigenous societies are known to be capable of identifying hundreds of edible and inedible plants and to be familiar with the properties of healing herbs. In recent decades studies have shown that forest inhabitants have knowledge of hundreds of plants with potential economic benefit to the world, including plants commonly used as contraceptives, cures for fungal infections, tooth ache and many other purposes.[4] Furthermore, archaeologists have stumbled across numerous examples of a prehistoric ability to know and to care. Ancient graves provide evidence of the use of herbal cures, and the long-term tending of wounded and disabled members of the community. The extended period of dependence of the human infant upon its mother appears to have led to the extension and preservation of a body of human knowledge vital to the care of loved ones. Cooperation between humans and with nature was more fruitful than the competitive and self-seeking game of hunting. As Asen Balikci[5] has shown, nomadic societies have rarely based their survival upon hunting alone. Where this has occurred, as in the Netsilik Eskimos, it was only possible with exceptionally high rates of infanticide and senilicide.

Hunting was only able to develop into warfare and trade on the basis of communal provision of necessities, underpinned by the development and preservation of a common body of knowledge. It is impossible to over-stress the dependence of the human group on the 'steady state' subsistence economy based on knowledge of, and cooperation with, the natural world.

Settlement to agriculture entails more work in the form of planting, weeding, harvesting and storage, but becomes essential to support male-centred 'economic' activities of warfare and trade. The gatherer/hunter societies had a sounder relationship with the environment. They inhabited a world where food and the other necessities of life were available in abundance. So long as family size did not outstrip the capacity of the mother to provide comfortably for each child, intelligent humans remained in control of their relationship with their food supplies. Wide birth spacing secured a comfortable relationship with the land: short birth spacing resulted in larger families, greater strain on the environment and more work for all adults, particularly women. Hence women's shared control over their fertility, through segregation of the sexes and observance of various taboos associated with sexual activity, was an essential element in the hunter/gatherer economy. There is very little evidence to suggest that countless generations of women put their brains on the back burner in order to live in a permanent state of near-starvation while they waited for man-the-hunter to get his act together.[6]

As Pierre Clastres[7] demonstrates in his study of the Guakaki of the Paraguayan tropical forests, foods are not gathered on the basis of chance findings. In certain cases highly favoured foods are the product of 'a sort of cultivation'. The 'guchu' larva, which grows in half-rotten tree trunks, is very rich in fats. It is eaten in large quantities by all. Even a baby at the breast will nip off the heads of larvae with its fingernails. The favoured food is 'cultivated' by cutting down the palm tree, leaving an 8 cm stump. The rest is cut into 30 cm sections, ideal for the larvae to feed and grow. In this way the food source is established for later collection. After many months of travelling the group will return to the site of cultivation, giving a pattern to their travels. Each larvae bed is the 'property' of the people who cut it, and no-one else touches it. The harvest is shared and eaten collectively. This small example demonstrates the potential range of skills and knowledge developed by indigenous peoples in their differing habitats across the globe.

Settlements and farming

The evidence suggests that people had the technological ability to farm long before they decided to exploit their knowledge and settle down to the annual cycle of sedentary cultivation. Limitation of family size appears to have provided a more rational means to the maintenance of a lifestyle based upon sufficiency, high productivity and a pleasing variety of work patterns. Settlement to farming entails increased workloads, involving considerably more labour than the planned collection and preparation of food in season. The underlying motivations for settlement are examined more fully in Chapter 6. Whatever those reasons may have been, the 'achievement' of the Industrial Revolution in England was to remove from the worker the land with which he both supplemented his income and refreshed his spirit.

The nomadic lifestyle is highly egalitarian and cooperative. Although beautiful artifacts can be fashioned by nomadic peoples, they necessarily travel light and tread gently on the earth. Their wealth is in story, skills and tradition, in mime, dance, music, song and knowledge of the earth and the ways of the natural world. Some early forms of settlement may well have been enriched by these traditions, bringing them to peaceful exploitation of the land. However, settlements offer scope for development of inegalitarian social stratification: some families become dominant, in a position to exploit the rest of the people and demand tribute as in the example of the pharaohs of Egypt in Chapter 4. In Western society it is a commonplace necessity to 'work for' somebody else, accepting their orders on promise of rewards and punishments determined by the master/employer. To gatherer/hunters and early settlers on the land, the right of some to control the work of many is not so obviously a necessary fact of life. Slaves taken by force can be starved and beaten into cooperation with the master. However, slavery is not a sound long-term basis for human cooperation. Divorced from their traditional cultures, slaves become degraded human beings. Kept in ignorance of knowledge and learning, brutalised by ill-treatment, the slaves' best hope is in freedom to rejoin their original culture or full absorption into the host culture. Where neither option is viable, they may form a brooding underclass more prone to destruction than reconstruction of sound social and ecological relations.

It would be a mistake to dismiss pre-industrial lifestyles as forms of hand-to-mouth existence. For the majority of people most of the time, access to the land, its natural materials and a body of traditional knowledge handed down from generation to generation provided ample resources for provision of a pleasing lifestyle. In all viable societies individuals had the duty to learn and pass on a vast range of skills and knowledge. Skills included the selection, collection and preparation of food; the making of clothes and ornamentation; the birthing, rearing and education of new members of the group; collection and use of building materials, woods, metals, clays and animal materials (bone and hide) for shelters, tools and implements; basic health care, and the care of the infirm or elderly; the singing of songs and the telling of stories in order to learn and transmit to others the means of interaction between human companions and the group's common relationship with the land. Significantly, the learning process was not conducted under conditions of threat and punishment. The child or young person's pride in development of adult skills, coupled with the innate curiosity which is a central feature of what it is to be human, provided the essential motivation for effective learning. Classification of these activities into 'work' (something to be avoided) and 'leisure' (something to be desired) remains nonsensical, save in terms of Western economic thought.

The medieval guilds in England

From time to time powerful warlords succeeded in separating some people from their land and communities, pressing them into slavery on the land, in the military, in the construction of prestige buildings and in sailing the seas. However, most people remained attached to a particular place. All had an equal chance of maturing from innocent childish ignorance through adult responsibility to respect in the wisdom of old age.

In pre-industrial medieval England the countryside was dotted with farm-villages governed according to peasant traditions. In the growing towns trade guilds evolved a similar style of operation. Apprentices and journeymen were taught the craft and all its secrets, being brought to live in the same house as the master, as one of the family, without class distinction. The only distinction was in age and skill. Provided with meat, drink, lodging clothes and perhaps a small wage, apprentices were not regarded as a form of cheap labour. Their numbers were restricted, and often they might be sent abroad to learn the language in France, Holland and Belgium, the better to conduct their trade. Apprentices were trained to progress in their skills in order to become master in their own right, able to set up their own household.[8]

As Pauline Gregg explains, strict standards were enforced by the guilds, the craft or trade being operated within the household. It was essential not to break the rules as expulsion meant ruin. Many guilds included some women, others, like the silk weavers, were exclusively of women. Often guilds were exclusively open to men, although widows, wives and daughters of members were admitted in certain circumstances.

An early form of division of labour, the guild system led to industrialisation. Textiles were the key trades leading to development of the economy of employment, in which some worked for others for a wage. As trade in woollens became increasingly profitable, land was enclosed to provide pasture for sheep. At first, master clothiers took wool out to weavers who made or bought their own looms. Often the whole family helped with the weaving, done in their homes to supplement their incomes in kind from the land. One possible motivation for the performance of this form of 'work' for others may well have been the removal of access to common pasture and woodlands as lands were enclosed for sheep pasture and other purposes.

The introduction of wage slavery

The earliest wage arrangement occurred when the master clothier bought several looms and put them in a shed or outhouse, perhaps near his own dwelling. Weavers would leave their own homes to gather with others at a 'place of work' where they would remain for an agreed time for a stated wage. 'Here is the factory system in embryo: the employer owns the raw material, the instruments of production, the place of production; the worker owns neither raw material nor instrument, nor does he use his own home'.[9]

The wage arrangement was the final step in removing the worker from land and culture. Workers cease to be responsible for the allocation of their time or the nature of the tasks undertaken when at 'work', i.e. in 'employer's time'. Through this fundamental shift of responsibility the employer, however benevolent, assumes the role of master over a slave. The employer can give or remove responsibility for a task, while the employee renounces, for the period of employment, a fundamental aspect of what it is to be human, the right to self-determination of action and its attendant responsibilities.

The contrast between the guild system, in which apprentices are taken into the family home of the master, and the wage arrangement, where workers leave home to sell their labour for a specified time, cannot be overstressed. The former arrangement is keyed into culture and community. The latter represents the first step towards the creation of a parasitical economy capable of disregarding the needs of the land and community upon which it nevertheless remains utterly dependent. Significantly, in their 'free' time workers remain in their own homes and communities where they continue to undertake tasks essential to the survival of their families. Within so-called 'developed' economies, half of all adult hours of work continue to be unpaid time spent in service to home and community. Even today, these hours of 'informal' work remain essential to the operation of the formal economy. The arrangement contrasts starkly with the pre-industrial world in which the individual was fully responsible for all their actions as an adult member of the community. Today, as worker, consumer, householder, investor or parent, the individual embarks upon many courses of action, the outcomes of which lie beyond their sphere of knowledge and responsibility.

From economic democracy to work slavery

At the onset of industrialisation workers left home for only a part of their lives to sell their labour for a wage. For the rest of the time their household continued to provide a substantial part of their material necessities directly from the land. A study of the lead mines of the northern Pennines in the early industrial revolution explores the many differing payment arrangements for workers in the mines. The author of the study notes that most mining families had smallholdings from which they could supplement the cash incomes from the mines. Furthermore, the production of food, including the pasturing of cows, was a source of pride and satisfaction to the families, and an opportunity for the younger and older members of the family to make a contribution. Hunt cites a number of studies of the continued production of subsistence food in upland lead-mining areas, listing rhubarb, potatoes, turnip, cabbage, lettuce, onions, carrots, plums, raspberries and currants. Collection of peat and 'craw' coal for fuel was safeguarded by certain Enclosure Acts, relieving the pressure on the cash wage. Up to the mid-nineteenth century 'most miners lived in scattered dwellings, valuing smallholdings more than easy access to places of work'.[9]

Similarly, the clothing areas were populated by people dependent upon old-established smallholdings:

> and it is likely that many families had clung to their bits of land through various changes, whittled down and insufficient for a livelihood in themselves, perhaps, but a useful supplement to industrial earnings. It could well be that, with garden and field, crops and animals, the clothing worker made the best of both worlds, and was better off than a factory worker proper on the one hand, or a peasant on the other. In practice it all depended on a combination of the two. But so long as he kept some open space to call his own, there can be no doubt that the worker who lived within touching distance of his trees, his crops, his bees and his animals was far removed from the proletarian created by a later age.[11]

In England, as across the world, many recognised the vital role played by the right of access to the land in assuring economic, and hence political, freedom. As Gerrard Winstanley powerfully explained, if the rich 'hold fast this property of Mine and Thine, let them labour their own land with their own hands. And let the common people, that say the earth is ours, not mine, let them labour together, and eat bread together upon the Commons, Mountains and Hills'.[12]

Historians have argued that the loss of common rights to the land was essential, a price worth paying along the path towards improved farming technology and material progress. In words with an uncannily familiar ring, the dispossessed were informed that things had to get worse before they could get better. Such an approach cut no ice with the much maligned Luddites, concerned as much with the loss of traditional rights to land, livelihood and village culture as with hatred of the machines which they smashed.[13]

The theft of the land

Total dependence upon a money wage turned human beings from responsible adults into wage slaves. It continues to be argued that workers 'voted with their feet' to leave the land and enter into industrial employment. However, while evidence for this vacuous assumption is spectacularly thin on the ground, details of the degraded conditions under which people were forced to work for the profit of others cover miles of library shelves. Local historian Ian Dewhirst has described conditions of life and work in nineteenth-century Keighley in graphic detail. He quotes from the work of a local vicar, published in 1805:

> This parish [Keighley] lies immediately North from that of Bingley, in the course of the Are, with little which can interest the eye, the memory or the imagination... Before the introduction of manufactories, the parish of Kighley [sic] did not want [lack] its retired glens and well-wooded hills; but the clear mountain torrent now is defiled, its scaly inhabitants suffocated by filth, its murmurs lost in the din of machinery, and the native music of its overhanging groves exchanged for oaths and curses.[14]

As in many other areas of industrialisation, conditions of work in Keighley would have driven all but the most saintly to curse and swear. A witness to the Sadler Committee on factory conditions in 1832 was asked for his impression of the physical condition of children in Keighley. He replied:

> I have observed them in the Sunday-school, and at times in the street, living in the midst of them, that they have not that healthy appearance we see children generally have in the country; frequently without arms, without legs, and without fingers; and we can produce in Keighley 150 rickety, crooked-legged children, owing to their being over-wrought.[15]

Dragged from their beds early in the morning in all weathers, children as young as five or six years old were forced to creep under the machinery to free obstructions while machines were working. Long hours of work contributed to frequent accidents as children fell asleep at the machines, and to long-term deformities from standing to operate machines for up to twelve and thirteen hours a day.

Industrial progress was founded upon use of people in what amounts to forced labour. The practice, which has close similarities to slavery, dates back to the sixteenth and seventeenth centuries when coal mining became profitable. Total coal output rose from 160,000 tons in the mid-sixteenth century to two-and-a-half million tons by 1800 through the excavation of deeper mines, reaching as deep as 90 metres. However, in addition to drainage and general safety, labour was a problem. According to economic theory, people flocked to the mines to sell their labour because it was in demand. Although a nineteenth-century government report exposed conditions of mining labour at that date, little is known about earlier conditions. In the nineteenth century accidents were frequent and terrible at the deeper levels. Floods, explosions and gaseous fumes gave rise to stories of evil spirits in the depths of the mines. With these conditions to tolerate, it is scarcely likely that the mines were operated by a voluntary labour force responding to free market conditions.

Gregg speculates that mine owners probably employed 'rogues and vagabonds'. Justices of the Peace may well have directed the 'unemployed' to mining under the wide provisions of the Poor Law. Women and children were also employed, giving rise to degradation of mind and morals. Their plight, like that of so much 'labour' in ships, factories and mines, was determined by the very people who had stolen not only their land, but also their birthright of access to the common pool of inherited wisdom and knowledge. According to the Poor Laws, 'sturdy' beggars who 'refuse to labour, living in idleness and sin and sometimes by thefts and other crimes' should not be encouraged to beg. Rather, they should be compelled to labour for the necessities of life.[16] Hence those displaced from the land by speculating landlords became a pool of exploitable labour, their 'idleness' justifying their oppression.

By the mid-eighteenth century some three-quarters of the population of towns were already engaged in some forms of non-agricultural pursuit. Activities included industry, shipping, trade, commerce, transport, insurance, docking, shipping clerks, customs officers and carters. 'Yet ... the country still pressed in on the town, no-one was far away from open country and few families were completely cut off from the land'. As iron and coal mines disfigured the landscape, wild areas remained accessible, and there was still continuity from generation to generation in the country areas.[17] The countryside continued to supply workers for domestic service and the many practical tasks essential to maintain the new merchants and industrialists as they embarked upon the profitable business of economic development.

Progress to economic servility

Despite the existence of excellent texts providing elegant reviews of reality, economic historians have persisted in the view that industrial progress was essential, an inevitable condition of permanent advance. In *The Village Labourer 1760-1832* the Hammonds explain that popular resistance to enclosure had much in common with the fierce resistance to the introduction of spinning and weaving machines, the 'symbols of the engines of the Industrial Revolution. History has drawn a curtain over those days of exile and suffering, when cottages were pulled down as if by an invader's hand, and families that had lived for centuries in the dales or on their small farms and commons were driven before the torrent ...' [18]

However, the suffering wrought by enclosure and dispossession was not limited to one generation. The commons were the 'patrimony of the poor'. However needy, the commoner's child was born with a spoon in his or her mouth. Each child arrived in a world in which they had a share and a place.

The civilisation which was now submerged spelt a sort of independence for the obscure lineage of the village. It represented, too, the importance of the interest of the community in its soil, and in this aspect also the robbery of the present was less important than the robbery of the future. For one act of confiscation blotted out a principle of permanent value to the State.[19]

Although at times wretched, ill-clothed and ill-fed, peasants had yet to lose their status, before they were converted into the casual, drifting figures of the urban proletariat. Within the peasant community in England, the hope of re-establishing its independence remained until the English aristocracy destroyed the promise of such a development when it 'broke the back of the peasant community'. The enclosures brought a new system of classes. The peasant had rights and status, sharing in the fortunes and government of the village, 'standing in rags but standing on his feet'. The labourer had 'no corporate rights to defend, no corporate power to invoke, no property to cherish, no ambition to pursue'. In fear of the masters, the labourer faced a future without hope. Until the time when the Hammonds were writing,

> no class in the world [had] so beaten and crouching a history, and if the blazing ricks in 1830 once threatened his rulers with the anguish of his despair, in no chapter of that history could it have been written, 'This parish is at law with its squire'. For the parish was no longer the community that offered the labourer friendship and sheltered his freedom: it was merely the shadow of his poverty, his helplessness and his shame.[20]

Quoting movingly from the *Annals of Agriculture* 1784-1815, the Hammonds explain the growth of drunkenness among the labouring classes as a direct result of loss of autonomy and access to land. However hard they worked, labourers could never control their own destinies. They had become wage slaves.

Work and motivation

For families dispossessed of rights of access to the land, acceptance of waged work for the parents and children became the only means of obtaining a liveli-hood. Children were sent from the countryside to seek work as domestic servants (a major source of employment throughout the eighteenth and nineteenth centuries), clerks, dockers, navvies on canals and railways and casual workers on the land. In the absence of traditional forms of livelihood, work on terms dictated by the employer came to be demanded as a right. Good conditions, and prospects of better pay through specialised training and experience, gilded the lily of a servile status. Within a couple of centuries all forms of service to the community, including medical care, nursing, politics and education came under the 'work-for-wages' rule. Despite the apparent status implied by the term 'salaried employment', the 'educated classes' became the servants of the business community. Only a very select few with independent means could consider risking the loss of their livelihood in the event of a clash of interest with their employing body.

Nevertheless, when forced to adapt to changing circumstances people continued to exercise natural human ingenuity and imagination, specialising in different skills and adapting their individual talents to make the best of their circumstances. Throughout the developed world people are classified by what they 'do' for a living, meaning what they are paid to do. However, people's reasons for working are by no means so simple.

Work

In their best-selling book *Your Money or Your Life*, Dominguez and Robin have explored this issue in the USA. There are many definitions of work. Kahlil Gibran regards work as 'love made visible'. To E. F. Schumacher human work has three purposes: it provides essential subsistence requirements, it provides the opportunity for all of us 'to perfect our gifts like good stewards', and it enables us to cooperate with others 'so as to liberate ourselves from our inborn ego-centricity'.

On the other hand, an economist would define work as something people do not want to do; hence the need for a money reward to compensate for 'the unpleasantness of the work'. Quoting from Studs Terkel, Dominguez and Robin note that in this sense work can be regarded as a form of 'violence — to the spirit as well as to the body'. For many people, work involves ulcers, disputes, frustrations, nervous breakdowns and a daily round of humiliations. The object of the exercise is to survive the day. Nevertheless, the 'walking wounded' search 'for daily meaning as well as daily bread'.[21]

In their chapter entitled 'Love or Money: Valuing Life Energy — Work and Income', Joe Dominguez and Vicki Robin raise such questions as, 'Did we win the Industrial Revolution?' or 'What is the purpose of work?' They conclude that, given a certain degree of income security, earning money is merely one, not necessarily the dominant, reason for seeking employment. Satisfactions derived from work include: enjoyment, duty, a sense of service, acquisition of new skills, prestige, status, socialising, personal growth, a sense of achievement, creativity and fulfilment. Dominguez and Robin argue that these satisfactions are not dependent upon receipt of a money wage. Often, identical tasks continue to be undertaken in home and community without monetary reward. Furthermore, Richard Douthwaite quotes research demonstrating that satisfaction derived from work can be reduced when the worker is reduced to employee status:

> In a goldmine of a book, *The Market Experience*, Professor Emeritus Robert Lane of Yale University describes an experiment in which students were paid to do a boring task and got more pleasure from it than a control group that was unpaid. However, when another batch of students was paid to do interesting work, they found it less rewarding than those who had done the same task for nothing. In fact the paid group doing the interesting job got even less enjoyment than those who had been happy to do the boring task unpaid

because they thought it was useful. Lane quotes from a study by F. Thomas Juster that shows that, almost regardless of the nature of their work or their social class, people prefer their jobs to most of their leisure activities.[22]

In theory labour is an unsatisfying activity to be avoided if possible. In practice, work is often regarded as a worthwhile activity, providing satisfaction in its own right and not merely as a means to an end. Curiously, while the capitalist employs others to make commodities for profitable sale in order to accumulate personal wealth, workers normally prefer occupation to idleness. Nevertheless, monetary reward remains the dominant motivation for seeking employment among the poorer classes.

Work and leisure

Thorstein Veblen published *Theory of the Leisure Class* in 1899. He observed that capitalists do not accumulate wealth because of its ability to satisfy physical wants. Rather, acquisition of wealth through industrial production is a predatory activity, indicative of prowess and achievement in hunting and warfare. The rich accumulate and consume wealth in ways that display that wealth, demonstrating power, honour and prestige. They secure their position as the 'leisure class' through 'conspicuous consumption' of wealth and gentlemanly leisure pursuits, while studiously avoiding menial labour. Under capitalism occupations rank from absentee ownership at the top of the scale to creative labour, the most repulsive and vulgar at the bottom of the scale. Women's work receives low reward, if any, and ranks below that of men, offering even the most menially occupied man some comparative status. As Veblen explained, types of employment fall into a hierarchical gradation of respectability, from the most to the least predatory:

> Those which have to do immediately with ownership on a large scale are the most reputable ... next to these in good repute come those employments that are immediately subservient to ownership and financiering, such as banking and law. Banking employments also carry a suggestion of large ownership, and this fact is doubtless accountable for a share of the prestige that attaches to the business. The profession of law does not imply large ownership; but since no taint of usefulness, for other than the competitive purpose, attaches to the lawyer's trade, it grades high in the conventional scheme. The lawyer is exclusively occupied with the details of predatory fraud, either in achieving or checkmating chicane, and success in the profession is therefore accepted as marking a large endowment of that barbarian astuteness which has always commanded men's respect and fear... Manual labour, or even the work of directing mechanical processes, is of course on a precarious footing as regards respectability.[23]

Wealthy absentee owners live in large cities, spending their time with lawyers, accountants, stockbrokers and other advisers. They buy and sell stocks and bonds, manipulate financial deals and engineer schemes of sabotage and fraud.

Detached from the life of the natural world, the soil and any practical pursuits connected with the sustaining of life, all activities of wealthy capitalists, their food, clothes and lifestyle, are concerned with impressing their importance upon others. Their prestige is visible, the predatory nature of their activities disguised under the veneer of respectability.

Theory of the Leisure Class provides an entertaining account, by no means dated, of the ways in which the leisure class displays its wealth and prowess. Veblen shows that conspicuous consumption entails conspicuous waste. The housing and possessions of the rich are ornate, largely useless and prominently displayed. Practical and useful artifacts affordable by the common people are considered vulgar and tasteless. Furthermore, a substantial citizen must dress and display his wife as a symbol of good taste, providing her with many servants in order to demonstrate her value as an ostentatious trophy of beauty and uselessness. Villas on the coast, yachts, elaborate chateaux, all rarely used but prominently visible, are vital as demonstrations of respectability.

Veblen's entertaining accounts of the antics of the rich leads to his observation of great significance. The culture of wealth acquisition is based upon envy and discrimination. Hence one of the most important guarantees of a growing economy is emulation. The very classes of people who perform the arduous, menial tasks for little pay might be expected to be discontented, posing a threat to the status quo. Indeed, the economically secure elements of the working class, those with marketable skills essential to maintain the fabric of society, might pose the greatest threat. Their instincts of workmanship, coupled with the associated traits of logical thought, ability to cooperate, mutual aid and general humanitarianism might lead them to push for socialism, dismissing the leisure class. Emulative consumption neatly forestalls the danger. Deprived of access to traditionally spiritually uplifting and socially acceptable occupations on the land, the poor live in a state of 'chronic dissatisfaction'. They are therefore drawn onto a treadmill of emulative consumption, or 'consumerism' as it has more recently been called.

The object of accumulation is to achieve high rank in comparison with the rest of the community. So long as the comparison appears distinctly unfavourable, the normal average individual lives in a state of chronic dissatisfaction. Once a target level is achieved, it becomes essential to widen the gap between oneself and the average standard. Hence workers are caught up in a treadmill of emulative consumption, their very response perpetuating their misery. They believe they could be happy if they could acquire more and more. So they go into debt, increasingly dependent on moving up in their jobs to secure more income. The only way in which they can transcend their chronic dissatisfaction is to please their employers. Hence they will never engage in any disruptive or radical activity.

However, in his earlier writings Veblen was optimistic that the values associated with the instinct of workmanship, the acquisition of dignity and happiness through good work for the majority of people, would triumph over the predatory, pecuniary values of business. Veblen's contemporaries, the guild socialists of the first two decades of the twentieth century, sought to create forms of industrial organisation capable of re-introducing a socially and spiritually sound work ethic.

Guild socialism

The guild socialists sought to abolish the power of absentee owners in the management of industry. They noted that jealousies, feuds and competition in the higher ranks of industry led to apathy and indifference in the lower ranks of large organisations. Individuals lost all life-giving interest in their work, which became merely a means to an end. As Arthur Penty, a leading guild socialist, explained:

> From a mercantile point of view it matters little whether the population be engaged in the production of food or motor-cars. But from a national point of view there is all the difference in the world, since the production of food guarantees a nation's future while the production of motor-cars does not. Yet when we remember how big business dominates national policy we cannot be surprised that, being, as we saw, heedless of its own future it should be equally heedless of that of the nation. If, therefore, one aspect of the return to fundamentals is a return to the principles of justice, honesty and fair dealing, the other aspect is a return to the land; to a life lived in closer contact with the elemental forces of nature.[24]

Concern with the mental, moral and spiritual aspects of work remained the distinguishing feature of guild socialism. Guild socialists sought an end to capitalist exploitation of the work of others. They rejected the notion that intrinsically unsatisfying work could result in production of any value save in money terms. Where the exercise of human free will and self-expression is removed, work is degraded into unsatisfying toil. Satisfying labour is spiritual in conception. By contrast, 'the philosophy of capitalism is materialist from beginning to end. It bases itself on the maxim that 'the greatest benefactor of humankind is the man who makes two blades of grass grow where one grew before', caring nothing for the soil from which it springs, nor the texture of the grass when it appears'.[25]

In the founding years of 'Old Labour', guild socialists sought to detach the trade unions from the system of wage-slavery. Their vision was to provide opportunity for all to give useful and worthwhile service to the community freed from the necessity to produce a profit for an employer. Control of agriculture, industry and community services would cease to remain in the hands of profiteers and status-seekers. Instead, all who worked would assume responsibility for their work, cooperating within a network of 'national guilds'. Decision-making would be decentralised on a subsidiarity basis to the lowest practicable level. The watchword 'service' would replace that of profit and a scramble for a greater share of it. Guild socialists deplored the acceptance by the Labour Party and the trade unions of the necessity to sell their labour to the highest bidder in order to maintain the corrupt, socially divisive and environmentally destructive capitalist system. In similar vein, more recently Douthwaite notes that satisfaction from employment is highest where the firm is owned and controlled by those working in it.

Conclusion

A particular barrier to constructive thought on the subject of work is the familiarity of the word. Ingrained within its meaning is the notion that work for an employer for money is an essential and worthwhile activity. Hence people in the so-called 'developed' world face a considerable problem of understanding what it might be like to live in a society fundamentally different from our own. Emulative consumers remain pre-occupied with quality housing, status cars, high-class holidays and 'society weddings', living under the illusion that they can be 'king' if only for the day. Women shop until they drop, convinced that glamour brings status. In the home, the last bastion of personal control over life, kitchen and home crafts are despised and rejected in favour of convenience foods, packaged, denuded of dirt, feathers, blood and guts. 'Ready-made' homes and gardens, furnishings and clothes are bought off the shelf, their source and their ultimate disposal as waste a matter of no concern to the consumer. And finally, the family and the body itself assume secondary importance to the necessity to work for money. The child in the womb is aborted if it conflicts with the economic pursuits of the individual as worker and consumer.

In the meantime, Westernised elites in Third World countries continue the work of destroying socially and environmentally sound traditions. In the name of progress, ecologically and socially sustainable patterns of cooperation based upon mutual respect and traditional practices are swept aside by predatory males seeking to establish themselves as the 'leisure class'. The imposition of taxes, the enclosure of land and the denial of customary means of communication remove traditional livelihoods and associated self-esteem. When piped water is introduced, the village women no longer meet together to communicate and share collective decision-making. Instead, they accept low-paid work to pay for the telephone and to meet all the other bills -convinced, perhaps, that their loss of control over their working lives makes them 'better off'.

NOTES

1. Lee, Richard B. (1968) 'What Hunters Do for a Living' *in* Richard B. Lee and Ivan DeVore (eds) *Man the Hunter* Chicago. Aldine. p36.
2 Lee, op. cit. p37,
3 Bailey, Robert (1989) 'The Efe: Archers of the African Rain Forest' *National Geographic* Vol. 176. No.5. Nov: 664-686.
4 Myers, Norman (1985) *The Gaia Atlas of Planet Management* Gaia Books.
5 Balikci, Asen (1968) 'The Netsilki Eskimos' *in* Richard B. Lee and Irven DeVore (eds) *Man the Hunter* Chicago. Aldine (1975 edn).
6 For an exploration of the issues raised in this paragraph see Lee, Richard B. (1979) *The !Kung*

San. Men, Women and Work in a Foraging Society Cambridge University Press. Also, Wilkinson, Richard D. (1973) *Poverty and Progress* London. Methuen.

7   Clastres, Pierre (1972) 'The Guakai' *in* M. G. Bicchieri (ed) *Hunters and Gatherers Today* Holt, Rinehart and Winston.

8   Gregg, Pauline (1976) *Black Death to Industrial Revolution* London. Harrap.

9   Gregg, op. cit. p151.

10 Hunt, C. J. (1970) *The Leadmines of the Northern Pennines in the Eighteenth and Nineteenth Centuries* Manchester University Press.

11 Gregg, op. cit. pp151-3.

12 Quoted in Gregg, op. cit. p180.

13 Bull, Angela (1980) *The Machine Breakers: The Story of the Luddites* London. Collins.

14 Quoted in Dewhirst, Ian (1974) *A History of Keighley* Keighley Corporation. p10.

15 Quoted in Dewhirst, op. cit. p18.

16 Gregg, op. cit. pp260-8.

17 Gregg, op. cit. pp298-9.

18 Hammond, J. L. and Hammond, Barbara (1913) *The Village Labourer 1760 - 1832* New York. Kelley (1976 edn). p104.

19 Hammonds, op. cit. pp103-4.

20 Hammonds, op. cit. p105.

21 Quoted in Dominguez, Joe and Robin, Vicki (1992) *Your Money or Your Life: Transforming Your Relationship with Money and Achieving Financial Independence* New York. Penguin. pp220-1

22 Douthwaite, Richard (1996) *Short Circuit: Strengthening Local Economies for Security in an Unstable World* Totnes. Green Books. p45.

23 Veblen, op. cit. p156. See also Veblen, Thorstein, (1923) *Absentee Ownership and Business Enterprise in Recent Times* London. George Allen and Unwin.

24 Penty, Arthur, J. (1921) *Guilds, Trade and Agriculture* London. George Allen and Unwin. p75.

25 Reckitt, Maurice B. and Bechhofer, C. E. (1918) *The Meaning of National Guilds* London. Cecil Palmer (1920 edn). p20.

Chapter 6

Money

ECONOMISTS, AND ESPECIALLY MONETARISTS, tend to overestimate the purely economic, narrow and technical function of money and have placed insufficient emphasis on its wider social, institutional and psychological aspects. However ... money originated very largely from non-economic causes: from tribute as well as from trade, from blood-money and bride-money as well as from barter, from ceremonial and religious rites as well as from commerce, from ostentatious ornamentation as well as from acting as the common drudge between economic men.

Glyn Davies (1994)

In *A History of Money*, Professor Glyn Davies notes that the man in the street is willing to admit ignorance of the economics of imperfect competition and the theory of free markets: nevertheless, 'he feels himself equipped and more than willing to take sides in the great monetarist debates of the day'. Professionals and amateurs alike launch into lengthy debate on monetary affairs and monetary theories in the quest for answers to perplexing questions of economic uncertainty, inflation, unemployment, stagnation and recession. Is it possible, Davies wonders, that control over the money supply could provide remedies for all these ills?[1]

This chapter reviews the origins of money and the money economy with a view to seeking answers to Davies' question. Money is the life-blood of the formal economy. It is therefore of crucial importance to understand exactly what it is and how it came into being. In order to grasp the essential characteristics of the institutions which govern the checks and balances of the money system, I have followed Veblen's lead (see Introduction). The formal economy is modelled upon the successful predatory raid. It is parasitical upon cooperative activities, including agriculture, the industrial arts, the cultural arts, the caring professions and the sciences, which together produce real wealth.

Hunting[2]

The origins of the formal economy lie in prehistoric hunting of the type practised by the Efe hunters of the rain forest (see Chapter 5). On the whole, hunting is an uneconomic activity, prestigious but highly wasteful in terms of time and energy expended relative to rewards gained. However, hunting offers rich returns to the individuals concerned in terms of kudos and access to the produce of the human group: as an activity it is highly 'serviceable to the individual', to use a Veblenian phrase (see Chapter 1). Man the hunter has a central place in anthropological and archaeological accounts of the origins of human civilisation. Nevertheless, recent evidence suggests that his activities were subsidised by the ingenuity of the cooperative human group based upon the mothers and their dependent children.

The very earliest tools are unlikely to have been weapons necessary to kill large, fast-moving and dangerous animals. Gathering plants, eggs, honey, insects, fish and small burrowing animals would require sticks for digging and knocking down, rocks for breaking tough shells and sharp-edged rocks for cutting roots and tubers. Containers for carrying collected foods for sharing are likely to have been the key tool and the basis of early social and economic links between individuals. Food sharing appears to have begun between mothers and dependent infants, being extended as adult females included other adults. Females sharing with their male siblings seem to have given rise to generalised sharing with other males. In other words, the pair-bonding of hunter-males and their mates is less likely to have given rise to cooperative activity than the extended period of childhood dependence upon the mothers.[3]

As Professor Tanner (1981) explains, hunting was made possible through the ability of collectors to create an economic surplus. As the mothers raised the children, providing food and education over the extended years of childhood, they developed the intellectual and emotional skills which make us human. Hunting is the product of social pressures, owing very little to natural instincts. Conscious observation of the half-consumed carrion of larger animals would suggest its potential value to humans, not only as a source of food but also as useful materials, bones for needles and pins, and skins for clothing, thongs and containers. However, for a group of humans to deliberately set out with the intention of killing large animals, considerable preparation was necessary. A high degree of motivation was required to expend thought and energy on this unnatural activity on a regular basis.

It is likely that with the failure of oestrus, making females fertile all year round, groups which excluded adult males from their daily collecting activities would be more successful in spacing their births and raising healthy children.[4] However, subsidising healthy males while they sat around camp all day would be less attractive than encouraging them to engage in an activity likely to bring in some return, however uneconomic. The wasteful expenditure of energies on the hunt could enable adult males to take advantage of their natural inability to produce young by developing the physical skills associated with speed and strength. The impractical practice of hunting would bring in a little extra, while providing an interesting diversion. This happy division of labour had the effect of incorporating men within human society. The occasional contribution of each hunter justified his membership of the human group.

Warfare and trade

Prehistoric Man appears to have resembled the eternal William. As recipient of the generosity of cooperating society and the natural world, he was free to wander the countryside making half-educated guesses as to the nature of the universe and his place within it. If the conclusions were wildly inaccurate this did not, at the time, matter a great deal. As the Mothers continued to indulge his whims he, like William, invented increasingly plausible reasons for *not* taking responsibility, coupled with an over-weaning desire for praise and status for what little he did achieve. Hence the elaborate celebrations following a successful hunt. The unfortunate result was that in prehistoric times Man established his own version of his relationship to society and the natural world. He has been perfecting it ever since.

Through ceremony men devised ways to deny their physical, social and economic dependence upon their productive mothers and sisters, who formed the core of human society. Male imagination devised social forms to mark the entry of new adult males to their exclusive social club. Often the female life-cycle was imitated. However, male society was at pains to exclude the female and the feminine, exalting the difference between the sexes and emphasising the significance of male roles in society. The physiological and psychological skills of strength, speed, aggression and control of fear were praised and encouraged. Emotion, intuition, affection and other female traits were denigrated. While women kept human society together, men retreated to their secret stores of ceremonial objects associated with the hunt. They developed rituals and ceremonies from which women were normally excluded. Such rituals were designed to establish the basic social truth that men were prestigious and women were expected to provide for them. Male aggression, violence and competitive behaviour would seem to have preceded settled farming.[5]

Evidence of violence between human beings dates back well into prehistoric times. The preconditions for warfare and aggressive competition lay in the ability of woman-based society to cooperate with the natural world in the provision of basic subsistence. Furthermore, anthropologists have discovered a close link between trade and warfare. The sport of killing one's neighbour was refined into merely threatening violence while demanding some reward or trade-off. As Marshall Sahlins notes, among tribes and clans which existed throughout the world until very recent time, seemingly voluntary exchanges took place under threat of personal violence or open warfare. Refusal to give or to accept was tantamount to declaration of war, implying the denial of an alliance. Normally, people arranged a treaty, coming to an arrangement of peace and exchange. Hence, in Sahlins' view, the development of markets and towns represents a triumph of human wisdom and intellect over the folly of war. The desire for possession of *things* overcame the attractions of using force and violence. Men had to lay down their arms and resolve their differences through exchange. Nevertheless, unsuccessful transactions continued to result in war.[6]

Social historians accept the 'fact' of man's violence towards his fellow men. In his struggle to progress to civilisation, trade presented a rational alternative to violence. However, the economic bedrock of human society remained rooted in the cooperative activities of gaining subsistence and rearing the next generation. Trade was no more productive than warfare. Trade, like warfare, depended upon the ability of human society to provide for its subsistence needs. The mothers and the natural environment continued to support man in spite of, and not through, his evolving politico-economic activities.

Two problems faced the successful tribe. First, the trade or plunder of non-essential material goods — beads, flints, feathers, shells, skins, salt, metals and decorative artifacts — could only remain very small-scale if most people continued with a nomadic lifestyle. Large quantities of superfluous items could not be carried from place to place. Second, a sedentary lifestyle enabled societies to increase their populations, creating extra strains upon human and natural resources.

The story of the development of trade and civilisation is one of destructive violence motivated by individual greed and the desire for power. The orthodox version of this story disregards the part played by cooperation within families and communities, and with the natural world, in the rebuilding after destruction and in the maintenance of supplies of food, fodder, shelter, clothes and fuel, coupled with the rearing of generations equipped with physical, intellectual and emotional skills. Armies could lay waste crops, destroy cattle and kill human beings as the few sought power and wealth at the expense of the many. However, powerful rulers could not create the sustaining life forces upon which they remained dependent. Civilised Man created a fantasy world in which Mother, in the form of society and nature, gave him everything he wanted, cleared up the mess after him, and applauded his every action. The formal cash economy continues to operate upon premises identical to those established by the Efe-style hunters of prehistory.

Sharing and wealth

The foregoing exploration of non-monetised societies provides vital clues as to the true nature of money. In his study of stone age economics Sahlins observes that forms of trade necessary for establishing peaceful relations between men did not normally involve exchange of staple foods. 'Food is life-giving, urgent, ordinarily symbolic of hearth and home, if not of mother'.[7] Food is readily and necessarily shared, while bark cloth, beads and other luxury items can be used in the process of 'balanced gift-giving', the earliest form of trade. In most social settings, the giving of an equivalent money return for food is considered unseemly, altering the relationship between the giver and the recipient. Even in Western society, if invited to a meal at a person's house it would be most inappropriate to offer money to the host. Throughout human history food has remained a 'delicate barometer', a mechanism for starting, sustaining or destroying (by exclusion) social relations. Food is not shared with enemies.

In societies across the world, even where money transactions take place, food may be shared, but not bought. 'Food has too much social value — ultimately because it has too much use value — to have exchange value'. Food, taken from the earth, is not classed as wealth. Rather, it is regarded as 'holy food', to be freely given. Within a community the sharing of food may normally be linked with cooperation in the necessary work of the household economy. On occasions food may be exchanged for money or other forms of wealth *outside* the community or tribe. Nevertheless, trade presupposes provision of subsistence necessities from within the home community.

Trade, through its facilitator, money, does not have its origins in the provision of a subsistence minimum. It has always been concerned with the acquisition of wealth and power by individuals who premise their actions upon the continued provision of basic skills and materials by society and the natural world. The formal economy is parasitical upon its foundations in the social and the natural.

As civilisations came and went, war lords and robber barons minted precious metals into coins, using them to bribe people to part with their time and their possessions. Money was useful as a means to secure power over others, while the ostentatious show of wealth displayed that power. However, for most people most of the time, subsistence requirements over their lifetimes and those of their families came directly from the land and their own labours. The formal economy of money and trade was the preserve of the rich and powerful, only occasionally impinging upon their everyday lives. On the land and in the farm-villages where most people lived, money was not used for everyday transactions. Where it was used, the underlying threat of force was never far away. For most people, access to the land was of far more significance than access to a money income. The evolution of Western civilisation into the global economy has, for the first time in human history, brought money into the daily lives of the majority of people.

Types of money

Money is a generally acceptable means of exchange. From ornamental feathers to blips on a computer screen, quite literally money can be anything commonly considered acceptable as currency in exchange for goods and services. As we see in the Appendix, the role of money in economic theory is obscured by theoretical conventions which assume that money has no part to play in the processes of production, distribution and exchange save that of pure facilitator.

For most of pre-industrial history this was probably an accurate description of affairs. Bands of marauders or traders seized goods from each other or bartered peacefully. Where trade took place a common currency, such as precious metals which could be measured by weight, performed a useful role in facilitating exchange. Nevertheless, such trade remained, in essence, barter: money merely provided a useful measure, a convenient medium of exchange, a store of value and a standard of deferred payments. The creation of money, the expansion or contraction of its supply and the manipulation of its availability for specific purposes had no part to play in the everyday labours of ordinary people. The relationship between people and the land which supplied them with their livelihoods was largely unaffected by the getting and spending of money.

As trading in luxury items expanded, money became a vital tool in the conduct of that trade. However, the trade which formed the precursor of the formal economy as we know it was far more closely allied to piracy on the high seas than with the provision of a subsistence minimum for all. Privateering is the basis of modern economic activity. The getting and spending of money is not ethically neutral: it is a highly political activity which takes place outside the democratic processes of government. The transformation of money from a neutral arbiter of exchange to the bottom line determinant of economic relations was dependent upon the development of banking.

Early banking and debt-finance

By and large, up to and including the Middle Ages, money acted as economic textbooks suggest: it facilitated barter. Whether it took the form of gold or silver, coined or uncoined, it was virtually entirely credit-based. While money was a useful commodity for facilitating trade, it had virtually no role or place in *initiating* production and distribution. Money was used in the exchange of non-essential luxury items and provisioning for war: it was not normally associated with access to everyday subsistence.

The story of economic development presented in school history books gives rise to the powerful misconception that money and banking were probably instrumental in facilitating production of and trade in basic subsistence requirements. The formal education system conveys a fundamentalist belief that the division of labour, enhanced by new technologies and scientific advances, put more clothes on backs and food in stomachs than ever before in human history. In this context, studies of money and banking are premised upon the supposition that the role of finance was to facilitate production and distribution of essential wealth and luxuries. Closer examination reveals an identification of money and banking with state power and the interests of private individuals at the expense of the community and the mass of the disinherited and powerless. The rise of the money economy is closely associated with denial of people's traditional rights of access to the means of putting clothes on their backs and food in their stomachs. The fundamental transition from pre-industrial to industrial economic activity is associated with the introduction of 'creative accounting' by the early bankers.

To examine the development of banking it is necessary to consider its origins in trade, itself more closely allied with warfare and private piracy than the hallowed halls of commercial banks and the cushioned environment of their university training grounds would seem to imply. From the Crusades through the wars with Spain, gold and silver were seized or acquired by trade under veiled threat of force. Successful ventures sailing the high seas brought home to speculators rich rewards in terms of precious metals or spices and other oriental goods capable of fetching high prices in terms of silver or gold. Accumulated gold required safekeeping, initially undertaken for a fee by goldsmiths.

English goldsmiths were centrally involved in the development of two key concepts fundamental to industrialisation, investment and sound money. Investment of accumulated wealth, or 'savings', was necessary to acquire further wealth through profits. When a ship put to sea in order to trade it represented an investment from which profits might be expected. The financial process involved bore little resemblance to domestic and local trade as, for example, between brewers, bakers and carpenters. Where goods were produced by guilds and domestic producers for sale in a local market, finance was not essential to the initiation of production. Equally, where money merely aided barter, the quality of the money was of little importance. However, where the function of money involved a time element, the soundness of the money became significant. In the Middle Ages, London goldsmiths played a key role in the development of finance and international trade by ensuring that coins were not debased, through the London Goldsmiths' Company.[8] Before considering further the role of goldsmiths in the evolution of modern financial institutions, two further developments require attention, the Treasury tally and bills of exchange.

The Treasury tally

'Minting and taxing were two sides of the same coin of royal prerogative',[9] Davies explains, as he explores the close links between monetary and fiscal policies. Until the Royal Mint was moved to the Tower of London in 1300, the royal treasury and the Royal Mint were literally part of the king's household. The king's need of money to finance his government and fight his wars gave rise not only to careful control over the minting of coins so as to prevent debasement of the coinage but also to an early form of extension of the money supply, the tally system. As Davies explains, the use of a notched stick or 'tally' as receipt for taxes paid persisted in Britain long after banking methods and cheap paper money rendered them redundant. Predating the founding of the Bank of England, the tally system gave evidence of payments on notched sticks, providing a model for modern banking methods and the use of paper money.

As in private business affairs, the first tallies were used by the Exchequer as simple receipts. Commonly made of hazel, about nine or ten inches long, the tally would be notched according to the size of payment agreed: a straight indented notch the width of a man's hand would represent £1,000, while the groove for £1 would just take a ripe barley corn. On registering the agreed tax or other cash payment in this way, the stick would be cut in half long ways, so that the two parts could match up or 'tally' at a later date. The larger section, including the uncut handle or 'stock', was retained by the creditor (the Exchequer), the smaller part or 'foil' being kept by the debtor (the citizen). Hence the historical derivation of government or corporate 'stock' and the term 'counterfoil'.

However, the Exchequer tally grew to be far more important than a straightforward record of tax-collection and receipts. While usury remained strictly forbidden, the tally became a convenient mechanism for circumventing such prohibition, functioning as an early means of raising loans and extending credit. The tally acted as a 'wooden bill of exchange, and a sort of dividend coupon for royal debt'. As the right to claim *future* taxes was sold in this way, the discounting of tallies (payment of ready cash at a discount below the full value of the tally) led to the development of an embryo money market in London. In this way the total volume of credit grew upon the foundation of Exchequer debt (in effect, borrowing against future taxes). Towards the end of the Middle Ages the demand for money was rapidly outgrowing the European supply of silver and gold. Under these circumstances the use of the tally 'effectively increased the money supply beyond the limits of minting'.[10]

It is worth considering the embryonic stages of the development of profitable investment in some detail. Throughout the Middle Ages annual taxes were raised, originally in kind but later in cash, to maintain the royal household. As the year progressed, it often became clear that extra taxes, beyond those agreed in the spring, would have to be raised in the form of 'aids' and 'subsidies' to pay for wars and ransoms to consolidate royal power. In the twelfth century church, state and finance were 'almost inseparably interconnected', service to the Exchequer being rewarded by the position of bishop.[11] Thus the Divine Right of kings lent an aura of respectability to high finance from its inception.

Once the debt owed to the king had been agreed and registered on the tally, the stock held in the Exchequer could be used like money in payment of a debt by the king. The king's creditor was then entitled to collect payment from the king's original debtor. In this way, the exchequer became a clearing house for writs and assignments, increasing the flow of money while economising on the use of coined precious metals.

Dividends and discounts

In a similar way, tradesmen who supplied goods to the royal court were paid in *tallia dividenda* or dividends which could be redeemed at the Exchequer, leading to the later system of dividend payments on government stocks and bonds. Redeemable at the Exchequer, tallies distributed in this type of transaction reduced the use of coinage. The use and discounting of tallies facilitated arbitration between various spatial and time preferences, while avoiding the sin of usury. The system offered the potential for the exercise of considerable skill and imagination. For example, cash payments could be made to the Exchequer in anticipation of taxes. If the tally issued represented a greater amount than that actually paid in, for example by twenty-five per cent, it became a reward for the loan: the growing practice of discounting disguised interest payments. In these various ways the wealthy devised means to reward 'productive savings', creating profitable debt on the basis of the desire of the crown to meet its expenses in peace and war.

Fiscal and financial effects of the Crusades

Distant wars and foreign trade had far reaching effects upon English financial history. The Crusades, lasting from 1095 to the mid-fifteenth century, involved the conduct of war over unprecedented distances. The sending and equipping of armies involved payments for supplies, equipment, allies and ransoms, for which money had to be safely and quickly transferred. Hence the Knights of the Temple and the Hospitallers acted as semi-banking intermediaries in the transfer of capital financed through heavy forced loans and taxation.

The conduct of war gave rise to trade in luxuries. Carpets, rugs, drugs, fruit, jewels, glass, perfume and finely-tempered steel were included in return cargoes as ships returned from carrying armies to the eastern Mediterranean. Hence the drain of real resources in the form of the export of knights and their retainers, camp followers, armour, horses, equipment and shipping was matched by a drain in cash and bullion to service the distant campaign and pay for the new luxuries from the east. The value of medieval money therefore retained a high degree of stability.

European financial institutions evolved from the first recognisable 'banks', which were concerned with foreign exchange, first in Italy and France and then in the Low Countries. The transfer of large amounts of capital necessary to finance the Crusades gave rise to the development of financial techniques capable of facilitating the growth in volume and variety of goods traded, including an escalation in the use of bills of exchange. In the quest to avoid the penalties of usury while creating new credit, 'fictitious' bills of exchange were circulated. Some of these were mere domestic deals posing as foreign. Often the bills represented credit unattached to real goods and services. 'In this way the constraints of a limited supply of gold and silver money were being overcome by the extension of paper credit, just as in the more backward use of wooden tallies for such purposes in England'.[12]

Knights Hospitallers and Knights of the Temple

The banking techniques later developed in England were learned from foreign conduct of quasi-banking and foreign exchange and from the specialised services of the orders of international chivalry, the Knights of the Temple and Hospitallers. Founded to provide hospitals and medical care for the casualties of the Crusades, the two orders became formidable economic and political forces in Western Europe and around the Mediterranean shores. Their commercial, military and financial activities laid the foundation for the key institutions of industrial development.

The two orders of knights owned ships, depots and storehouses, keeping their own private armies and occupying strong points and castles at key ports and inland towns. Therefore they were in an excellent position to arrange the safe transfer of valuable goods, specie and coins. Significantly, they were also able to avoid the necessity for moving specie and coins by arranging bilateral or trilateral offsetting transfers.

As kings and merchants placed vast deposits in their safe-keeping the knights increased their already vast resources by lending to creditworthy borrowers, disguising the interest element of such deals through the use of foreign exchange and bills of exchange. Gifts included large estates, in Europe and in England. As contacts were made through war and trade, knowledge of machines and techniques flowed to Europe from China and the Middle East. According to Davies, it is no coincidence that the first windmills and watermills for fulling wool were built in England on estates belonging to the Templars. Industrial innovation was premised upon commercial and financial operations.

From chivalrous myth to financial reality

Tales of the Crusades circulating in twentieth-century school textbooks include the 'damsel in distress' theory for the fall of Jerusalem, and the discovery of the imprisoned Richard by his faithful servant Blondel playing Richard's favourite tune and listening for his master's response in song. However, money, not chivalry, lay behind these events. The conduct of the Crusades required repeated, urgent and heavy demands for cash, raised through subsidies, tithes, taxation of personal property and other forms of taxation. Failure to provide sufficient funds led to the fall of Jerusalem, while Richard I's Third Crusade turned out to be 'a most expensive adventure'.[13] The conduct of war led to increasing indebtedness, in its turn leading to the growing significance of the role of money. The royal prerogatives on the minting of money and raising taxes were inextricably interconnected.

Before setting out Richard I effectively privatised publicly owned assets, selling as much as possible to supplement the taxes. He granted patents and charters to persons, guilds and towns, in return for cash, so that he could buy allies, ships, armies and munitions. His capture on the return journey led to demands for a ransom of the fantastic sum of 150,000 marks, i.e. £100,000, which far exceeded the whole of the average revenue of the kingdom. Much of this sum was quickly raised through further taxes on incomes, property and production, supplemented by further sales of royal offices and privileges and by generous gifts, including 'the proceeds from the whole of the year's wool clip by the Cistercian monks from their sheep-rich lands'.[14] The latter example illustrates an early phase of the trend to profitable use of land for financially lucrative production.

The Golden Hoof

Markets in medieval times existed primarily for the exchange of surpluses resulting from unpredictably benign weather conditions. Normally basic crops met the needs of the local community outside the sphere of monetary exchange. From time to time famine prices for foodstuffs occurred, but normally medieval markets were thin. Transport of bulky agricultural products was slow and difficult, limiting the volume of goods available in a specific place at a particular price. Storage facilities were equally limited. Where feudal ties remained strong, payments might be made in money or in kind. These payments tended to remain stable, although if feudal dues were paid in kind the market value of the part of the harvest received by the knight, lord or bishop would be subject to considerable variation. Wool was a major exception to this rule.

The development of wholesale trade in wool and other luxuries was heavily dependent upon credit. Even when the woollen clothing industry remained technically a domestic system, as the trade developed each stage of production was dependent upon the wholesale extension of credit. Extension of credit was the essential prerequisite for sales of land and of rents, while foreign exchange and 'fictitious' bills of exchange also facilitated the extension of credit essential to the conduct of profitable trade.[15]

Bills of exchange

The development of money, banking and financial institutions was crucial to the destruction of traditional patterns of communal obligations, simultaneously offering individuals the opportunity to gain power over land and communally produced resources. The desire of kings to fight wars to consolidate their wealth and power provided opportunity for profitable investment and speculation. Minting, taxation, production for profit and trade were inextricably intertwined. As individuals fought for control over land and resources, the powerful dispossessed the weak in the quest for profitable investment at the expense of the common good. The financial mechanism of debt provided the impetus for wealth creation, which in turn gave rise to industrialisation. Expansion of the use of bills of exchange and modern banking institutions drove industrial growth through debt creation and the requirement for debt repayment.

The bill of exchange, developed in connection with foreign exchange and distant wars, provided the basic model to be elaborated upon by a variety of financial instruments. The practice of offering a bill of exchange indicating a *future* intention to pay fundamentally altered the role of money in the economy. The use of a paper receipt to transfer ownership of real wealth in the form of gold or specie appears no more than a commonsense transaction. If merchant A in London wanted to buy cloth from merchant B in York he faced a dangerous six day journey during which he risked losing the gold. It seemed sensible for merchant A to leave the gold in safekeeping, sending a bill of exchange to settle his debt to merchant B. In this way the debtor, merchant A, agreed to pay an agreed sum at a fixed *future* date to the holder of the bill, merchant B. In effect, money is being invested in a profitable venture on the basis of *financial* viability. Control of resources is moving from the community into the hands of financial institutions. At this point, money ceases to be a mere facilitator of exchange, becoming instead the lifeblood of economic growth, its flow regulated by financial institutions and upheld in law.

The next step is for the creditor, merchant B, to use his bill to settle his debts to a third trader by signing his name on the bill. The bill could be passed from hand to hand until arrival of the fixed date on which payment was promised. The holder of the bill on that date could present it to the original debtor who had issued the bill. In this way, there was no need for the gold to leave the vaults at all. However, in the course of its journey the bill might fall into the hands of, say, a shipbuilder who needed the money to buy timber and pay workers' wages. The bill of exchange could be used to borrow from a goldsmith or rich landowner, the lender holding on to the bill until it was due for payment.

The significance of this development cannot be overstated. It placed production of goods for the market onto a production-for-profit basis, revolutionising the relationship between manufacturer, worker and consumer. It was now possible for a manufacturer of woollen cloth, for example, to lay claim to resources in order to produce goods for distant markets specifically for the purpose of personal financial gain. The manufacturer might receive an order for woollen cloth worth £1,000. Note that at this point, although a deal is struck no goods exist: we are starting to use a money system which works over time.

To meet the order the manufacturer needs to buy wool from a farmer, to hire labour to convert the wool into cloth and to pay for transport to the commissioning merchant. His lack of money might prevent him from meeting the order. However, the buyer could offer a bill of exchange, promising to pay £1,000 on the date when the goods were due to be delivered. Now the woollen manufacturer could present the bill to a goldsmith in exchange for gold. The goldsmith would not pay the full amount, charging a discount against death, bankruptcy or other failure of the manufacturer to meet his order. The key development here is that the manufacturer is in a legally enforceable state of debt to the goldsmith. He must meet his future obligation in order to remain in business.

Banking in England

Domestic banking in England evolved as a means to support the nation's enterprises in war and trade. Throughout its evolution, short- and long-term debt provided the crucial controlling influence over banking development. In the process the desire of the rich and powerful for more riches and power took precedence over traditional checks and balances protecting the rights of the poor. The monarch's constant need for money to fight wars gave rise to a tax farming system during the Stuart years, from 1604 onwards. Through this system a group of rich individuals paid sums of money to the king in advance as a licence fee, conferring the right to collect for him the various taxes and customs dues, transferring the agreed amount to the king on a monthly or quarterly basis and pocketing generous expenses. In this way rich and influential middlemen made loans to the king in anticipation of collection of local revenue, placing the burden of the formal cash economy upon local communities throughout the land. This early business community carved out the rules of the game of finance, forming 'a kind of collective banking syndicate, being able to lend on a scale that no one individual (prudently) could'.[16]

However, it was the goldsmiths who were the key players in the development of English banking. Merchants set out to make money for themselves, and to the extent that they were successful they required safe storage for their gold and silver. Until 1640 the Tower of London was considered the safest place for storage. However, gold, 'the sinews of war', was essential for the purchase of warships and the support of foreign rulers. Charles I's seizure of the gold of the leading merchants in 1640 in an attempt to finance his side in the Civil War led to the practice of merchants depositing their gold with London goldsmiths for safe keeping.

At first, goldsmiths agreed a small charge for storage of gold, issuing a receipt to the merchant. Soon the receipts began to circulate, taking the form of the first banknotes. Also, a merchant who had deposited gold with a goldsmith might write a note to the goldsmith asking him to pay a third person a certain sum, the earliest form of paying by cheque. In general practice, bankers found that only about one note in ten was presented for payment of gold. It was therefore possible for goldsmiths or 'bankers' to lend out nine or ten pounds for every pound of gold deposited with them and charge high rates of interest to borrowers of these notes. Although the charging of interest on fictitious loans appears fraudulent, the process of loan-making itself is more significant. By lending to 'sound' business people engaged upon 'profitable' ventures the early bankers were on course towards establishing a political economy based upon greed and scarcity. Loans were not issued in cases of altruism or necessity. Rather, resources were mortgaged to private profit.

The Bank of England

In 1688 the Dutch William of Orange was invited to take the British throne. William's acceptance was motivated by the desire to counteract the power of France. At that time, Holland was the world's leading commercial and banking centre. Antwerp was Europe's major port and the Dutch East Indies were the richest and most profitable of all colonial possessions. The invitation to William of Orange was the eventual outcome of the earlier Anglo-Dutch Wars, marking Britain's growing economic and commercial power.

Anxious to wage war at once, William sought £1,200,000 to meet his expenses. The emerging business community of the London goldsmiths, merchants and rich financiers, aware of the dangers of lending large sums to individual monarchs, proposed that the financing of wars should be taken out of the king's hands. Royal revenues from estates and parliamentary grants should be spent on the upkeep of the royal staff and palaces. The demands of the London business community and the monarch's need for money to fight a war led to the Act which established the Bank of England.

It is worth considering in some detail the stages whereby the personal royal debt of a powerful individual ruler was transformed into a public or 'national' debt controlled by parliament. The historical process of political economy has traditionally been portrayed as a gradual democratisation of the political and economic process. More realistically, we can see that the development of national banking removed traditional patterns of mutually supportive obligations by consolidating power in the hands of a few. The vast riches which flowed from colonisation of distant lands enabled the many to be bought off and appeased by the patronage of the rich. The education of the educated classes presented a world view which conveniently forgot the barbarism at home and abroad which accompanied the rise of Western civilisation.

The Bank of England was established for the mutual benefit of the business community of the City and the monarch of the day, as the latter sought to wage a long war against Louis XIV, the most powerful ruler in Europe. In the final thirty years of the seventeenth century the need for cash to fight wars vastly outstripped the ability of goldsmiths or new forms of taxation to provide it. Davies quotes Chandaman's figures to show the increases in financial demands being made by the government. In the fifteen years from 1670 to 1685 net fiscal revenue came to £24.8 million. In the fifteen years from 1685 to 1700 it more than doubled, reaching £55.7 million. Between those same periods net borrowing jumped seventeen fold 'from a total of just £0.8 million in the first period to £13.8 million in the second'.[17]

Hence there was a perceived need to tap new sources of long-term borrowing through some form of perpetual loan. The Bank of England came into being as a means to make finance available at a rate of interest which the government could afford, yet fully acceptable to the lenders because of the other benefits attached to the arrangement. Whereas even a long-term loan would place an unacceptable tax on the already over-taxed population, a *permanent* loan would merely necessitate additional taxation to cover a fraction of the loan in the form of the annual interest or service charge. It was a 'sprat to catch a mackerel'.

In 1694 Parliament passed the Ways and Means Act and confirmed the existence of the Bank of England through the Royal Charter of Corporation in July. A group of rich families agreed to lend the king the sum of £1,200,000, in return for payment of interest at 8% annually. The Act imposed taxes on everyday goods (the real economy), including beer, ales and vinegar, in order to raise the £100,000 payable in interest.

Six of the rich merchants who raised the £1,200,000 became directors of the Bank, which was allowed to issue bank notes to the value of £1,200,000, the value of the loan made to the king. The notes were issued to people who wished to borrow money from the Bank. Like all banks, the Bank made a profit by charging interest on the loans. However, in the first years of its existence the Bank had no gold to back its note issue, beyond the £100,000 provided each year from taxation. The wealth of the Bank's directors, who guaranteed the issue, and the trust of borrowers, who rarely sought to exchange their notes for gold, secured the institutional framework of the Bank of England. The shareholders owned the company jointly, creating a joint stock company, offering greater security than an individually owned firm or partnership of goldsmiths or merchants.

National debt and the South Sea Bubble

The Bank of England, guaranteed by the government, became the main source of loans for large firms and companies, including the East India Company and the Hudson Bay Company. The Bank was used by the government to raise new loans from the public, usually for the purpose of waging costly wars. From the War of the Spanish Succession (1701-13), the War of Jenkins' Ear and the War of the Austrian Succession (1739-48), to the Seven Years' War (1756-63) fought in India, Canada, the East Indies and Europe, the National Debt rose, reaching £20 million in 1696, £50 million in 1713, £78 million in 1748, £138 million in 1763 and £249 million in 1784.

Since the population of Britain in the eighteenth century was around six million, such vast debts might appear potentially disastrous. On the contrary, however, they represented the mechanism whereby Britain gained control over the resources of many and distant lands across the world. Thus loans to the government or to private individuals were profitably invested in seizing the land, property and persons (as slaves) of peoples around the world. Beneath the story of the golden triangle (guns and whisky to Africa, slaves to the Americas, sugar and cotton to Europe), the imposition of the British Raj in India and the many other steps on the march of 'progress', lies the steely motivation of the debt-based money system.

Profitable investment became the order of the day. Inspired by the success of the Bank and the profits of its shareholders, landowners invested money in developing their estates, creating the Agricultural Revolution which turned land from a commonly managed food-producing resource to a privately-owned profitable investment. By 1695 joint stock companies were evolving as profitable investment opportunities, producing arms, gunpowder, coal, iron, tin, lead, linen, glass, paper and silk. Domestic investment was largely governed by smaller, often local, banks.

However, it was the South Sea Bubble which established England's unique form of banking system. Founded in 1711, the South Sea Company sought to break the Spanish monopoly of trade with Central and South America. Following Marlborough's success in the War of the Spanish Succession, the South Sea Company gained the monopoly right to send 4,800 African slaves to the Spanish Colonies and to trade in other commodities. Although its trading activities were only moderately successful, the company attempted to take over the National Debt, exchanging its stocks for government bonds. The company sought to privatise or 'ingraft' the national debt into its company shares, through widespread corruption, including the bribing of members of parliament and the government. After widespread speculation in junk companies 'formed for the most unlikely or most vague purposes — perpetual motion, coral fishing, to make butter from beech trees, to extract silver from lead, gold from sea water, and ... "for carrying on an undertaking of great advantage which shall in due time be revealed"', the South Sea Company became bankrupt.[18]

Following the crash, from 1720 to 1780 the Bank of England emerged as the guardian in law of the money supply, and also of the financial concerns of the government of England. The development of the form and methods of operation of the banking system and the legal structure of companies was influenced by the South Sea Bubble, not only in England and Wales (less so in Scotland) but also overseas. Joint stock companies not specifically authorised by law were outlawed. In due course (1858) limited liability of individuals was guaranteed in law. Through this legislation, individuals could exploit human and natural resources for personal gain irrespective of the common good of society as a whole, and were not even subject to personal financial penalty if their business failed.

Debt and development

However, the legal guarantee of the right of financial institutions to create money out of nothing for the purpose of profitable investment remains the single most significant development underlying industrial 'progress'. Since wealth is customarily accounted in money terms, the definition of money and the process by which it is created are issues of crucial significance. However, as Galbraith (1975) explains:

> The process by which banks create money is so simple that the mind is repelled. Where something so important is involved, a deeper mystery seems only decent ... The coin on deposit served no less as money by being in a bank and being subject to transfer by the stroke of a pen.
> Inevitably it was discovered ... that another stroke of the pen would give a borrower from the bank, as distinct from the creditor of the original depositor, a loan from the original and idle deposit. It was not a detail that the bank would have the interest on the loan so made. The original depositor could be told that his deposit was subject to such use — and perhaps be paid for it. The original deposit still stood to the credit of the original depositor. But there was now a new deposit from the proceeds of the loan. Both deposits could be used to make payments, be used as money. Money had thus been created.[19]

The development of financial institutions followed from the early discovery that money could be created as a debt at the stroke of a pen in order that the debt could be reclaimed with interest. The mortgaging to the banks of land, plant and machinery, and future production fuelled the search for increasingly profitable investment.

Inexorably, as the industrial revolution progressed, common resources were made scarce in order to be allocated according to the mechanism of individual personal greed. Increasingly divorced from the real world of ecologically sustainable sufficiency, the financial markets continue to expand global purchasing power, using speculative instruments, including option trading, short sales, non-trading derivatives, hedge funds, non-deliverable currency transactions and index futures. As a result, financial wealth commanding control over real resources is now concentrated in the hands of a minority elite. Business forecasters, academic economists and G7 leaders, afraid to send the 'wrong signals' to the financial markets, bombard public opinion with 'glowing images of global growth and prosperity. The economy is said to be booming under the impetus of the free market reforms. Without debate or discussion, so-called 'sound macro-economic policies' (meaning the gamut of budgetary austerity, deregulation, down-sizing and privatisation) are heralded as the key to economic success'.[20] While the need to earn money dominates all levels of decision-making, from the individual to national governments and beyond, the question 'what is money, and where does it come from?' hangs unspoken in the air.

Conclusion

Over the last two decades of the twentieth century the share of increased productivity going to labour fell, while that going to profits via shares was vastly increased. The inevitability of the trend to this unsustainable situation was predictable from the early decades of the industrial revolution. Writing in 1945, Massingham described Cobbett's hostility to the commercialisation of agriculture and the spread of industrialism:

> He [Cobbett] prophesied that this financial 'THING' would destroy the stable agriculture of a thousand years... He foresaw that the debt system would become a millstone round the neck of the nation and so it has become. He dreaded that, as taxation increased to feed an insatiable Debt, so security in and responsibility for property would result in a loss of property for the many and too much of it for the few.[21]

At the time, Cobbett was considered 'a stupid and sentimental impediment in the path of progress'. However, by the mid-twentieth century it was becoming clear that a 'secondary economics' based upon manufacturing and the import of cheap foods from abroad was undermining the primary economy of agriculture.[22] As the misuse and corruption of money has displaced all other values, socially and ecologically useful work like tilling the soil, preparing the food, making clothes and tending the sick are undervalued and poorly paid. High rewards go to those in powerful but non-essential positions: the wagers of war, the dealers in international finance, the creators of artificial scarcity and the purveyors of the skills and knowledge of how to control access to the common cultural inheritance. On the whole, consciousness of the distorting effects of money values upon the real-life economy has evolved outside formal educational and research institutions. We take up this story in the following chapters.

NOTES

1   Davies, Glyn (1994) *A History of Money from Ancient Times to the Present Day* Cardiff. University of Wales Press (1996 edn.). p4.

2   A recent report on the work of Chris Stringer of the Natural History Museum, London, shows that gatherer-hunters enjoyed a healthy diet. 'For most of our evolutionary history, our fore-bears got their food from a wide variety of sources: women gathered herbs, fruits and berries, while men supplemented these with *occasional kills of game*, a way of life still adopted by the world's few remaining tribes of hunter-gatherers... Then, about 9000 years ago, agriculture was invented — with devastating consequences.' (Emphasis added.) McKie, Robin and Tredre, Roger, 'It's True. We're all getting too big for our boots.' *The Observer*. 8 March 1998.

3   See Leakey, Richard (1981) *The Making of Mankind* London. Michael Joseph. p92. Also, Tanner, Nancy M. (1981) *On Becoming Human* London. Cambridge University Press.

4   See e.g. Wilkinson, Richard (1973) *Poverty and Progress* London. Methuen, and Tannahill, Reah, (1980) *Sex in History* London. Hamish Hamilton, for detailed evidence to support this assertion.

5   For more detail see, for example, Bettelheim, Bruno (1955) *Symbolic Wounds: Puberty Rites and the Envious Male* London. Thames and Hudson. For a psychiatrist's desperate plea to eradicate irresponsible competitive (juvenile) behaviour in all adults by changing human nature itself, see also Dinnerstein, Dorothy (1987) *The Rocking of the Cradle and the Ruling of the World* London. The Women's Press.

6   Sahlins, Marshall (1974) *Stone Age Economics* London. Tavistock.

7   Sahlins, op. cit. p215.

8   Davies, op. cit. p146.

9   Davies, op. cit. p146.

10 Davies, op. cit. p149.

11 Davies, op. cit. p148.

12 Davies, op. cit. pp155-6.

13 Davies, op. cit. p157.

14 Davies, op. cit. p157.

15 Davies, op. cit. p172.

16 C. Wilson, quoted in Davies, op. cit. p249.

17 Davies, op. cit. pp256-7.

18 Davies, op. cit. p268.

19 Galbraith, John K. (1975) *Money: Whence it Came, Where it Went* Harmondsworth. Penguin. p29.

20 Chossudovsky, Michel (1997) 'Global Financial Crisis' Unpublished e-mail memo.

21 Massingham, H. J. (1945) *The Wisdom of the Fields* Collins. London. p19.

22 Ibid.

Chapter 7

The new world trade order: GATT and the World Trade Organisation

by Alan Freeman

Think of the world economy, and two household names come to mind: the International Monetary Fund and the World Bank, the two supranational bodies created by the Bretton Woods Treaty of 1947 when the allied powers constructed the post-war economic world order. It is less well-known that these two have been joined by another. The World Trade Organisation (WTO), formed in 1994 as a result of the 1986 'Uruguay Round' of negotiations under the General Agreement on Tariffs and Trade (GATT), has emerged as the third pillar of the post-war economic order. Although generally presented as a simple continuation of GATT, it has in fact inaugurated a fundamental change in the organisation of world trade.

The sleeping policeman of the new world order

The GATT has been transformed from an ineffectual chamber of commerce into a powerful device for restructuring the world market in the commercial and financial interests of the leading powers, the core requirement being to maintain the supremacy of the US economy in the face of the largest trade deficit in world history.

The WTO is supposed to expand world trade, generally perceived as a positive and harmless general benefit to all nations. But whatever the free trade rhetoric, its actual role is to integrate the non-aligned and former Eastern bloc nations into an unrestricted market for the products of a select club of advanced nations, to suppress national sovereignty in favour of institutional guarantees for the systematic plunder of this market, and to grant this same club immunity from every competitive threat which might result.

The control of trade has emerged from the entrails of the world market to claim its place, alongside financial blackmail and debt-slavery, as a primary instrument of advanced-country domination.

The new trade agenda

The WTO enshrines a radical new agenda in world trade. Its cornerstones are:

a) liberalising 'services' through GATS (General Agreements on Trade and Services) covering one-fifth of all world trade ($1 trillion). This is an *institutional* change masquerading as trade reform. Since financial services are treated as a 'commodity' it encapsulates a legal obligation to free capital movement, overriding the legitimate right to national economic sovereignty. Moreover the definition of exports has been extended in the case of services to include production by foreign-owned subsidiaries in the host country. Trade regulation has thus been extended for the first time to the internal market régimes of member states.

b) a decisive new trade category of Intellectual Property Rights (IPRs). IPRs have as much to do with trade liberalisation as the free transport of slaves. They *outlaw* trade in products embodying any technology less than twenty years old — that is, almost everything — except as specified by the current owner of the technology. They are an absolute monopoly of the advanced countries: 0.16% of world patents are currently owned by Third World residents.[1] They make the owner of a technical process a separate legal entity distinct not only from the labourer but also the factory or farm owner and the original inventor. They transform the ownership and control of technology into a marketable instrument of domination. They set in concrete the principal market mechanism that impoverishes the Third World, namely the transfer of technological super-profit through trade.

c) large-scale anti-dumping (AD) actions as the preferred protectionist device of the USA, EU and Australia/New Zealand, a practice baldly described by the World Bank as 'a packaging of protectionism to make it look like something different'.[2] As Hoekman and Kostecki remark (p178): 'AD is not about fair play. Its goal is to tilt the playing field'. Before 1986, anti-dumping actions were exceptional events. By 1992 they were universal advanced-country practice. 1040 anti-dumping actions were initiated by the industrialised countries between 1985 and 1992, over half directed against either Eastern Europe (132), the Third World (137) or the developing Asian countries (297). The non-industrialised countries — three-quarters of the world's people — initiated a grand total of 91.

d) the consolidation of a system of trading blocks — 'Free Trade Areas' around the dominant capitalist countries: the European Community (EC), North American Free Trade Organisation (NAFTA) and the Asian Pacific Economic Co-operation (APEC) countries — with specific exemption from the measures imposed on all other WTO members. Though Article XXIV of the GATT proposes stringent conditions that a Free Trade Area must satisfy, these are never applied. As of 1990, only four working parties (of a total of over fifty) could agree that any regional agreement satisfied Article XXIV, three of these before 1957. 'The GATT's experience in testing FTAs (Free Trade Areas) and customs unions against Article XXIV has not been very encouraging... It is not much of an exaggeration to say that GATT rules [on regional agreements] were largely a dead letter' (Hoekman and Kostecki: 219). In short, the advanced countries do what the hell they like.

From consensus to compulsion

This disparate series of changes is being cemented by converting a treaty organisation — the old GATT — into a supranational enforcement organisation that imposes and legislates not just trading relations but the internal property, tax and subsidy régimes of its members. Moreover since the WTO now organises by far the greater part of the world economy, its capacity to organise its members to act in concert provide it with an economic power that can exact a very high price from any country that declines to become a member. It is, in effect, the legal embodiment of the world market.

GATT held protracted 'rounds' of multi-party negotiations aimed at the mutual reduction of specific tariffs, subject to consensus. In effect, it was a brokering organisation for extending the bilateral arrangements which the big players would have made in any case to a slightly wider circle of participants. 'In instances where the choice was between risking serious conflict and attempting to enforce the letter of GATT disciplines — for example on regional integration or subsidies — the contracting parties generally "blinked". In large part this reflects the nature of the institution, which is basically a club. The club has rules, but its members can decide to waive them, or pretend not to see violations.' (Hoekman and Kostecki: 3)

Although historians see the GATT as the principal vehicle of trade liberalisation, this was in large measure because the major powers, under US hegemony, wanted to liberalise their own trade in any case to secure a share of exported US capital during the period when it still enjoyed industrial supremacy. GATT simply invited the others along for the ride.

The WTO marked two decisive changes. Firstly it moved from 'result-orientation' to 'rule-orientation'; trade was now governed by laws and formulas instead of targeted commodities. This extends to legal trade regulations which the WTO obliges member governments to write into their own laws. Most significantly, these rules are now policed.

'Formerly the GATT was not an international organisation (i.e. a legal entity in its own right) but an inter-governmental treaty. As a result, instead of "member states" GATT had "contracting parties"... The WTO is an international organisation that administers multilateral agreements pertaining to trade in goods (GATT), trade in services (GATS), and trade-related aspects of intellectual property rights'. (Hoekman and Kostecki: 23)

If a member country breaches a WTO regulation, an enforcement process is triggered and consensus is required not to implement sanctions but to *prevent* them. If a Third World country seeks exemption to protect its industries or agricultural producers from competition from the technologically more advanced Northern countries, it faces co-ordinated, punitive trade sanctions from all WTO members.

The reconstruction of the world market

What makes such threats effective is a systematic expansion of GATT and the WTO which has culminated in the re-establishment of a global world market previously sundered in two by the outcome of the Russian revolution, two World Wars and the Chinese revolution.

GATT was a minority club with a mere 23 signatories. The balance of forces was so weak that it proved impossible to establish the international trade organisation (ITO), called for in the Bretton Woods agreements. In the 1949 Annecy Round of negotiations a mere 11 countries took part. China withdrew in 1950 and the US, which had followed a fiercely protectionist stance between the wars, abandoned the attempt to secure congressional ratification of the ITO. Though the initial 1947 agreement secured a 21% reduction in US tariffs, the next three rounds secured only a further 8.4% reduction.

The term 'free trade' has never appeared on GATT's formal agenda. The GATT-1947 preamble calls for 'raising standards of living, ensuring full employment and a large and steadily growing volume of real income and effective demand, developing the full use of the resources of the world and expanding the production and exchange of goods'. The principal mechanism was to reduce tariffs and eliminate discriminatory treatment.

No planned economy took part until 1967 when Poland joined, and the Third World countries succeeded in neutralising or blocking the application of the GATT trade agreements to themselves through the non-aligned movement and the 1964 establishment of UNCTAD — the United Nations Conference on Trade and Development — which was formed to press for trade measures to benefit developing countries. The Kennedy Round of 1963 involved 74 countries and was spun out for four years. The practice of picking and choosing which GATT regulations to implement was so widespread it was nicknamed 'GATT à la carte'. The Tokyo Round of 1973 involved 99 countries but lasted six years and was obliged to legalise preferential tariff and non-tariff treatment in favour of developing countries.

While the developing countries were drawn into GATT's orbit, access to a separate economic system in the USSR and Warsaw Pact countries offered them an important degree of autonomy. Though governed (and impoverished) by the world market they could veto many imperialist proposals, imposing selective controls on trade to protect domestic producers, and limiting the drain of capital brought on by unequal exchange, because they could always resort to (or threaten) trade with the Soviet or Chinese blocs instead. The 'Third World' — a term coined by Mao Tse-Tung — took part in trade negotiations, but acted collectively to veto or water down measures that damaged domestic producers, offsetting — though not overcoming — the impact of the world market on domestic accumulation.

By the end of the Uruguay Round, which began in 1986 and ended a gruelling eight years later, the scene had changed utterly. There were now 128 member countries including most former Eastern European countries. The former USSR no longer presented an effective alternative outlet or supplier. Aggressive 'threat-based' US policies, the debt crisis and the draconian intervention of the IMF with its structural adjustment, export-oriented programmes, produced the 'neoclassical counter-revolution' (Todaro 1994:85). Keynesians were replaced on the leading world financial institutions, and wave after wave of neoliberal advisors and political regimes came to the fore in development economics and in the Third World countries themselves. Resistance gave way to capitulation; the new order had arrived.

'Divergence, big time'

What are the material consequences of this new economic régime? The most fundamental point to grasp is that *free trade produces inequality*. The neo-classical doctrine of convergence predicts that in consequence of trade, the disparities between trading nations should disappear over time. The nearest adequate term for this idea is 'cretinous'. No serious known fact supports it.

Characterising 120 years of the world market as 'Divergence, big time', senior World Bank economist Lant Pritchett (1997:12) goes on to examine its more recent phase:

> From 1980-1994, growth per capita GDP averaged 1.5 per cent in the advanced countries and 0.34 percent in the less developed countries. There has been no acceleration of growth in most poor countries, either absolutely or relatively, and there is no obvious reversal in divergence ... taken together, these findings imply that almost nothing that is true about the growth rates of advanced countries is true of the developing countries, either individually or on average. (Pritchett 1997:14)

The dogma which informs the notion of convergence — the theory of comparative advantage — is false. It predicts that all nations will gain from trade. In fact in all trade there are losers and winners, and the greater the extent of the market, the wider the divergences between them become.

This can be offset after a fashion by technical change, so that even with widening differences between nations, the absolute living standards of many nations can for certain periods improve, and this did happen to a degree after World War II. It was facilitated by the absence of generalised multilateral trade regulation, which meant individual nations could to a limited degree determine their own relation to the world market and offset some of its most damaging effects. A small number — the 'four tigers' for example — were even able, on the basis of large capital inflows and (ironically for free-trade dogma) highly-regulated internal markets, especially labour markets, to begin catching up with the advanced powers.

With the Reagan era and above all the arrival of the WTO, this window of opportunity vanished. Now, not only are relative differences between nations accelerating but a growing number of people face absolute declines in living standards, starvation, and ruin. Already in 1990 *Socialist Economic Bulletin #3* calculated that:

- relative impoverishment had become the normal condition of three-quarters of the human race; by 1988 the proportion of the world population in market economies falling further behind the industrialised countries in GDP per capita reached 75% compared with 46% in 1967;
- a striking rise in absolute impoverishment; over the same period, the number of people living in countries registering an absolute decline in GDP per capita had risen twelve-fold, from 71 million to 808 million.

The chart below shows the ratio between the GDP per capita of the richest 25% and the poorest 25% of countries since 1970. It speaks for itself.

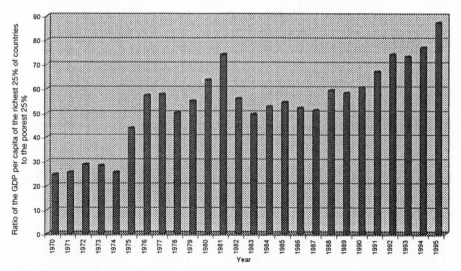

Source: World Bank World Development Indicators 1995. GDP per capita in $, Atlas exchange-rate method.

If unrestrained, the social conflicts generated by such an explosive differentiation would rapidly destabilise market relations. The nation-state provides an institutional framework to contain, ameliorate or suppress such antagonisms — fiscal redistribution, labour mobility, social solidarity in general or, if need be, repression. When conditions of relative uniformity in living standards are found in a single nation, they thus arise not from the *extension* of the market but from the social and political counter-reactions which it generates and the external, political limits to which these give rise.

In world trade these institutional factors mitigating the destructive solvent effects of the unrestricted market are largely absent. Nor can they be overcome by the geographical expansion of the richer nations; the prodigious redistribution of wealth required to create a genuine social solidarity is far beyond the threshold acceptable to the holders of private wealth, or indeed the competitive survival of their business. The absorption of the very small territory of East Germany, with a mere 17 million not very poor people, has driven the richest country in Europe from surplus to deficit for over a decade, called forth one of the greatest fiscal transfers since Marshall Aid, and with more unemployed than in the Weimar Republic, has still not resolved the resulting rampant antagonisms.

The only ultimate solution is the abolition of all national barriers, but the market acts in the opposite direction, as is evident from the explosion of new nations that accompanied — and resulted from — the new trade era imposed by the USA via the WTO, as the disintegration of Yugoslavia and of the former Soviet Union bears vivid testimony.

The formation of any larger blocs or units of the rich nations is a consequence of, and depends on, the extent to which they can unify their own classes around the plunder of the poorer nations. What they require, therefore, is access to the markets of these nations without any reciprocation. Free trade is not only a myth, but a lie.

The world market thus itself calls into being nation-states and just as surely pitches them into conflicts whose result, twice in the last hundred years already, has been global war. This sets absolute limits on what it can achieve. It is therefore one of the principal modern forms in which the market throws up barriers to itself, alongside the creation of social classes. In particular, it leads to a remarkably persistent division of the world which has lasted more or less since the early 1870s to the present day, between a small bloc of very wealthy nations with a near-monopoly over technology, finance, commerce and the means of warfare, and everyone else in the world. This is the actual empirical consequence of the formation of a world market; what has to be grasped is that it is not an accident or deviation from the way the market works, but on the contrary represents the highest development to which the world market can attain.

The WTO as institutional policeman

The re-consolidation of a universal world market is the surest guarantee of the impetuous descent into mass starvation and poverty of the mass of the world's peoples. The only escape for any nation except the small club of leaders is to except itself, in one way or another, from the general functioning of the market. This is why the old GATT could not be an enforcement agency and why the new WTO *has* to be an enforcement agency.

The WTO is now the third arm of the IMF and the World Bank, who work in consort to impose a complete institutional policy framework on the world. The banks impose open markets and free trade as a condition of credit and debt relief.

But free trade is defined to mean a definite institutional régime which overrides the economic sovereignty of all but the largest players. This includes not just full capitalist property rights and the free movement of capital but extends to taxes, subsidies or *any* measure that can be construed as 'unfair competition' — that is, any element of state provision.

The original GATT agenda sought to avert a repeat of the interwar breakup into hostile trading blocs, and prioritised 'non-discrimination' and 'reciprocity'. Non-discrimination states that members must make the same trade concessions to all others as to their 'most-favoured nations'. Reciprocity states that there should be, in some (usually poorly-defined) sense, an equality of loss, which implies an exchange of reductions in barriers. These principles could apply in a small club where they extended essentially bilateral agreements to a wider circle. But in any wider reduction the losses and gains for all partners cannot possibly be the same; there are losers and winners. This is why GATT functioned as it did, as a negotiating forum whose decisions were quite easy to avoid or bypass.

With enforcement and 'rule-based' tariff reductions it becomes impossible to ensure that all parties benefit. Therefore, everyone seeks exceptions to the rules. The industrial powers have established two systematic procedures for imposing their exceptions: (1) the recourse to anti-dumping legislation, and (2) the GATT provision that exempts 'trading blocs' from most GATT regulations. The Third World and transition countries have in contrast lost almost all exceptions they could previously resort to. Moreover, the application of reciprocity is by nature asymmetrical between large and 'small' nations where 'small', it should be remembered, has to be translated into the language of money — in which India is one-fifth the size of the USA. As Hoekman and Kostecki (p163) note: 'fundamentally, it is a fact of life that small economies (i.e. most developing countries) have little to bring to the negotiating table'.

This is the background to two further principles which have risen to prominence with the WTO: 'fair competition' and 'market access'. Under fair competition any non-market production — or indeed, any element of subsidy — of any good for export is immediately in violation of WTO principles.

But the market access rule involves the most far-reaching consequences of institutional enforcement because of the role played by services, which characterise the new stage of capital exports. 50% of the global stock of foreign direct investment is now in services.

Most service activities can only be provided locally, so to reach foreign markets a service provider must locate in the host country. On US insistence, the WTO now provides that services provided by a foreign-owned subsidiary constitute exports and must be able to compete on a 'level playing field' with domestic producers. If generalised, this principle would mean, for example, that a US health company in the UK could initiate a GATT action against the UK for unfair competition by the NHS.

This position is not yet settled. The G-10 group of larger developing countries opposed it vigorously, supported by UNCTAD which proposed to define trade in services as occurring only when the majority of value added is produced by non-residents; a *labour-*, in fact *human*-based criterion. It embodies the simple principle that a nation's residents should determine what happens in their own economy. The US proposal, a *property*-based principle, asserts that the economic right of the owner overrules the political rights of the people.

In 1990 Martin Khor Kok Peng (Mihevc: 37) accurately predicted that: 'the [Uruguay] Round is an attempt by transnational companies to establish sets of international laws that would grant them unprecedented unfettered freedoms and rights to operate at will and without fear of new competitors almost anywhere in the world.' By 1994 the institutional structure for this vision was in place.

Caging the Owl of Minerva: intellectual property and the freedom of trade

There has been a global world market before — at the turn of the twentieth century. When history repeats itself, it either brings new elements into being or transforms old ones so much that they become something else. The reconstruction of the world market has brought with it a new development in property relations: TRIPS or Trade-Related Intellectual Property Rights, which seek to establish a world-wide market in knowledge. In a notable new conflict between the forces and relations of production, the words 'extension of trade' for the first time take on the actual meaning 'restraint of trade'.

Intellectual Property Rights (IPRs) emerged as a central aspect of a general US campaign on trade which Bhagwati (1993) designates 'Aggressive Unilateralism'. This centred on section 301 of the Trade and Tariff Act of 1974, a keystone of US trade legislation. Sections 301 to 306 of this act were further elaborated in 1984, and further changes to sections 301 to 310 were introduced with the Omnibus Trade and Competitiveness Act of 1988.

Section 301 raised hackles because it provided for mandatory action in pursuit of the enforcement of GATT-agreed arrangements, even when GATT procedures had not been exhausted. The US thus set itself above the same international legal framework from which it drew justification for its actions and the claims that its partners had trade obligations to it. The 'Super 301' and 'Special 301' provisions raised this to a new level. Bhagwati (1993) records that:

> Super 301 required the US Trade representative to prepare an inventory of foreign trade barriers, establish a priority list of countries and their unreasonable practices, and then set deadlines for their removal by the foreign countries, and, should they fail to comply, for decisions on retaliation by the United States. Special 301 is similar in its time-bound approach but is addressed specifically to intellectual property rights.

He goes on to remark that:

> Section 301 is characterised by the (wholly distinct) fact that it enables the United States to unilaterally make demands for trade concessions by

others without offering any matching, reciprocal concessions of its own that others might demand in turn.

IPRs fall into three categories: trademark goods (designer and brand products), copyright goods (artistic materials) and patent goods (industrial processes and their products). Copyright law has been significantly extended to include software. Bringing these three categories together signifies, essentially, a generalised alienation of mental products and their transformation into a distinctly marketable entity. A patent, a copyright, or a trademark embodies the right to produce 'something' defined not by what it is or contains, but by the knowledge or information that distinguishes it. Software, the most advanced form of IPR, involves hardly any material product at all. What is actually sold is the legal right — or licence — to use the software in your own production processes.

IPRs, like GATS, defined trade barriers in terms of the internal legal régime. The USA explicitly sought, and through the WTO achieved, changes in the internal structures of its trading partners and rivals to harmonise their copyright and patent laws with its own, with a view to stamping out what it characterised as 'piracy'; the production of copies. It abandoned the existing, bilateral structure for intellectual property safeguarded by the United Nations body known as the World International Property Organisation (WIPO) precisely because of this need. WIPO operated on the old GATT principle of non-discrimination; as Maskus (1993:82) delicately explains:

> the prevailing policy principle in WIPO is national treatment, which requires countries not to discriminate between domestic and foreign firms in IPRs. However, this principle does not prevent the level of protection from being weak if a particular country so desires.

The USA sought to ensure that the country's desires would not enter into the matter. Prior to the Uruguay Round, India provided a seven-year patent protection for pharmaceutical production processes and none for pharmaceutical products; as a WTO member it becomes obliged to extend protection on both products and processes to twenty years. In plain English, the legislation makes it illegal for India to cure its sick, and deprives the Indian people of the sovereign right to do anything about it.

This illustrates our second point: this extension of the market demands a restriction of production. US manufacturers were concerned, not to protect the US markets against floods of fake Gucci watches and pirate CDs, but to prevent other countries making these same or comparable products themselves for their own use. In 1989 the US exported $58.8 billion worth of goods sensitive to IPR, being 16.1% of its total exports, whilst Brazil exported $2.0 billion, that is, 0.2% of US imports, and imported $2.4 billion, that is 13.1% of its own imports.[3]

IPRs thus created a new category of commodity: knowledge itself. The US compelled the world to make the communication or application of privately-owned knowledge a crime. Imitation was transformed from the sincerest form of flattery into the newest form of theft.

The universal nature of this change, by no means restricted to a small hi-tech sector, is demonstrated in the transformation of agriculture, the occupation of more than half the people of the world. Among its profoundly reactionary consequences is an end to the self-sufficiency of world agricultural production. Producers are now obliged to abandon natural production from their own seed and pay premium prices for genetically engineered seeds; indeed these seeds are neutered so that they do not reproduce.

It must be stressed in case of misunderstanding that this change, like all new social institutions, is transforming earlier institutions into something entirely new. As a means of providing authors, artists, musicians and their publishers with an income, or as a means of providing a modest return to permit inventors to ply their personal guild or craft activities, the old copyright and patent laws were by and large unexceptionable because they conferred the income from creation onto specific *persons*. But social institutions that are specific to persons become something entirely different when the titles to the incomes concerned are alienated, or made generally alienable, and bought and sold by *corporate bodies*. At that point the institution actually becomes corrosive of the very relations it was established to protect and is in this case indeed becoming one of the principal devices for crushing the small inventor, the musician, the writer and the small publisher, gradually subordinating all personal creativity to the impersonal rule of capital.

This process is exceptionally evident in the pop music industry, for example where the modern merchandised artist not only submits to being made into a highly-tailored 'product' but surrenders the rights to her or his own identity in return, to the extent that, for example, George Michael was moved to characterise his contract with Sony as a 'slave contract'.

An historical analogy is the right to property in land. At certain points in history, particularly when expressed as laws of inheritance, land ownership conferred rights not only on lords but on serfs and free peasants, and secured the attachment of these persons to their means of livelihood. It acted as an important guarantor of income from the soil; it provided a general social *right to land*. But once the ownership of land was alienated, though it was part of a generally progressive development, it not only became something entirely different, but indeed became the principal means for destroying the rural population, as is evident from the highland clearances and the last four centuries of Irish history.

The move to the universal alienation of intellectual products is not, however, part of a generally progressive social development but is on the contrary one of the highest expressions of the internal limits which the commodity form places on itself. It is riven by a fundamental contradiction: in order for knowledge to be a marketable thing, it is necessary to enforce ignorance. If a secret becomes universally known, it is no longer a secret but just something everyone does, like walking or breathing. If one wanted to make walking a specialised activity, one would have to cripple the majority of humans. In the same way, to ensure that knowledge is marketable, humans must now be prevented from using it; that is, fetters must be placed on the free development of their potential. The marketing of knowledge implies, by its very nature, restraint on its diffusion.

In consequence, the enforcement of IPRs entails the imposition of a monopoly. Originally this was limited to the quite specific aim of allowing the inventor to recover the costs of her or his research, as Hoekman and Kostecki (p146) explain: 'Patents or copyrights grant an inventor or author a temporary monopoly over the use of the invention or the reproduction of a work, and prevent competitors from sharing or using their knowledge without payment'.

The modern tradable patent or copyright agreement is a very different instrument. It is not aimed at the inventor or author, but on the contrary at the current owner of the right to exploit the inventor's work, who generally usurps the inventor. Any software writer (and, increasingly, any writer) who enters employment as such, signs away all rights to the fruits of her or his mental labour by consigning copyright to the employer.

A device initially intended to protect a specific person — the originator of a work or at most its immediate reseller — has become a means of alienating that knowledge from this specific person, and making it a marketable object. Microsoft does not trade in the ideas of Bill Gates — not even the most dedicated nerd does $8 billion worth of thinking — but, in a certain sense, the ideas of *everyone but Bill Gates*, to which however Bill Gates has obtained the exclusive rights.

IPRs are justified in terms of reward for the work of innovation. But there is no reason to suppose, even in terms of orthodox theory, that the granting of a monopoly in a product should generate a reward that is in any way related to the work of creating the product. IPRs are a legal monopoly: a licence to print money. The language itself used to describe their motivation is quite explicit about this:

> If an innovation has economic value but is also easily imitated, competing firms would copy and sell it, earning a share of the potential profits. In perfectly competitive markets, enough duplication would emerge to eliminate all profits... Intellectual property rights attempt to correct this problem by providing an exclusive right, or monopoly, to the innovative firm to sell or use the product or technology. Patents, trademarks, copyrights, and other IPRs limit market access to the innovation and raise its price. (Maskus 1993:72)

To grasp how vast are the amounts of money involved, we cite a single fact: a fortnight before the release of Windows 95 at a world price of $99, 'pirate' copies better than Microsoft's own release were available on Moscow's Arbatskaya for $3. The difference of $96 represents a rent which Microsoft is only able to levy as a result of IPR protection of its licence. With worldwide sales approaching 30 million copies, this difference overall amounts to the GDP of a small country.

Indeed the contradiction implicit in IPRs is coming to a head in the growing conflict between Microsoft and the US Justice Department, which seeks to prosecute it for monopolistic practices. However Mike Elgan, writing in *Windows* magazine for January 1997, explains:

> Critics call Microsoft an unstoppable monopoly that snuffs out competition and innovation. They say government action is needed to protect the industry and the users... Why don't Microsoft's antitrust critics just sue the company? Because they'd lose. In order to win such a suit, they'd have to demonstrate that Microsoft's revenues are growing faster than other software vendors. They're not. (Elgan 1997:59)

Microsoft's fortunes do not arise from a monopoly of any particular product, for example operating systems (OS). As Elgan points out: 'The argument for splitting Microsoft leans heavily on the idea that owning an OS gives a company an unfair advantage in selling applications compatible with that OS. But Microsoft dominates the Macintosh applications market even more thoroughly than it does the Windows market'.

All Microsoft has done is vigorously implement the very principles which the US imposed on the rest of the world, and indeed logically, if the US government has a basis in law to prosecute Microsoft, the world has a basis in law to prosecute the US government. If Microsoft's $38 billion fortune is accepted as the fruit of a private monopoly, what does this say about the even more gigantic fortunes amassed by US, European and Japanese corporates in their hi-tech world trade in IPR-sensitive goods?

Microsoft's huge fortunes do not lie in any monopolistic practice distinct from the rest of the industry, or indeed distinct from the monopolies conferred on the industry by IPR legislation. They arise because Microsoft brought a universal standard into being, which others were compelled to use simply because it was a standard. Microsoft's super-profits arise not from imposing a standard, which on the contrary was welcomed by the industry, but because 'normal' copyright protection makes it illegal to copy this standard freely. If the duration of a software licence were legally restricted to, say, two years, the vast fortunes of the software industry would melt like dew in the tropical sun, third parties could quickly start fixing the (many) bugs in its products, and users would reap the benefits of cheaper and better software.

But equally, if the duration of all IPRs were restricted in the same manner, three-quarters of the world would no longer be maintained in a state of enforced backwardness to hold the growing trade deficit of the USA in check.

The market in dominance: IPR, technical change and the source of inequality

The new legislation is a product of a distinct phase in the development of technology, which is in principle no longer embedded in particular objects and processes. When the diffusion of knowledge was restricted by physical constraints, industrial knowledge did not pass rapidly from one producer to another because the real secrets of an industrial process were tied up in expensive equipment, specialist training, in 'know-how'. The mere invention of a process was really only a tiny part of the creation of a new technology.

Increasingly, however, the governance of automated systems resides in reproducible components — a piece of software or indeed a genome, which even reproduces itself. The divorce between the knowledge of a process, and the process itself, has turned technical innovation into an easily transmissible thing. The cost of *reproducing* a technical advance is an ever-smaller proportion of the cost of *producing* it in the first place.

This interferes with an essential element of the motor of capitalist development. Technological change under capitalist conditions gives advanced industrial producers, selling into the same market as a backward producer, an excess or 'super-profit'. If it costs me $20 to produce a product, and it costs you $5 to make the same product on account of your access to advanced machinery or software, then since we both sell our product for the same world price, you make $15 more than me for each item sold. The motor force of capital movement is the search for these surplus profits, and this is what drives innovation.[4]

The root cause of inequality is that given a free market in goods and capital, this surplus profit accumulates in the advanced nations. Clearly, if I do succeed in making my $15 excess profit, unless I am particularly profligate, I can re-invest it in further innovation so that by the time you have employed my new technology, I am already installing even more advanced equipment. This *unequal exchange* is the root of the growing gap between rich and poor, particularly when the state in the advanced nations acts as a military and legal guarantor of such capital transfers. The process of accumulation and technical change literally sucks the lifeblood from the poor nations.

But if the technology can be passed on in a disk or a seed, the physical guarantees of this capital transfer are removed. The natural basis of superprofit is eroded and must be supplanted by a new, legal basis.

This world *market in knowledge* is a major and profoundly anti-democratic new stage of capitalist development. In this new and chilling stage, the application or even the communication of knowledge is itself a violation of property rights. The WTO is transforming what was previously a universal resource of the human race — its collectively, historically and freely-developed knowledge of itself and nature — into a private and marketable force of production and, with the general imposition of IPRs in genetic material, removing the natural basis of the reproduction of food and with it the independent self-sufficiency of the planet.

Human rights vs property rights:
The world trading system and its contradictions

Much of the policy debate has little contact with reality. It is widely assumed that :

a) universal free trade is inevitable;

b) globalisation is synonymous with it;

c) trade can be extended without limit.

This gives many policy debates a very peculiar aspect, since they revolve around whether to endorse or reject something that is not actually happening. Whatever is going on, it is not free trade. No rich country chooses it, and no poor country is offered it. Insofar as the barriers to trade are destroyed, the basis of trade is undermined because the accelerated concentration of wealth which results incessantly destabilises the political and social order.

Universal dogma to the contrary, all parties do not gain from it, not even the whole of a single nation. On the contrary, as Pritchett shows, the winners are few and the losers are many; and even in the winner states, the beneficiaries are unable to form a social class capable of advancing the nation as a whole.[5] A striking proof is the very fact that the rich have erected such an armoury of defences against competition from their poorer rivals. *If* the gains from free trade are so universal, why do even those who gain the most circumvent it on such a scale?

The terms in which the policy dilemma is always presented — as a choice between free trade or autarky — are thus simply out of touch with the real options. A reaction against autarky is both justified and understandable — it was directly responsible for the collapse of the Soviet Union. But, in the new world order at least, autarky is not a choice but a punishment. Rule-based, enforceable trade regulation means that sanctions — cutting a country off from the world market — are a regular instrument of policy. The very nations which for decades rejected sanctions against apartheid as an unworkable infringement on commerce, now deploy them both as regular policy — for example against Iraq and Serbia — and use the threat of them, alongside debt servitude, as an instrument for securing favourable terms in trade negotiations.

Sanctions can be an effective threat because it is today almost impossible to survive outside of the world economy. But it is currently impossible to take part in the world economy except through trade. Thus when any nation takes practical steps to defend the welfare of its people against the new world economic order, its immediate need is not to leave the world market, but to avoid being thrown out of it. Nations are no longer free to determine for themselves what relation they will have to the rest of the world. The obligations of multilateral trade treaties have deprived them of a vital freedom: *economic sovereignty.*

The fundamental choice is therefore not whether to orient the domestic economy into or out of the world market, but to find a foreign policy which defends the right to an independent domestic policy regardless of trade obligations.

In the old GATT days the G-10 countries, at least, could to a limited degree choose how to take part in the world market. The rich nations were not cohesive enough to dictate to them. The non-aligned movement, UNCTAD, GATT 'à la carte' and the very fact that trade agreements were bilateral, all gave them limited freedom of action which let them offset, though not overcome, the destructive impact of trading from behind.

This freedom of action has been removed. Thus whatever its economic form, the new world order is essentially a new *political* order. Though measured in money, the true cost of its restructuring is human, social and environmental. The doctrine of free trade, especially when extended to services, finances and knowledge, amounts to the following: that humans do not have the right to intervene in, and control, any aspect of their lives which has become a marketable instrument. But as everything becomes a commodity, *all* human and social relations are being marketed. The recent world conference on global warming shipwrecked on precisely the USA's insistence on its right to trade in pollution. It is only a matter of time before the human genome itself is patented and, if the literal meaning of IPRs is applied, the commercial ownership of a human and all her descendants in perpetuity will become a legally enforceable right. In short, the general extension of trade, quite contrary to Hayekian utopia, is synonymous with a general loss of freedom.

Twenty years ago such human rights as care when ill, dignified old age, employment rights, education, and unfettered access to knowledge were so widely accepted that they entered constitutions and charters of universal rights. Today they are unfair competition. The universal market is in direct formal contradiction with human rights.

To produce one dollar's worth of output, an Indian worker must now on average work eighty times longer than her or his American counterpart — twice as long, incidentally, as in 1980. If a band of military adventurers arrived on India's shores, set up a prison camp and forced the local people to work under these conditions, it would probably provoke armed rebellion. Now the Indian government is obliged to impose the very same relations in the name of freedom.

This principle, of the unequal exchange of labour, has always underpinned trade on account of concentration of advanced technique in the hands of the advanced producers. However a new factor is the remarkable extension of the commodity relation into spheres previously limited by the directness of human interaction — services, communication, and technical knowledge — or by the directness of the relation to nature and its reproductive processes — agriculture. This among other factors has propelled education, health, the care of the young and the old, the environment and access to the fruits of knowledge into the frontline of resistance.

As long as the battle is kept out of the political terrain, these rights are surrendered without a shot. If it is *illegal* for a nation to determine its relation to the market, then it has no choice but to surrender human rights, because the market overrides its sovereign right to provide them. The conversion of social relations governed by politics into economic relations governed by private contracts has a paralysing effect on resistance because it hides the true relations of constraint which the contracts embody, making these contracts appear as the fruit of uncontrollable and impersonal forces offering no option but surrender.

But one cannot opt for something that isn't there. The problem facing most actual trading nations, above all the poorer ones, is to decide their relation to a world market which the WTO has transformed into a weapon against them.

The choice on offer from the WTO, the World Bank and the IMF is liberalisation, that is, surrender. It means:

a) opening the domestic economy to demolition by the cheap products of the dominant powers regardless of the consequences for local environment and industry, with no reciprocal rights to sell into the advanced countries;

b) surrendering collectivised welfare provision in the interests of free competition;

c) dismantling all protection for people and lands which might be deemed in restraint of the free movement of capital;

d) dismantling all protection over conditions of work or pay;

e) abandoning any public claims on the intellectual heritage of humanity.

Resistance is not only feasible, but no other option is practical, as country after country discovers, usually to its cost. Ironically the countries held up as examples of market success — the 'Four Tigers' — are now suffering its most destructive effects. On the other hand, when an economy as small as Cuba has managed to hold out, against all the odds and for a remarkably long time, against the destruction of its social policies at the hands of the market, why should it be so difficult for any larger countries?

The alternative in the first instance does not lie in the adoption of any economic nostrum but in re-asserting the sovereign *political* rights of all humans over their own activities and their results: to decide for themselves how they will arrange their production, their welfare, their lands, their education, and their means of informing themselves.

But this in turn requires a political effort, since it calls for an alliance with sufficient weight to counter the rich and powerful nations. The basis for such an alliance is not the imposition of a specific economic strategy or nostrum, since each nation needs the right to determine its own economic strategy. The basis for an alliance is the defence of this right itself: the placing of the *right of economic self-determination* squarely on the agenda of free and equal relations between peoples.

REFERENCES

1   Mihevc (1995).
2   Hoekman and Kostecki (1995).
3   *UN Yearbook of International Trade Statistics* cited in Maskus (1993).
4   The impact of this surplus profit will vary depending on circumstance. If the world price is sufficiently high for me to continue producing even for a diminished return, or for me to

continue producing provided I pay my workers one-hundredth part of the wages that you pay, then I will stay in business but probably with a much reduced share of the total profit on this type of commodity. If the price sinks low enough, then it will drive me into ruin. However, the one thing I cannot do, once there is a world market, is sell the same product as you at a different price from you. The formation of a universal world market, with more or less unified prices, imposes on me the transfer to you of the value which my labours produced. That is what a world market consists of; the purpose of the WTO is to impose it.

5   The Institute for Policy Research (1997) reports that of the largest 100 economic entities in the world (counting nation states), 58 are global corporations and the sales of one alone — Wal-Mart Inc — exceeds the GDP of 158 nations including Poland, Greece and Israel. Yet the combined employment of the top 200 corporations amounts to only 18.8 million people.

Bibliography

Bhagwati, J. (1993) 'Aggressive Unilateralism: an Overview', in Bhagwati, J. and Hugh Patrick (eds) (1993) *Aggressive Unilateralism*, Ann Arbor: University of Michigan Press; reprinted in King, Philip (1995) *International Economics and International Economic Policy*, New York and London: McGraw-Hill.

Chossudovsky, M. (1997) *The Globalization of Poverty, Impacts of IMF and World Bank Reforms*, Penang: Third World Network, and London: Zed Books.

Elgan, Mike (1997) 'Justice Department: Hands Off Microsoft!', in *Windows* magazine, Manhasset, NY: CMP Press.

Freeman, A. (1997) 'The Poverty of Nations', in *LINKS*, June 1997.

Hoekman, B. and Michel Kostecki (1995) *The Political Economy of the World Trading System: from GATT to WTO*: Oxford: Oxford University Press.

Institute for Policy Studies (1997) *The Top 200: The Rise of Global Corporate Power*. Washington.

Maskus, Keith E. (1993) 'Intellectual Property Rights and the Uruguay Round', in *Federal Bank of Kansas City Economic Review*, first quarter 1993, pp11-23; reprinted in King, Philip (1995) *International Economics and International Economic Policy*, New York and London: McGraw-Hill.

Mihevc, J. (1995) *The Market Tells Them So*. London: Zed Books.

Pritchett, Lant (1997) 'Divergence, Big Time', in *Journal of Economic Perspectives*, Summer 1997, pp3-17.

Todaro, M. P. (1994) *Economic Development*. New York: London.

World Development Indicators (1995), Washington: World Bank.

Yearbook of International Trade Statistics (1995), United Nations.

Sources and resources

Author's e-mail <a.freeman@greenwich.ac.uk>. Web-page <www.greenwich.ac.uk/~fa03>.

Socialist Economic Bulletin, available from Ken Livingstone, M.P., House of Commons, Westminster London SW1.

LINKS magazine from Post Office Box 515, Broadway, NSW 2007 Australia (e-mail <links@peg.apc.org>, web page <www.peg.apc.org/~stan/links>.)

Chapter 8

Guild socialism revisited

THE *LATIFUNDIA*, A PROPERTYLESS PROLETARIAT, predatory vested interests, the wage-system, blaspheme the Doctrine of Creation... Until the
Churches become aware that the fair price, the social dividend, regional self-
government, the family farm, a repopulation of the land, craftsmanly labour
and a functional not a State ownership are at bottom religious questions,
their inspiration and leadership are except for the few devout nul and void.

Massingham (1943)

Massingham belongs to a well-established body of political economic
thought which has been studiously neglected by mainstream education
and research over the decades since World War II. In this chapter we examine
guild socialism and its allied economic theory, social credit, a familiarity with
which is assumed by Massingham in his *The Tree of Life, Wisdom of the Fields* and
other writings.[1] The ideas reach back into the rich soil of Celtic Christianity, travelling forward through the protests of the common people at enclosure of the land
and the subordination of their culture to the encroaching value-system of the
successful raiders of the past.

The development of the predatory economy in which money replaces all other
values has enabled a minority to gain exclusive control over wealth and economic
power through their domination of the processes of production and distribution.
The system dispossesses the majority, including future generations, whose right to
life is threatened by ecological devastation and social turmoil. Orthodox economic
theory provides the elites of industrialised nations with a scientific justification for
their exploitation of the planet and its peoples. Hence mainstream dismissal of
alternatives *as* 'alternative', 'new', 'heterodox' or 'heretical', to be studied by the
mainstream for their curiosity value and the occasional instructive insight for the
perpetuation of the *status quo*. To date, there has been little prospect for dialogue.

Social credit themes

The common ownership of the cultural inheritance

Douglas and the guild socialists[2] adopted Veblen's line of thought, as introduced in Chapter 1 and amplified in subsequent chapters. The industrial

revolution had been made possible through inventions of tools and processes which were the product of the combination of human cooperative ingenuity with the common cultural inheritance of knowledge and skills acquired over untold past generations. The 'progress of the industrial arts' was, however, being 'sabotaged' by finance and business enterprise. Veblen looked back to the origins of economic activity in institutions associated with hunting, warfare and trade, in which desire for prestige and competitive advantage was the dominant motivation. Policy-making based upon profit and privateering was not conducive to the common good. On the contrary, the economic system was parasitical upon the goodwill and cooperation of men and women prepared to give service to the community and wishing to protect their environment. Under the system of competition for private gain people were forced to work in unpleasing conditions, producing armaments for export and 'fashion' items designed to be consumed, discarded and replaced.

Douglas examined the role of money in this circular process of production and distribution. He noted that money had a crucial role to play in determining what was produced and how it was distributed (i.e. who obtained a money income with which the products of the economy could be bought). If the present system was properly understood, it could be analysed and adapted to provide for the common good.

As Douglas observed, the financial system was determining the use of the community's resources on the basis of a competitive game played out by business and financial interests. Ordinary people were reduced to mere pawns, dependent upon wage-slavery for an income, in a system which was beyond their comprehension and control. Douglas was convinced that ordinary people were capable of comprehending how the system works in order to seek change. Nothing has changed since Douglas wrote his first article, entitled 'The Delusion of Super-Production', and his first book, *Economic Democracy*, in 1919. Indeed, his work accurately anticipated the economic and social instability which would flow from unrestrained global capitalism. We therefore follow Douglas as he observes that the first stage in the re-assessment of the role of money in the real economy is to distinguish between real and financial value.

Financial credit and real credit

In *The Control and Distribution of Production* Douglas noted that capitalism is based upon a financial accounting system that is only tenuously associated with the real world. Under orthodox economic theory a constant increase in financial wealth can be manufactured regardless of the practical requirements of society and the physical realities within which the economy exists. We can illustrate this point by taking the example of a product commonly found on a modern supermarket shelf — apple sauce. The processes of production of this product involve taking natural resources in the form of materials and energy and combining them through labour. The real cost of the final product includes spent energy, materials and labour, all of which have been deducted from the real wealth of the community during the process of production. However, the productive process distributes money incomes and creates profit in the financial sense, providing the illusion that a quantifiable measure of real wealth has been created. There is no guarantee that the process will have enhanced the real wealth of the community. As in Douglas' day, the financial system remains incapable of providing any real life measures of wealth-creation or dissipation.

As Douglas explained, through the productive process some material resource which happens to be lying about can be turned into something else. By 'a process of arithmetical legerdemain known as cost accounting the value of the original matter which we may call "a" is now $a+(b+c)+(d+e)$, "b" being labour, "c" being overhead charges, "d" selling charges and "e" profit, and that the wealth of the country is increased by this operation in respect of a sum equal to $(b+c+d+e)$'. With the aid of the banking system credits are now created to reflect the increased 'wealth', minus any loss or depreciation of capital machinery.[3]

However, in the productive process power is dissipated, tools depreciate, and food, clothing and shelter are consumed by the workforce. The resulting net gain, if any, to the community from this constant increase in production is currently measurable only in terms of the peculiar cost-accounting financial system which drives the productive mechanism. Hence the necessity to draw a distinction between real value (or credit) and financial value (or credit). Real credit comprises the potential supply of goods, i.e. the real wealth of the community. Financial credit is merely the supply of money. There is no necessary correlation between the two. Hence services undertaken outside the financial system, for example housework, may add real value, but do not register in financial terms.[4] Natural resources form a vital part of the real wealth of the community, but do not count until or unless brought onto the market.

Incomes and real wealth-creation

The person who works for money does not necessarily produce benefit to the community as a whole, although they may bring profit to their employer and the employing firm's financial investors. A person who works in home or community may well give essential service to the common good. However, in many instances they do not receive direct financial reward. Hence a person who spends their life giving voluntary care to children, the chronically sick, disabled or the homeless is deemed to make no recognised contribution to the economy. They therefore fail to qualify for pension rights. Meanwhile, scientists who design land-mines and military aircraft for profitable export to corrupt regimes receive high salaries during their working lives and can buy the right to handsome pensions.

In the Douglas analysis, incomes should be distributed on the basis of the common cultural inheritance, i.e. the common ownership of the real resources of the community. The natural environment and the skills and knowledge of how to use the resources which flow from that environment rightly belong to every man, woman and child in the community. To regain community control over real resources it was necessary to review the ways in which incomes are distributed. Douglas proposed two mechanisms to regain community control over finance without resorting to violent revolution: the national (or social) dividend and the 'Credit Scheme'.

The national dividend

The national dividend, payable to all citizens, was the most well-known and understood of Douglas' proposals. Douglas classed all dividends from investments as unearned income. On this basis he argued that the common cultural inheritance belongs to all, and should be distributed to all in the form of a financial dividend. Douglas' proposals for a national (or social) dividend involved the payment of a basic income by right of citizenship to every man, woman and child, regardless of any income from employment, past or present. The basic argument was that, freed from the dictates of the profiteers, individuals could assume responsibility for distinguishing 'good work' (to use a later phrase from Schumacher) from bad (i.e. socially and environmentally destructive), and be empowered to avoid the latter.

Advocates of the national dividend recognised that changes in the educational system would be essential in order to prepare people for a working life based upon service rather than wage-slavery. Furthermore, from the outset Douglas and Orage recognised that the introduction of a 'National Dividend for all' would require political support which was unlikely to be forthcoming from capitalist or labourist political parties. It was therefore necessary to explore other mechanisms for converting money from master to useful tool. Although payment of a national dividend could not be accommodated within the conceptual framework of orthodox economics (which we examine in the Appendix), it could be introduced at any time given the political will and an understanding of the true nature of money.[5]

The guild idea

Economic rights and the community

The main point of attack by guild socialists was upon the exploitation of common knowledge, common resources and cooperative work for the profit of the few rather than use for the majority. Profiteering would not end until the control of industry was taken from the 'functionless' or 'passive' property holder and restored to the real producers and consumers who form the community. Property and other rights are relative to the welfare of society. Industry, including services, arts and the professions, should always be responsible to the community.[6]

Hence industrial democracy is a matter of responsibility to the community as a whole, not merely a question of the rights of the workers within a particular industry. 'According to this theory, rights have no absolute validity, but are granted to an individual by the community in order that he may render it certain

useful services, and are therefore properly terminated when he ceases to do so…
(I)t is the divorce of property rights from any clear concept of function which has
led to so many of the ills of modern industrialism'.[7]

Guild socialist writings on the Guild Commune and civic sovereignty gave rise
to the Douglas/Orage Credit Scheme, which derives from the observation that
workers' control of discrete industrial units would merely result in worker profiteering and the re-emergence of capitalism. In order to prevent guilds from
operating purely in their own interests it was essential they remain answerable to
the community.

The Credit Scheme (outlined in the Appendix) gave recognition to the significance of finance as providing checks and balances over the processes of
production and distribution. Combined with the socio-political theories being
evolved by guild socialists at the time, the financial mechanisms proposed by the
Scheme offer an intriguing potential to adapt existing economic institutions and
practices to socially and ecologically sound ends. Ahead of their time, the
proposals offer valuable insights which can be adapted by socially and ecologically sustainable ventures of the present day. The first step is to define the type of
organisation — i.e. the 'guild', 'firm', 'industry', or 'productive organisation' —
within which the scheme might be applied.

The guilds as productive organisations

The guild idea originated in urban industrial towns. Hence guild socialists
looked to the trade unions as the main institutions of reform. However, the term
trade union was expanded to encompass professional, caring and artistic bodies.

Guild socialists took issue with the conventional view that society's wealth lay
in the production of material artifacts. They could see that the manufacturing
sector of the economy drew from and was dependent upon the wider community
of workers, artists, inventors, consumers and citizens. The Credit Scheme was
designed to reconcile the interests of all categories with particular reference to
personal incomes.

Guild socialists noted that within the capitalist political economy the right of
access to income was dependent upon participation in the productive process,
either as wage-labourers or by virtue of ownership of private property in the form
of land or capital essential for production. The contrary view was that, whatever
the nominal system of economic interaction, all members of the community were
in reality dependent upon certain common factors. These common factors were
inherited from the past and held in trust for the future. They included the land and
natural resources, the fabric and infrastructure of buildings and communications,
artistic traditions and the full range of 'intellectual property', the knowledge of
skills and process built up by countless generations of the past. Furthermore, all
types of production were dependent upon the 'increment of association', that is,
on collective forms of association in order to give service to the community in a
wide variety of ways.

The underlying philosophy

Guild socialists opposed the view that capitalism marked a stage in the evolution of the industrial economy en route to a world of plenty for all. They witnessed the degrading horrors of industrial employment in the satanic mills and the desecration of the countryside in the name of 'progress'. In their view the arts, architecture, music and culture of the Middle Ages were not the product of an unjust and exploitative economic system which had inevitably to be replaced in the name of progress. On the contrary, medieval concepts of the guild, the Just Price, learning, sound farming practice and good work provided clues for a viable alternative to a centralised capitalist system based upon private profit and the abdication of responsibility for actions save under threat of force.

Guild socialists recognised and condemned the range of measures whereby the discontent of the urban proletariat was dissipated through the promise of higher wages and personal advancement, the offer of tawdry baubles and artifacts as symbols of advancement and the provision of mindless leisure pursuits. As emulative consumerism replaced countryside knowledge and skills, the common people became dependent in their daily lives, as never before, upon decisions made by unknown bureaucrats controlled by the rich and powerful. The 'servile state' endorsed the removal of rights and responsibilities from the common people. Political pressure for ameliorative legislation on working conditions, trading standards and welfare benefits paid for by taxation was no substitute for removal of common rights and their attendant responsibilities. Centralisation of decision making on a national and international scale, whether by the state or big business, gave power to the few while dispossessing the many. The occasional chance to vote in democratic elections was no substitute for economic democracy. In common with other schools of socialist thought at the time, guild socialists were aware that times had changed. People had been removed from their traditional communities, and novel measures would be necessary to take account of current realities.

With uncanny perception, guild socialists anticipated the spread of wage-slavery into all aspects of social interaction through the wholesale monetising of relationships. They noted that the money system was the driving force behind the exploitation of social wealth for private gain. It was therefore necessary to review the methods whereby money was created and people obtained access to an income.

Guild socialists proposed a fascinating variant upon the theme of worker control. They envisaged a system in which the watchword 'service' replaced 'profit' and a scramble for a greater share of it. Although ownership of each 'industry' would be vested in the state, each guild would be individually administered. Modelled upon trade unions, guilds would, however, consist of all workers in an 'industry' — managers, unskilled workers, clerical, manual and so on. Payment would be on a service basis, continuing through sickness and idle times, rather than as remuneration for hours worked or in relation to productivity. The vision was to include all types of work essential to human existence *without* placing them directly upon a wage-slavery payment-as-reward-for-obedience footing.[8]

The sharpest contrast between the orthodox view of economic relations and guild socialist theory lies in its acknowledgment of the communal basis of wealth creation. Flowing from this comes the recognition of the necessity of community control of distribution of rights of access to shares in wealth, through incomes. The guild idea was not limited to traditional industries like textiles, mining, fishing, building and so on. The list also incorporated agriculture, domestic service, the civil service, professions, including law, medicine, education and all 'profession of ideas, as distinct from the actual production and distribution of concrete wealth'.[9] Hence the system was able to recognise the work of priests, preachers, artists, craftsmen, journalists and authors as an essential contribution to the common wealth, rather than a drain upon it or a luxury to be afforded *after* the creation of material wealth.

Guild socialists poured scorn on the idea that new ideas and inventions could be brought forth through the carrot and stick of the wage-slavery system, or could be owned by individuals to be used for private gain. In order to encourage the free play of 'idle curiosity' essential to new discoveries, certain guilds would exist to manage the work of inventors, pure scientists and any other groups, including 'housekeeping women', who are normally excluded as economic agents.[10]

The freeing of the arts, sciences and caring professions from dependence upon the patronage of the rich and powerful appropriators of communal wealth was a key concept of guild socialist theory. Like any other social movement, however, guild socialism was riven with dissent and conflict when it came to proceeding to practical measures. The pursuit of private gain has, to date, proved a more attractive cause than communal welfare for all, being simple to explain and easy to enforce through legal measures backed ultimately by the threat of force. Taking a more optimistic view of human nature, guild socialists embarked upon a series of experiments which met with varying degrees of success. Although the Credit Scheme was not implemented, it encapsulates all the key features of guild socialism and the reform of finance which would be necessary to secure community control over the twin processes of production and distribution.

The role of finance in production and distribution

Although local, national and international trade existed in the Middle Ages, *production* for financial profit was rare. In the guilds, prestige attached to quality and excellence in standards and workmanship. Trade was conducted on a personal level, and pursuit of financial gain for its own sake was roundly condemned. Trade took place after goods had been produced in an economy based upon barter-like exchange: money was not necessary to embark upon the productive process. Equally, it was normal for cottages to have land attached. So long as most families had access to the foods, fuels and natural materials of the wooded wastelands, money was not necessary for everyday survival.

By the processes outlined in previous chapters, money came to dominate production and distribution. Guild socialists noted that as industrialisation proceeded money became essential to initiate all economic activity. Without money, people, land and machinery could stand idle, despite the need for goods and the desire to create them. Goods already created could be destroyed according to the dictates of the money system, despite the desperate need of people for the essentials of life. While many a learned tome was written on ways to make the exploitative system work *better* by ironing out booms and slumps in what was, by implication, a fundamentally sound system, guild socialists asked some uncomfortably perceptive questions about the nature of money and the relationship of the money system to the real economy.

They noted that the bulk of money comes into existence as debt created by the banking system. Under the capitalist system the state and large corporations operate to the same financial agenda. Therefore nationalisation of the banking system would change nothing, as was proved by a study of other industrialised nations where a comfortable relationship between a state banking system and private capitalists is perfectly possible. Whatever the system, money comes into existence *in order* to initiate production. Furthermore, it is through production that incomes are distributed, providing necessities for members of the community. The object of the exercise is to produce a profit for the initiators of the productive process. However, profitable production is not necessarily socially just or useful to the community. The production of junk, including armaments for export, and the infrastructure which facilitates trade in these items, are profitable. The money system generates incomes, but at the price of the destruction of the countryside, the demotion of home to a mere dormitory and the degradation of work to wage-slavery. However gilded the cage, capitalism enslaves the common people.

The alternative proposed by the guild socialists has not lost its relevance with the passage of time.

The key element in the guild idea was its relationship to existing institutions. Guildsmen did not advocate the wholesale scrapping of the familiar social and economic framework, still less the creation *ex nihilo* of new, unfamiliar structures. Proposals were based upon well-tried and tested practices in trade union democracy, the consumer cooperative movement, banking and finance.

Although short-lived, the guild idea was based upon a sound blend of theory with practice, offering insights into alternatives to socially exploitative and environmentally destructive capitalism.

Background theoretical observations

Guildsmen sought to create an economics of sufficiency by replacing a financial system based upon debt, privateering and the necessity for constant economic growth with one based upon community control of the issue of credit. The Credit Scheme envisaged a gradualist, decentralist reform of the financial system underlying industrial economy. The theory was based upon Douglas' book *Economic Democracy* and the numerous articles circulated through *The New Age*, many of which appeared in book form in *Credit-Power and Democracy* and *The Control and Distribution of Production*.

The desire of the guildsmen to make use of established economic institutions is encapsulated in the Douglas/Orage Credit Scheme, known also as the Draft Mining Scheme. The selection of one particular industry enabled the proposers of the scheme to root their ideas in the everyday realities and practicalities of the day. However, the scheme is readily adaptable to a variety of differing times and circumstances. The core proposal is to bring under democratic control the credit-issuing agencies of the community. The scheme could be adapted across the economy, liberating the processes of production, distribution and exchange from the blight caused by the privatisation of investment and its basis in profiteering.

The A+B theorem

In devising the scheme, Douglas and Orage noted two significant changes occurring since the introduction of industrial productive measures. First, production takes place over *time*. The division of labour and other forms of specialisation mean that from the initial primary production of raw materials to the final retail outlet, a commodity may pass through the hands of several different firms. Secondly, *money* is an essential element both in the production of commodities and in their distribution. *At each stage of production* money is invested. The money invested at each stage is spent on labour, machinery, energy, raw materials and part-processed goods. *At each stage* that money goes out into the community, to be spent on goods and services existing *at that point in time*. When the finished product reaches the market, its price must reflect the accumulation of costs incurred since the first stage of production. There is no necessary correlation between the volume of *commodities* available for sale and the quantity of money available for their purchase *at one point of time*.

In practice, money invested in the present Period A is distributed as incomes now, in Period A. However, those incomes must be spent on commodities produced in the past, Period B. It follows that money must constantly be invested in future production, so that income can be distributed to workers (in the present period) and the present supply of commodities bought. The system ceases to function if present incomes are not sufficient to buy existing goods at the cumulative cost-prices incurred as they moved through the stages of production from raw material to finished product. In this case productive employment is not available and unemployment ensues, resulting in a deficit of purchasing power. It is therefore imperative to keep up investment, producing a constant flow of goods onto the market, whether they be wealth or waste, so that incomes can be distributed.

Inherent flaws in the system — for example the failure to account for certain accumulated elements of depreciation, including the consumption of energy in the productive process — give rise to successive periods of boom and slump.

Traditionally, economists sought means to overcome observed failures of the system through supply-side and demand-side measures (to use later terminology). All of these measures failed to take account of the relationship of the debt-based financial system to the processes of production, income distribution and exchange.

Money which enters the system of production and distribution as a debt/loan (1) belongs to the bank *and is controlled by the bank* in the sense that the *bank* determines how it will be invested on grounds of profitability. Also (2) although the bank creates money as a loan, the loan does not go out of existence once it is repaid by the original debtor *but* (3) the repaid loan must be rapidly re-loaned in order to maintain production, *since it is through the productive process that incomes are distributed*. Point (3) is the key to the purpose behind the Credit Scheme. The financial system is a man-made institution which has developed historically in a such a way that incomes are dependent upon participation in the productive process, the initiation of which is dependent upon money entering the system (being invested) as debt, on the basis of profitability to private individuals and institutions. It is possible to imagine money entering the system as *credit* rather than debt, through a banking system controlled by the local community.

The Just Price

There is no natural law to dictate that banks and other financial institutions should retain absolute control over the money system in its present form. Central to the Douglas proposals was the realisation that complex calculations relating to the supply and flow of money were taking place every day throughout financial and business enterprises. Given the political will, such calculations could be engineered in order to bring a sufficiency of the products of industrial invention to all citizens. The production and consumption of superfluous waste could be phased out, and access to 'good work' made available to all. Douglas proposed two main means for the community to introduce money into the economy. The national dividend could operate at national level, while the Credit Scheme would devolve financial controls to the most local level feasible, although operating through a central clearing-house. Both necessitated complex calculations in order to maintain a stable relationship between real wealth and the money supply through the operation of the Just Price.

The Just Price involves the setting up of a National Credit Office (NCO). Using returns from relevant government departments, the NCO can compute, on a quarterly or yearly basis, the total value of the nation's assets, production and imports, and the total value of all assets consumed in the previous period. By maintaining a steady ratio between purchasing power in the hands of the community and real wealth (the actual and potential capacity to supply goods and services) the Just Price can be achieved. Through these mechanisms the necessity for a constant increase in debt-driven production is removed. It is no longer necessary to maintain prices (and therefore incomes) at a level high enough to recoup accumulated past costs.

All new money can then be fed into the system as consumer credits, i.e. as a national dividend, or as producer credits. In time, all new money will flow into the system through producer-owned guilds as the Credit Scheme is widely adopted. It was envisaged that removal of economic uncertainty, fear and want within each nation would remove the necessity for the competitive struggle for foreign markets. Hence chances of war would be reduced to a minimum. In future, competition would be for excellence of quality and durability, with necessities being locally supplied on the basis of the choices of local individuals.

Local employment

The Credit Scheme could be applied to any institutions providing employment within a local area. Wherever people work together for money, whether in industry, the arts, education, farming, medicine, retailing or any other essential service, their pooled financial resources could provide the basis for recovery of control over their own work. Guild socialists adopted a reformist approach, seeking to unite all who work as producers of goods and services within a locality with each other, and with local consumers. Through a gradual dispossession of the 'profiteers' and absentee bureaucrats of the centralist state, local communities could reclaim control over their own resources.

The practical proposals, designed to apply to the mining industry of that time (1920), envisaged employers and trade unions working together at local level to meet the needs of the community and provide good work for its producers (all the workers, including the managers).

The Credit Scheme — main features

The Credit Scheme was designed to form a neat transition from capitalism to local economic democracy for all *without* resort to revolution or industrial buy-outs by the state. The latter would merely perpetuate capitalism: compensated capitalists would transfer their capital to other industries, or take it abroad. The case for communal credit control rests on the argument that capitalism can be defined as 'the improper use of capital' through 'its monopoly of the Real Credit of the industry' coupled with 'the power to fix prices'.[11] As credit-power is concentrated in the hands of a few, prices rise faster than the effective demand for the commodities to which the prices are attached. The result is unbalanced, wasteful distribution and consumption of wealth, coupled with the constant quest for control over new markets and resources by the credit-mongers.

Rightly, the control of credit (i.e. financial power) should reside with the local community rather than in private hands. Productive capacity derives from general social progress and the common inheritance of intellectual and natural resources, including physical energy sources. In relation to the whole, individual effort makes a minuscule contribution. While the community as a whole creates wealth, financial power is the key to effective control of that wealth. Therefore the community needs to take direct control over finance. State control of the existing system (which has not changed over the decades since the original proposals) would not alter the mechanisms responsible for the exploitation of the many in their homes and places of work by the distant and unaccountable few. However, state endorsement of the revised financial mechanisms would be essential in order to recognise and harmonise the legality of the financial system (see Chapter 2).

'Sooner or later ... the time will come when such a scheme will be all that stands between Chaos and Order in industry. For it is *impossible* that the present system should continue'.[12] The proposals for a labour-capital partnership based upon the prediction by the original authors of the Scheme remain as relevant today as when they were first debated eight decades ago. Moreover, the widespread destruction of natural resources and social capital which has occurred through the development of global capitalism over the intervening decades has not served to diminish the relevance of the proposals.

The two key aspects of the Scheme are (1) the communalisation of credit and (2) the fixing of prices. The means proposed for the achievement of these ends are capable of variation and adaptation according to the needs and resources of the particular industry, the locality in which it operates and the economic, social and environmental circumstances of the wider community. The adaptations require careful consideration and explanation when adapted to practical circumstances. However, they comprise relatively simple adaptations of the existing system.

The draft Scheme was not intended as a blueprint for immediate action. Rather it was designed as a spur to lateral thinking on alternatives to continued dependence upon a global financial system which is inherently unstable, socially unjust and environmentally disastrous. Already, in some isolated instances, forms of financial action similar to that envisaged in the Draft Scheme have been adopted. For example, young unemployed people have pooled their giro cheques in order to develop a housing cooperative in Hull. Similarly, any group of people working together in an institution could contemplate seeking to control their own work through first taking control over their combined earning-power. A local school, for example, where 50 staff average incomes of £20,000 each, dispenses £1 million per year. That represents a lot of financial wealth which could, to put it simply, be banked in a local community-controlled bank. Applied in a number of employing institutions within a locality, some variation upon the draft Scheme offers considerable potential for lateral thought.

It is possible to drive a car without understanding its mechanics. Similarly, it is possible to act as an economic agent without a full understanding of exactly how the financial system operates. However, internal combustion engines and financial institutions are both man-made. It follows that financial institutions can be observed and adapted to serve socially useful and ecologically sustainable ends. If this is not the case, and finance is truly beyond the control of the community, we must accept that it is beyond the wit of humankind to stop the progressive desecration of the planet's life-support systems.

An analysis of guild socialist economics

The Credit Scheme was designed to prompt discussion of practical means whereby the community could regain control over its resources. The underlying premise was that since society as a whole creates wealth, its just distribution could not be determined by individuals motivated by greed and operating on the basis of the creation of artificial scarcities. The proposed mechanisms of credit creation and price control would not serve to perpetuate business-as-usual among the privateers. Since it would not perpetuate economic growth in conventional terms, it could be dismissed as utopian nonsense. However, the alliance of producers and consumers within the legal framework of local and national government could provide a more rational basis for socio-economic interaction than the present free-for-all based upon irrational market forces operating at global level.

Social philosophy

Orthodox economic theory and mainstream financial practice was founded on the premise that Rational Economic Man could make hard-headed, practical and objectively sound decisions about the use of the world's resources on purely selfish grounds. The harmful effects of economic and military conflict have been sustained by the belief that it is women's role to supply the necessary emotional cushions outside the 'real' world of male endeavour and intellect. From this flows the common antagonism, expressed by both women and men, towards the career woman. It is considered normal for men to be aggressive, competitive and self-seeking. Hence the depressingly dangerous claim that 'you can't change human nature'. Guild socialists, and those who followed their political philosophy, adopted a more realistic view of human nature. They discerned the value of the traditional peasant community way of life, in which men and women cooperated for the common good.

The Credit Scheme was founded upon the premise that the cooperative elements within society are essential for the creation of wealth, however defined. Home care, child care, knowledge, invention, education, the web of culture and the care of soils and countryside belong to, and are the responsibility of, all the members of the community. The pursuit of private gain by individuals at the expense of the local community and environment may be tolerated only in so far as it does not conflict with the common good over the long term. However, where the individual who benefits fails to justify their appropriation of wealth on the grounds of their personal contribution to social welfare, there can be no valid communal sanction of the appropriation. Furthermore, decisions of what should be produced and how it should be distributed are rightly determined by the community. Community control of the institutions of finance was essential if production and distribution policy formation was to be subject to community sanctions.

Monetary reform was seen to provide the key to the community's ability to exert checks and balances upon the actions of individuals motivated by greed and self-interest. Nevertheless, monetary reform alone cannot change fundamentally unsound relationships between people, nor between communities and their natural resource base. Financial reform necessitates a reappraisal of certain basic assumptions about motivation, sufficiency, the location of producers in relation to consumers, and the culture within which they operate.

Good work

The guild socialists argued that income should not be directly related to productive work within the formal economy as conventionally defined. Proposals to guarantee an income whether or not the worker/individual was 'in work' were justified on the grounds that the community, and not the individual, should take responsibility for 'industrial depression, sickness, accident or old age'.[13] The growth of social insurance, pension and workers' compensation schemes support the argument. Moreover, the case for a guaranteed minimum income independent of any employment criteria was considered 'of such obvious merit as scarcely to require demonstration'. Although cautious in his support for some of the guild socialist proposals, Carpenter's advocacy of the principle of an income guarantee is clear:

> The worker today is subject to vicissitudes over which he [sic] has virtually no control whatever. They are, furthermore, in no sense the unescapable visitations of an inscrutable Providence. Instead they are the normal accompaniments of modern industrialism. Hence to leave to the worker's individual 'thrift' or 'fortitude' the sole provision for a mine explosion, lead-worker's paralysis, or a world-wide business depression is as futile as it is unjust. These risks are as integral an element of the cost of production as fire or depreciation and must be assumed by [the community].[14]

Proposals for a national dividend based upon this line of argument were popular among the unemployed, women, artists, small farmers and many groups in society dispossessed by industrialisation. The concept was less popular among trade unionists and those in employment, and was dismissed as impractical, unworkable and theoretically unsound by the employing classes and academic theorists. Shorn of its multitude of irrelevancies, the basic objection to a national dividend was that if personal incomes ceased to be dependent upon production, production would stop.

The guild socialists held that certain types of socially undesirable and ecologically destructive forms of production *would* in all probability cease to provide attractive forms of employment. A guarantee of an income would end wage-slavery by removing the necessity for certain types of socially and environmentally unsound production. However, some dislocation could be expected as people transferred to less socially and ecologically degrading forms of production. A lot hinges on the definition of work and the relationship between work and money.

In line with guild socialist thought, Dominguez and Robin (1992) explore the link between work and money. They pose the question: 'What is the purpose, in your experience, of your paid employment?' To assist the inquirer, they list the reasons people give for going out to earn money. These include: earning money to provide necessities and comforts, security, tradition, enjoyment, duty, service, learning, prestige and status, power, socialising, personal growth, success, creativity and fulfilment, time structuring, and 'just cuz: because that's just what people do'.[15]

Hence it is possible to argue that the primary purpose served by *paid* employment is financial, to meet the need to obtain a money income. The financial function of *paid* work is its *only* function. The *personal* function of work — its emotional, intellectual, psychological and even spiritual purposes — can be equally well served where there is no financial reward. All that is required is that basic needs are met. Each task undertaken as a paid form of work can also be undertaken as a voluntary or leisure pursuit. Similarly, all forms of service to others and leisure pursuits can be monetised.

Moreover, as recent studies indicate, money rewards can reduce satisfaction gained from an occupation. Douthwaite[16] quotes a number of studies showing that the relationship between money and 'work' is highly complex, concluding that satisfaction from work is highest where the firm is owned and controlled by those working in it. Further studies, for example *The Overworked American* by Juliet Schor,[17] indicate that the option to work shorter hours for less pay would be considered desirable by many people in employment. However, in many large firms there is no option to work shorter hours. The choice, determined by a centralised, bureaucratic system, is between long hours, in which the intrinsic satisfaction derived from work is reduced, and unemployment with no income.

Equally, high salaries may not compensate for the abusive environment in a workplace dominated by individualism and competition. Lesley Wright and Marty Smye[18] found that competition between colleagues, the 'blaming culture', long, irregular hours and stress all stifle initiative and satisfaction at work. It can be in a person's best interests to seek out a more cooperative working environment, even where that means accepting a lower salary.

In short, people tend to seek out intrinsically satisfying work in which the money reward may not be the sole, or even the dominant consideration. The notion plays havoc with economic theory which assumes a positive correlation between the price of labour (wages) and the supply of labour (the number of hours people are willing to work). It is equally destructive of the notion that material rewards make up for being forced to undertake unpleasing and unsatisfying work which is necessary to produce essential goods.

Satisfactions and sufficiency

In theory, the more goods that are produced, the better off everybody will be. The more homes, houses, cars, household gadgets, clothes and holidays produced and consumed, the higher the Gross Domestic Product (GDP). The use of GDP as a indicator of welfare poses further problems. In theory the items (goods and services) produced can be listed and their money values totalled to provide a measure of wealth. In practice, car accidents and oil spills, which damage people's lives and the environment, appear in the national accounts as *additions* to wealth. The employment of the emergency services, insurance claims, hospital care, clean-up operations, replacement of vehicles and property, all feature as a plus, while the misery and long-term effects of personal and ecological disaster fail to register at all.

Even without disasters, the production of many goods and services involves ecological destruction and reductions in personal and public health. Disposal of waste materials generated by economic activity involves the discharge into the countryside of untold quantities of toxic substances, the effects of which cannot be evaluated by the simplistic money-centred accounting system. On a global scale, production of, and trade in, armaments ranks as an economically sound activity, despite damage to human health, welfare and happiness caused by use of the end product.

Furthermore, as Dominguez and Robin and others have observed, the net benefit flow from a high money income can be surprisingly modest. A prestige job often entails the cost of housing in a prestigious residential area, a status car, smart clothes, meals out for reasons of time, convenience foods, child care and frequent holiday breaks to relieve the stress. When these items are deducted from total earnings, alongside hours spent preparing for work and getting to work, the balance sheet looks good from the point of view of the global economy, but appears less decisively so from that of the individual concerned or the community as a whole.

The argument that rising industrial productivity, as measured in the money value of goods produced and exchanged on the market, is an indicator of general welfare is further confounded by the observation that a distinction can be drawn between 'external' and 'internal' goods. As Keekok Lee (1989) observed, a certain number of external goods which can be bought and sold are essential for survival. However, internal goods, like memories or the ability to speak Italian, are not exchanged on the market. Nevertheless, internal goods are as valid a form of wealth and welfare as external goods.

The 'developed' industrial economy is primarily concerned with the production of such items as cars, fashion clothes and armaments. At any point in time these are in fixed supply. People feel impelled to possess and consume them, indeed they are urged to do so by advertising and the media. In doing so, people find themselves engaged in a zero-sum game in which winners must be forever vigilant to maintain their foremost positions. 'Satisfaction is not derived simply from the possession and consumption of goods ... for this would entail the notion of sufficiency which it specifically denies'.[19] Internal goods require some minimal consumption of external goods: musical skills may only be exercised through possession of a musical instrument. However, the internal goods themselves become part of the person. Since their acquisition does not involve a zero-sum game, it is essentially non-competitive and can be cooperative. There are no losers, and all may be winners. The gaining of knowledge, and sporting, artistic, culinary or horticultural activities, are all encompassed within the category of internal goods. The ability to speak five languages can enhance a person's welfare without diminishing the welfare available to others. Moreover, such ability enhances potential total wealth, making skills more widely available to be taught. However, conventional economic theory demands more and more *production*. Internal goods are excluded from all economic calculations. Hence guitars and guns register as saleable output and therefore show as a plus. The deskilling processes of unemployment and intrinsically unsatisfying wage-slavery fail to register as a minus.

Conclusion

At first glance, guild socialist proposals to abolish wage-slavery and substitute intrinsically satisfying forms of cooperative work may appear utopian. However, it is not necessary to await a fundamental change in human nature in order to create an ecologically sound and socially just economy. As this chapter indicates, it is neither natural nor normal to conform to the model of Rational Economic Man by seeking to maximise monetary rewards as a means to secure material goods to the exclusion of all else. Furthermore, there is very little evidence that, were it possible to remove all but material satisfactions, the economy would continue to function.

The strength of the guild idea was its ability to collaborate with existing institutions. Reform movements often develop a doctrinal rigidity and mutual exclusiveness which stultify their growth. Those who developed guild socialist ideas avoided this trap:

> Partly because of its diverse origin, and partly because of its birth on English soil, where the ability to compromise amounts to a national genius, the Guild Movement has shown remarkable flexibility. Far from urging their theories as a wholly unique body of doctrine, its protagonists have gloried in its agreement with other economic and social tendencies, and have endeavoured constantly to work with them and through them.[20]

Guild socialist literature and debate spread throughout the 'developed' world, reaching the United States, Canada, Australia, New Zealand, South Africa, Japan, Russia, France, Germany, Hungary and Italy by 1922.[21]

However, in Britain and elsewhere, the guild movement failed to find a power base in the institutions of the industrialised economy. Certain ideas were subverted to the cause of capitalism and labourism, informing the creation of welfare state provisions as economic growth and urbanisation continued apace. Divorced from its roots in the countryside, REM's so-called developed economy now threatens to engulf the whole of humanity. Meanwhile, practical discussion of realistic alternatives to the REM economy has faded into obscurity.

NOTES

1   Note, for example, the quotation at the head of this chapter, taken from Massingham, H. J. (1943) *The Tree of Life* London. Chapman and Hall. pp195-6.

2   Certain groups and individuals developed some aspects of guild socialist theory, while others varied in their emphasis. For a detailed analysis see Hutchinson, Frances and Burkitt, Brian (1997) *The Political Economy of Social Credit and Guild Socialism* London and New York. Routledge.

3   Douglas, Clifford H. (1922) *The Control and Distribution of Production* London. Stanley Nott. pp45-6.

4   See Waring, Marilyn (1989) *If Women Counted* London. Macmillan.

5   The possibility of a 'citizen's income' has been debated in the UK in recent years by the Citizen's Income Research Group. See Resources for details.

6   Carpenter, Niles (1922) *Guild Socialism: An Historical and Critical Analysis* New York and London. D. Appleton and Co. p145.

7   Carpenter, op. cit. pp301-2. See Glossary for definition of 'function.'

8   Hutchinson, Frances and Burkitt, Brian (1997) *The Political Economy of Social Credit and Guild Socialism* London and New York. Routledge. pp19-20.

9   Hobson, S. G. (1914) *National Guilds: An Inquiry into the Wage System and the Way Out* London. Bell (1919 edn.) p163.

10   Hutchinson and Burkitt, op. cit. pp20-21.

11   Douglas, Clifford H. (1920) *Credit-Power and Democracy* London. Cecil Palmer. (1921 edn). p176.

12   Douglas op. cit. p211.

13   Carpenter op. cit. p312.

14   Carpenter op. cit. pp312-3.

15   Dominguez, Joe and Robin, Vicki (1992) *Your Money or Your Life: Transforming Your Relationship with Money* Harmondsworth. Penguin. pp228-9.

16   Douthwaite, Richard (1996) *Short Circuit: Strengthening Local Economies for Security in an Unstable World* Totnes. Green Books. p45.

17   Schor, Juliet (1991) *The Overworked American* New York. Basic Books.

18   Wright, Lesley and Smye, Marti (1997) *Corporate Abuse* London. Simon & Schuster.

19   Lee, Keekok, (1989) *Social Philosophy and Ecological Scarcity*. London and New York. Routledge. p205.

20   Carpenter op. cit. p306.

21   Carpenter op. cit. p117.

Chapter 9

Home economics

THE INTELLIGENCE WHICH has converted the brother of the wolf into the faithful guardian of the flock ought to be able to do something towards curbing the instincts of savagery in civilised men.

Huxley (1893)[1]

THERE ARE NO 'technical solutions' to this crisis [the globalisation of poverty]. Meaningful reforms are not likely to be implemented without an enduring social struggle. What is at stake is the massive concentration of financial wealth and command over real resources by a social minority. The latter also controls the 'creation of money' within the international banking system.

Chossudovsky (1997)[2]

The poor may be always with us, but never before have the rich cultivated such complete power over the everyday lives of the masses. How we spend our working days, what we eat, what we wear and what we know are governed by the mass markets operating through the mass media. Citizens of the developed world spend a large proportion of their waking lives attempting to secure a money income, then spending money and finally recovering from the stress and strain of their getting and spending activities. Meanwhile, the poor are increasingly marginalised. It is estimated that each week half a million children die as a result of structural adjustment programmes imposed to reclaim Third World debt. Most ordinary people hesitate, however, to venture an opinion on their role as economic agents. In this chapter we seek some insights into the choices open to the person in the home, street and shopping mall.

Home economics (a term first coined by the farmer-philosopher Wendell Berry)[3] recognises the planet as the home which human beings share with the rest of God's creation. It is based upon the idea of locality as home to the human community. Home is the place where we work, socialise, and care for the environment. Our homes are the locations where, every day, each one of us makes economic decisions, affecting the lives of others near and far, present and future.

Puzzles and connections

Nevertheless, we seem to have lost the ability to distinguish between making money and creating real wealth. When we act as economic agents we are dependent upon a flow of information and ideas, many of which are confusing and contradictory, providing a poor basis for exercising our options. For example, we have a hazy idea that by going out to work we are making a contribution to the real economy, in recognition of which we expect a financial reward. In some mysterious way our work appears to generate money.

Production and exchange do not make money: banks make money. The simple but fundamental truth can be illustrated by a concrete example. Imagine a producer/farmer in a system of single-stage production. She has access to land, which did not need to be bought, the use of a discarded second-hand spade, saved seed potato and a pile of discarded horse manure. In these circumstances it is possible for a producer/farmer to plant and harvest a potato crop at no financial cost. The harvested crop can be put in an old container and sold to a neighbour for £5. Has the producer created £5? Or any money at all?

The transaction may have increased the purchasing power of money in general, because more goods now exist within the economy. However, if there is no more money in the system, no further trade can take place until the farmer spends all or part of her £5, no matter how much real value (in terms of commodities) is subsequently produced through hard work. There is not the slightest reason to connect a strong *financial* economy with a strong (or sustainable) *real* economy. Money does not create wealth. Hard work does not create money.

By definition, paid employment in an industrial economy provides the employee with a money income. Very little more can be said on the matter with any certainty. Work undertaken for a money reward may add to the common good, or it may not. Certain forms of work create social or environmental costs far in excess of any calculable return, even within the terms of conventional accounting, though these calculations are rarely undertaken. Moreover, high rewards may go to tasks with dubious social value, while essential tasks receive little reward, if they are rewarded at all. Banking and legal services are highly rewarded while caring services in the home are rarely rewarded in money terms. Welfare-to-work and workfare programmes which make benefits and entitlements to a money income dependent upon the search for, and acceptance of, any form of employment regardless of the individual's preferences, highlight the contrast. The highly paid are said to require *higher* pay to make them work, while the poor must be deprived of incomes in order to make them work. The accepted definition of work is 'employment for monetary reward'.

The illogicalities of the debate come into sharp focus when considering the question of women's pay and payments for work traditionally undertaken by women. Women have always worked in the home, educating children, rearing children, growing food, preparing meals, cleaning homes, washing clothes, caring for the sick and undertaking the many tasks essential for everyday life throughout the year. In pre-industrial society the home was central to the economy of everyday life. As the industrial economy developed, it gradually undermined the home as the central economic unit. Originally founded on warfare and trade in luxury goods, the money economy crept into the home: everyday necessities ceased to be available from the land, and could only be had for a money income. Women continued to be responsible for the time-consuming physical tasks of housekeeping and home care. Often denied access to educational opportunity, women left it to men to pursue highly-paid work. Their options were (1) to marry a high earner, (2) to attempt to combine family care with low paid, insecure and casual work, or (3) to compete with men on equal terms by flouting social convention.

Option (3) creates unease not only among men but also among many women. The reason is not hard to find: somebody has to be there, at home, as the emotional cushion without which human society would cease to function. Rational Economic Man evolved because Mother could be expected to pick up the pieces, just as Mother Earth would clear up all the mess in the environment that his industry spewed out.[4] Human society is doomed if 'mother' ventures forth to join in REM's games. However, so long as the majority of women remain financially dependent upon men, as housewives or as low-paid workers, Rational Economic Man can use his intellect to make hard-headed decisions in the cut-and-thrust of his so-called 'real world' competitive economy. The knocks he sustains and inflicts only count if they register within the artificial world of financial accounting. Social and ecological disasters are of no account. If resources are to be spent on them, they must be justified in financial terms. Mother clears up the mess in the home and the environment, and requires no financial reward for doing so. A little praise now and then will keep her silently about her business.

As they battle to help victims and protect their local communities against the worst excesses of the cash-based economy, local politicians and pressure-group activists sense a fundamental fault in the system. Some seek highly-paid and prestigious jobs within the flawed system in the hope of effecting change for the better. Others devote themselves to voluntary work, constantly begging for money from a position of weakness. Like all good causes, care in the community and care of the environment are expensive luxuries which it is difficult to justify on orthodox economic grounds. Those who provide caring services free may be applauded, but when they come to claim a pension they have no proof of having made a contribution to the economy. Their claim is therefore rejected.

Flat earth thinking versus common sense

As the following exchange of views on the Internet indicates, few economists are prepared to challenge the theoretical assumptions which underpin the global economic system.

Question. Can anyone tell me why very few reputable economists have been prepared to discuss the sustainability of the capitalist system? A feature of capitalist economies is that they collapse if they fail to generate economic growth, but, with the exception of Herman Daly and one or two others, the handful of economists who have written on the matter deny that this means that such economies are unsustainable. Growth, they insist, can continue for ever because technology will enable the larger values of goods and services the process requires to be produced with less natural resources and fewer polluting emissions. This improvement in factor productivity will be helped, they say, by a growing emphasis in the market on quality rather than quantity. The value of the output, not its volume, is what counts ...

So why do economists have this blind spot? Does anyone have a convincing explanation for their reluctance to accept that economic growth cannot continue? I would have thought that the challenge presented by the need to design a truly sustainable economic system would be one that would appeal to many members of the profession.

Answer. In his book *The Sleepwalkers* Arthur Koestler notes that those who resisted most vigorously the idea that the earth revolved around the sun, and not the other way around, were those in the intellectual establishment — not only the church but also the universities. Why? Because they had spent their whole adult lives studying, explaining, defending and shoring up the very shaky intellectual edifice of medieval cosmology. They were therefore going to be the last to relinquish these outmoded ideas. The new cosmology had a much readier acceptance at the margins.

If this sounds familiar, it is because every department of the universities, the think tanks, the hospitals, the banks, the media, etc, are now filled with 'medieval cosmologists'.

As an illustration of this phenomenon take the alternative medicine movement: nowhere does it meet with more resistance than in the medical and pharmaceutical establishment, who not only have huge vested financial/power interests to defend, but have also made a huge intellectual commitment, an intellectual commitment which they are loath to admit is fundamentally misguided. And yet, in the face of official sneering, condescension, dismissal etc, about one third of the population now use alternative treatment.

I think those on the margin, i.e. most people, would have no difficulty in accepting that **unceasing economic growth is the short road to ecological and social disaster**, if only they were exposed to the issues and arguments. They would probably find it much easier than establishment economists to devise economic alternatives as well. **How an alternative economic agenda can be disseminated in the face of vigorous and unceasing propaganda for the growth economy,** is another matter.[5]

Mistaken belief in a flat earth had little practical significance for everyday life. The notion that the sun travels round the earth had no effect whatsoever upon the earth's ecosystems. Plants and animals grew despite the inaccuracy of the observations. Today, however, the spread of capitalism and industrialisation is affecting the ability of local and global ecosystems to sustain human life, threatening ecological and social disaster.[6] Faith in everlasting economic growth has more than mere academic significance.

In *Risk* John Adams (1995) coined the term 'Vogon economics' to describe the practice of reducing all values to the single concept of money-value in exchange. Using the example of the two bypasses threatening the house of Arthur Dent in Douglas Adams' *The Hitchhiker's Guide to the Galaxy*, Adams shows that cost-benefit analysis is the ultimate tool of unsustainable growth economics. Benefits of a bypass may be calculated in financial terms, and enjoyed by others who save time in transport and commuting. But can a meaningful market value be placed on the loss of one's house?

> If one's home is demolished the geographical centre of one's existence must be re-located. For some this experience will be more upsetting than for others. For many, surveys have repeatedly confirmed, the disruption of their web of friendships and the loss of cherished surroundings cannot be compensated for by any sum of money.[7]

The problem is not limited to homes. Economic growth destroys other buildings and landscapes with nostalgic associations, endangered species, security, health and life itself. Where recognised at all, these categories are evaluated in decision-making by reducing them to a cash value. For many in the Third World, there continues to be no compensation for loss of access to land. Adams describes the last announcement of the Vogon Constructor Fleet as they demolish the Earth to make way for a Galactic Hyperspatial Express Route. The Vogon explains:

> ... all the planning charts and demolition orders have been on display in your local planning department in Alpha Centuri for fifty of your Earth years, so you've had plenty of time to lodge any formal complaint and it's too late to make a fuss about it now.[8]

In Adams' view, the Vogon's irritability stems from the conventional belief that economic progress is necessary, and objectors are a nuisance. From road-building to analysis of the threat to the Earth of global warming, the rich and powerful justify their actions. Objections by the poor and powerless who stand in their path are barely heeded, and projects whose proposers are weak and powerless 'rarely get off the drawing board'.[9]

Possible ways forward

Grabbing power and riches from the rich and powerful appears an attractive option to the impatient, and an unrealisable dream to the apathetic. In practice, violent revolution rarely changes anything. Where successful, it merely causes power and riches to change hands. Hence large centralised systems, whether private or state owned, are run by a competitively selected hierarchy. Decisions are taken by a distant elite on the basis of Vogon economics, affecting ordinary people in localities which are no more than a dot on the map of the decision makers. The guild idea is to re-define wealth and re-evaluate its sources with a view to decentralising decisions on the use of local resources.

In guild theory the *potential* to create wealth is held in common. Land, knowledge, skills, energy and all necessary elements for the creation of material, intellectual and cultural wealth, are held in common. All that is made draws upon the common stock of wealth, and nothing can be made by an individual or group without drawing upon that common pool of resources. Certain productive activities may enhance the quality of the common stock, while others may reduce it. At issue is the right of individuals to draw upon the common stock.

The guild argument was that under capitalism a small number of individuals had drawn to themselves the power to determine the communal agenda. The determination of what is produced, and how it is produced and distributed, has been appropriated by a narrow elite. Entrapped in a gilded cage, essential workers are highly rewarded with consumer goods, while the general populace are allowed access to a limited amount of necessities and non-essentials sufficient to forestall social disruption and create an illusion of justice. In this way, acquiescence is achieved in a fundamentally unjust and ecologically unsustainable economic system.

Therefore the first step is to subject our perceptions of reality to the cold light of scrutiny. Does free trade mean 'freedom for people to choose how they want their world to be run' or does it mean 'freedom for the [transnational] corporations to pursue profitability ruthlessly'?[10] In keeping with guild socialist thought, Lord Beaumont concluded that there would be no place in a sustainable economy for the limited liability company, 'which is an ingenious invention to enable people to borrow money on the strength of an uncertain future and not be responsible for paying it back if their expectations are not fulfilled'.[11] We do not need to seek a change in 'human nature'; all that is necessary is to understand it a little better.

Corporate knowledge?

Vogon economics steals *both* the common *and* the goose, leaving the community in the position of having to beg for permission to use resources from the powerful corporations. Global finance and transnational corporations control money and investment, determining what is produced, how incomes are distributed and how markets are controlled. In financial terms, some of the largest corporations are more powerful than many national governments (see Chapter 7). As the activities of these massive corporations look set to destroy the planet's ability to sustain the human economy, our very perceptions of reality are determined by a mass media and education system powerfully influenced by the global corporate economy.[12] Knowledge, once held as common property, has become a saleable commodity in research institutions and educational establishments throughout the 'developed' world. Access to a university education is viewed as an investment in respect of future earning power. Much research in the physical sciences is funded by pharmaceutical and armaments companies, while social science research is heavily weighted towards maintaining the necessary infrastructure for Vogon economics to flourish.

Beneath a veneer of respectability, large corporations go to great expense to ensure that rational, informed debate of the social and ecological effects of economic growth does not occur.[13] Following the first meeting of the United Nations' Intergovernmental Panel on Climate Change (IPPC) in 1989, the Global Climate Coalition (GCC) was set up to discredit its findings. Funded by US oil, motor and energy companies, the GCC countered the call for a precautionary approach by the world's leading scientists in the IPCC, through funding scientists prepared to cast doubt on the findings of the IPCC. The hired scientists argued through the media that climate change had not been scientifically proven. Although their arguments served to cast doubt in the minds of the general public, they were not sufficiently sound scientifically to be used in the negotiations themselves. In negotiations they have argued that climate action proposals 'could add as much as a dollar to a gallon of petrol, cause 600,000 job losses annually and reduce US competitiveness worldwide'.[14] Despite presentation of evidence to the contrary, the arguments of the GCC fuel resistance to any change in the American consumerist lifestyle.

The practice of corporate lobbying was not invented by the GCC. In 1983 the European Round Table (ERT) of Industrialists was formed by a small group of top business leaders. The discrete body of forty heads of European-based multinationals plays a decisive role in policy making at Brussels and in the quest for economic integration of the member countries of the European Union. In a thoroughly researched article, Ann Doherty and Olivier Hoedeman (1994) demonstrated how the exclusive group of executives were 'orchestrating the present and future shape of Europe'. Policy groups within the ERT cover education, competition policy, infrastructure, Central and Eastern Europe, North-South issues, trade and GATT, environment and social policy. Their reports are 'eagerly received' by national governments and in Brussels... According to ERT Secretary-General Keith Richardson, 'access' is the key to the ERT's success:

> Access means being able to phone Helmut Kohl and recommend that he read a report... Access also means John Major phoning ... to thank the ERT for its viewpoints, or having lunch with the Swedish Prime Minister just prior to the Swedish decision to apply for EC membership.[15]

In sharp contrast other non-governmental groups, including trade unions, small businesses (a category into which 99% of European firms fall) and environmental groups may wait weeks or even years for an appointment. The

ERT has become part of the European Union apparatus, influencing European policies on the implementation of the single market, creating the Trans-European Network infrastructure scheme and structuring European education policy while whittling away social protection measures. The ERT agenda is clear:

> What industry cannot accept is that the pursuit of other objectives is used as an excuse for damaging the wealth-creating machine itself, whether by raising its costs or blocking its development. There can be no healthy society or healthy environment without a healthy economy to pay for them.[16]

In this way the ERT claims the moral high ground on behalf of the wealth-creating machine, setting an agenda with negative effects which cannot be checked by rational argument. In 1989 the list of negative effects drawn up by the European Environment Bureau, itself part of the European Commission, included 'large-scale waste transport, obligatory acceptance of products with less stringent controls, diminished opportunity for environmental taxes on the national level, and increased road traffic and resulting emissions'.[17]

The ERT has produced reports on transport (*Missing Links* 1984) and on education (*Education and European Competence* 1989). The former advocates the construction of Europe-wide infrastructure networks to facilitate mobility of resources. The latter criticises the European educational system's inadequacies in preparing 'human resources' for industry. It called for a major overhaul of education, condemning the present system which 'allows and even encourages its young individuals to take the liberty of pursuing 'interesting', not directly job-related studies which in many cases have little prospect of practical application'[18]. The more streamlined Japanese and US models are held up as favourable alternatives. The financing of social security measures is held to be an obstacle to economic growth. The ERT favours 'flexibility' in the labour market: this includes the shuttling of workers around Europe, seasonal contracts, flexible hours, job-sharing and part-time work.

In similar manner the Business Council for Sustainable Development (BCSD), supported by such industrial giants as DuPont, Dow Chemical, Ciba Geigy, Aea Brown Boveri, Chevron, together with ERT members Daimler Benz and Norsk Hydro, set about defending the necessity for unregulated free trade at the 1992 United Nations Conference on Environment and Development (UNCED) Earth Summit under a smokescreen of green rhetoric.

Countering Vogon economics

If there was a massive conspiracy to control the earth's life support systems, we could more easily fight to destroy the evil. Unfortunately, people at the top genuinely believe they are working for the good of the planet. Large firms (Shell, Siemens, ERT members, the World Bank) recruit intelligent youngsters, often with a fair share of idealism. As they work their way through life to the top, the firm becomes like a family, with a particular world view and ways of working.[19]

Those who feel uncomfortable within the accepted framework will leave. Those who stay ask few penetrating questions. Researchers employed by large firms are disconcertingly content to focus purely upon the science, trusting their employers with the ethical implications of their work. George Monbiot considers that many researchers appear to be 'idiot savants', brilliant in their specialism but incapable of viewing the broad perspective. He describes meeting a plant scientist who had been researching the genetics of a crop plant for four years. Asked what her work would achieve, she replied it would 'help feed the world'. When Monbiot pointed out that the plant was not a food crop, she was nonplussed.[20]

For the majority trained within the formal education system, perceptions are coloured by an underlying misconception that sound laws and safety standards have been fought for and won. It follows that whistle blowers are classed as alarmist, ill-informed cranks, while those who claim there are 'two sides to every question' are eagerly encouraged to present the case for dismissing precautionary measures as alarmist. Hence the frequency of occurrence of conversations along the following lines.

A Creepy-Crawly Tale

Mrs A and Mrs B talk in an English garden. Mrs A's two year old grandchild, Pip, plays on the lawn, drifting onto the flowerbeds from time to time.

Mrs A: 'I know I shouldn't use slug pellets, but have you *seen* the slugs and snails round here? They're climbing up the plants, the walls, the trees. They're everywhere.'

Mrs. B: 'I'm not surprised. Not many songbirds and other predators around here! They've all been killed off by eating the poisoned slugs. The whole ground will be contaminated.'

Mrs A: 'Yes, but what can I do? Those plants cost me a small fortune at the garden centre — as in a LOT of money! I'm not having them eaten by slugs. I pick up the pellets before Pip comes. It's safe enough.'

Mrs B: 'I see you've netted off the pond.'

Mrs A: 'Yes, can't have Pip falling in. Safety first! Can't be too careful with grandchildren around.'

At this point Mrs B did not have the heart to mention that four more chemicals commonly used by amateur gardeners had recently been added to the list of those totally banned from sale by the UK government on grounds of serious risks to human health. The substances contained dichlorophen, which can cause serious eye inflammation. The products banned were moss herbicides and lawn growth promoters sold in garden centre chains, including Boots Total Lawn Treatment. Other pesticides used for treating headlice and in dog and cat flea collars and lawn dressings were noted to have carcinogenic properties and had also been banned. 'Users have been advised not to dispose of these products on land, or down the sink, toilet or drains. Nor should they be put in domestic refuse bins because of the risk to refuse workers'.[21] Helplines were set up to dispose of the products. Mrs B could be forgiven for dismissing the matter from her thoughts. Reports of contamination in household products and foodstuffs have become so commonplace that the only 'rational' reaction is to dismiss each new one as yet another scare story of no particular interest.

Common knowledge

The examples used in the Creepy Crawly Tale were selected almost at random from an incredibly wide range of causes for concern about foods and household products already in daily use or about to come onto the market. Assessment of the issue as a whole reveals a wider problem, that of the de-skilling of the common people as they set about their daily lives. The formal education system concentrates on turning out human resources for multinational corporations; folk knowledge along with 'old wives tales' are dismissed as having no bearing on job-related studies. Such a process has proved a valuable asset in stripping the common people of their basic survival skills, making them totally dependent upon an information and legal system designed to meet the aspirations of global capitalism.

In the early 1970s Richard Mabey wrote in some amazement of the novel experience of eating a whole dish of wild vegetables. 'To be embarking upon such a strange and risky eating venture seemed — dare I say it — *unnatural*'.[22] Taught to accept attractive, shapely and regular products from which all traces of soil and evidence of the growing process have been removed, 'not only are we cut off from samphire [the wild succulent plant first tasted by Mabey], and many other delectable wild foods, but from first-hand knowledge of what food *is* and how it gets to us'.[23] His guide offers advice on how to find, recognise and prepare many of the 320 wild foods which grow in the British Isles.

The work of Mabey and others draws attention to the distinction between wild plants, traditionally known by and available to all, and plant products, available only for money. At least half of the exotic varieties of plant foods available on supermarket shelves in the developed world are naturally occurring weeds in other parts of the world. All the world's vegetable foods were once wild plants. In addition to their nutritional value, many wild foods have medicinal uses which date back long before the era of commercialisation. The common knowledge of how to prepare foods and medicines from these sources, invaluable in times of war and famine, is in danger of disappearing for ever as multinational corporations appropriate the knowledge for commercial gain. Brand-orientated marketing necessitates the introduction of the deskilled global culture, so that traditional products can be sold back to local markets under the guise of brand names for commercial profit. As an ERT member explains:

> A subsidiary well-rooted in the local markets will be able to mobilize indigenous resources and to commercialize them with a strong brand. Hindustan Lever (Unilever) scientists have considerably advanced substitute oils for soap-making. Over 70,000 tons of unconventional and previously neglected

indigenous (such as sal, neem, kusum, karanja etc.) have been adapted for making soap and other products.[24]

Such 'unconventional and previously neglected' substances had been used for centuries by ordinary people. Their commercial use involves taking the products out of the hands of local communities and placing them in the hands of a Western-educated elite who stand to profit and thereby provide a market for cars and other exports.

Large-scale production and transportation of foods and medicines removes knowledge and control of production methods from workers and consumers alike. Additionally, the growth, storage and processing of foods on a world-wide scale involves the use of a host of chemical additives if the food is to appear fresh and flavoursome at point of purchase. Ironically, legislation designed to prevent adulteration and contamination hits small farmers. Meanwhile the chemical cocktail found on common foods draws government advice to wash and peel fruit and vegetables, and restrict their consumption by children. Checks on the chemical contamination of processed foods become virtually impossible, due to the wide variety of sources of the individual constituents.

Each day the average New York household is prepared to buy and discard three kilogrammes of 'garbage'. Every kilogramme bought in this way throughout the 'developed' world can be represented in money terms as a cost to the consumers, for which they must undertake paid work, and as a profit to the companies concerned in the production and retail. Certain costs, including damage to worker and consumer health due to exposure to toxic substances, and environmental degradation due to unsound farming practices and waste disposal, remain wholly or partially obscured by a money system which was designed on the basis of competition and greed.

Home economics

Home economics is capable of respecting the earth as home to humanity. It is premised upon the belief that a distinction can be drawn between real value and financial value. The global economy is concerned with production of financial value as a means to power over real resources. Home economics explores the relationship between the financial economy and the real economy upon which it rests. It investigates novel concepts and presents familiar assumptions from a new perspective.

The financial illusion

Capitalism's fictional accounting system is best portrayed through examples taken from the food industry. Addressing the UK Food Manufacturers Federation's annual convention in 1971, Stephen King and Jeremy Bullmore noted gloomily, 'It occurred to us that there is, in fact, in the whole world, only one true Food Manufacturer. And though He may well be here, He is not — as far as we know — planning to speak'. They went on to observe that 'food in reality is not *made*.

Food, wonderfully and mysteriously, grows: in animals and fruit and vegetables and cereals'. Food 'manufacture' is concerned with enhancing the financial value of the product, rather than with creating the product itself.

Reliable estimates from the food industry established that, in the early 1970s, allowing for a healthy diet and varied menu, total UK expenditure on food '*need only have been £1,800m*'. Actual expenditure amounted to £6,363m. 'The population of this country could have been just as well nourished, just as healthy — *and spent four and a half thousand million pounds less than it actually did*'.[25] The processing, preservation and packaging of food adds financial value and provides paid employment. It is therefore accounted as a positive activity by capitalist economists. The social and environmental costs of production of the enhanced financial value are not accounted as relevant. Labour spent on dreary routine tasks of processing, packaging, transport, clerical administration and so on is regarded as a positive outcome. Costs of disposal of packaging, transport emissions and damage to health from environmental pollution and food additives are also left out of the calculations. Equally, no account is taken of the environmental costs of the agri-business growing methods necessary to produce standardised crops suitable for mass processing.

The availability of processed and packaged food serves both to deskill the population at large and to confuse the intellect. As an individual example, take apple sauce as a processed food product which registers in accounting terms as economic growth — 'we are all better off'. However, the extra resources, in terms of hours of work and materials consumed in its production, degrade the environment and add nothing to human welfare.

Apples grow well throughout the UK. It takes a few seconds to core an apple and pop it next to the roast in the oven. Within minutes the skin can be peeled off (and composted, no waste) leaving a delicious, flavoursome apple sauce to go straight onto the table. Yet, at the height of the apple harvest and during the following seven months during which apples are easily stored, supermarket shelves display jars and packets of apple sauce. Not only have these apples been stored and transported, often from the far side of the world, but the processing and packing, transport, distribution and retail processes involve work and environmental costs which add nothing to the quality of the product in terms of flavour, convenience or nutritional value. Nevertheless, all activity conducted within the formal economy is accounted in positive terms as 'economic growth'.

The 'food miles' phenomenon has been studied, for example, by the SAFE Alliance in its *Food Miles Report*.[26] In the 'real world' it is 'no longer economic' to supply organically produced fresh produce, un-processed, un-packaged and un-transported, to a local market. There is 'not the money to do it'.

A home economics analysis enables individuals to reassess the relationship between money and the real economy of social institutions underpinned by the environment. It enables us to re-examine our roles as economic actors, both from an individual household perspective and also within the institutions in which we work and conduct our lives as members of the wider community.

The evaluation of work

Since industrialisation the necessity to work to gain a money income has blunted perceptions of the meaning of work. Hence it is possible for people to rationalise their participation in activities which, were it not for the money income, they might not consider undertaking. The nuclear physicist claims that nuclear power or weapons are 'safe', the lorry driver declares that good roads are necessary and pollution problems are over-rated, while workers producing and farmers using toxic chemicals ignore the risks to their own health and that of their families and the wider community. Unsatisfying, tiring, stressful and dangerous work is accepted as necessary to survival, an opinion ratified by the payment it receives.

However, the vast majority of individuals in the 'developed' world rank as 'silent polluters'. Work in offices, hospitals, educational institutions, churches, shops and warehouses involves the use of products from polluting industries. At home and at work, we all use plastics, papers, inks, energy and create mountains of waste. Additionally the products we use and discard are transported daily over vast distances. The most silent polluters of all are parents and educators who prepare the next generation to accept the status quo without question.

The acquisition of a money income free of contamination by some aspect of the global economy is at present impossible. However, you and I can review our personal roles in that economy in order to adjust our decision-making in the light of our findings. The process may involve asking some uncomfortable questions about the working practices and end product of the organisation from which our incomes are derived.

Ethical consumption

Helga Moss, a Norwegian mother in her thirties, presents an arresting picture of her own role in the global economy.

> I do not grow any food, or weave or sew clothes; I have not built my house or made the furniture in it. Everything I use has been made by other people. It is like a global household. But of course, normally, you do not reflect on that. If you have the money you buy things in stores. When they are no longer useful, they become waste and will be disposed of by a public service. If I look around my flat I see hundreds of items whose history I know nothing about; in this respect I am a 'normal' Western urban individual.[27]

Moss suspects that if she scrutinised her purchases more critically there would be reasons to boycott most of the items she buys on grounds of their social and environmental costs. As things are, she has to buy all the things she needs, up to ten items per day. In making the selection she is usually in a hurry to return home to her children. She dismisses labels indicating that a product is environmentally friendly on grounds that 'greenwashing' is a capitalist ploy to make money out of people's concern for the environment. Nevertheless, every commodity purchased involves choice, and there are many things to be considered. Normally the price factor wins, and she prefers foods produced in Norway. In other respects, her choices are not very well informed. 'I feel guilty about this. I should do more, know more. I buy so many things! And I am always in a hurry. The task of becoming a conscious, informed consumer seems so vast'.[28]

In order to clarify what she would need to know in order to make informed purchases, Moss investigates the history of one commodity from its beginnings to the point at which it reaches her home. For the sake of simplicity she ignores the problems of disposal of packaging and of the end product when it ceases to function. Taking the example of a radio, she traces the product back to its source. The steps take her to the retailer, the wholesaler, the factory that produced the radio, the subcontractors who made the accessories, the machine factories that contributed to each process along the way, and the extraction of the natural resources necessary to supply the factory. An 'unknown number' of plants provide the multitude of components and materials which eventually make up the radio. In investigating the radio's impact it would be necessary to include an environmental impact assessment of the various production processes (their consumption of materials and generation of waste), including the transport arrangements between each stage. It would then be possible to draw up a diagram to illustrate the progress of the radio 'from cradle to my home'.

To complete the model, Moss shows it would be necessary to evaluate the human aspects of the radio's production, in order to assess the social sustainability of the model. Hence the workers have to be taken into account, first in respect of their working conditions and any health hazards, and second through their part in the web of consumption and production relations. Although the combination of factors in the model has become highly complex, it illustrates several key points.

1 The individual is delinked from nature and people as producers of commodities essential for everyday life. Ignorance regarding our relationship to nature in any concrete sense is profound.

2 Within the global market economy the people and ecosystems contributing to any commodity are invisible. However, all are utterly dependent upon 'a web of seemingly infinite concrete relations to the varying ecosystems and working people of the world'. Orthodox belief in the independent actor in the market and the 'self-made man' becomes untenable.

3 We are presented with a serious ethical dilemma. As would-be ethical consumers, we are constantly violating the very value system we seek to teach our children: care, sharing, solidarity and responsible action. Were we to try to live in harmony with the natural world, including all its plants, animals and people, we and our families would starve to death. Reduction of consumption to a bare minimum for survival would not reduce dependence upon the 'global

household', and would, under present circumstances, result in social exclusion.

4   Buying is a political act. 'It is an act in which my money carries the power and my moral judgement has to be suspended'.

Moss concludes that, through cash cropping for export, the peoples of the Third World, particularly women, contribute to our Western households with their labour power and their natural resources. As their environment is destroyed, people in the South receive very little in return for their efforts and their loss of access to land. Meanwhile, people in the North can buy large quantities of goods cheaply because of environmental and social sacrifices forced upon the South.[29]

As Moss indicates, the dilemmas she raises cannot be resolved by individuals acting in isolation. Home economics entails systematic study of the ethical implications of consumption in order that rational, informed choices can be made. These need not necessarily lead to a lowering of standards or a hair shirt existence. Home production and preparation of food and entertainment, the revival of the arts of conversation and story-telling and the revival of handicrafts may take time, but can serve to unite families and friends over the long term. To date, however, orthodoxy has succeeded in creating a series of isolated individuals with little option but to operate within the institutions of orthodoxy.

The evaluation of the role of money

The debt-based money system unites the activities of workers and consumers with common resources (natural resources and human knowledge) within countries and on a global scale. People are paid for the work they do, and spend their money on the products of the system. Normally money forms the only link between the activities of workers and consumers, setting aside all other ethical considerations. While it may be unrealistic to expect the system to adapt to pressure for change from the top downwards, it is possible to use the debt-based system creatively while exploring alternatives to it.

Creative use of the money system can take two forms. First, control over money can be reclaimed through ethical investment, credit unions and other forms of community action. Second, 'alternative' currencies and exchange systems can work alongside so-called 'orthodox' financial structures, giving rise to creative alternatives.

'The collective wealth which ordinary citizens and working people own through their various pension and insurance funds is truly massive', wrote Guy Dauncey in 1988. Nevertheless, decisions on the use of collective wealth reside in the hands of profiteers. Ethical investment offers a mechanism whereby individual or institutional savers can have a negative or positive effect upon business and industry. Traditionally, members of the pacifist Society of Friends (Quakers) have sought to avoid profiting from investment in the arms industry (negative effect). More recently, ethical investment funds have been set up to enable savers to finance environmentally sound projects, including organic food and farming, green energy and fair trade ventures in the Third World. The scope for making connections between personal and occupational pension fund investments and their ethical impacts is considerable.[30]

Credit unions were first formed to provide people with access to savings, freeing them from dependence on loan sharks in times of hardship. Members of a church, employees of a company, or any group with a common local bond, may form a credit union. The essential element is trust and mutual cooperation. The non-profit-making credit union is owned and controlled by its members, offering loans at low rates of interest on the basis of mutual support. However, legal restraints ensure that the savings of the union must be deposited in a conventional banking or savings institution. The concept has the capacity for considerable adaptation. In some countries unions may invest in local businesses.

Other forms of exchange include LETS and WIR-type initiatives. LETS (Local Exchange Trading Systems) enable people to exchange goods and services locally without using bank-created money, in a form of collective barter. The original *Wirtschaftsring* (WIR) was founded in Switzerland in the 1930s, and continues to this day. WIRs enable local businesses to trade together using chits instead of conventional money. Frequently, local cooperation of this type involves both the local authorities and voluntary organisations, including churches.[31] On occasions businesses, such as railway companies, have created financial credit on the basis of the real credit of their services, issuing railway money certificates. Often the production of organically grown local food for local consumption is only possible through community support of this type.[32]

The role of churches and other institutions

The aim of home economics is to develop the potential to free local economies from exploitation by the global economy, to 'short circuit' the economy over which local communities have no control. A great deal of work has already been done in documenting the scope for developing local diversity and autonomy. In *Short Circuit* Richard Douthwaite[33] records the emergence of grassroots economic action in finance, food, farming and fuel, providing models capable of adaptation to an infinite variety of local geographical, social and cultural circumstances. Illustrated by examples from across the world, *Short Circuit* has been translated into several languages and is available in many countries. It provides an excellent resource for individuals, groups and institutions seeking mechanisms for change.

Progress is greatest where people come together to pool resources and ideas. As the guild socialists noted, the most effective means for change is through the regeneration and adaptation of existing local institutions, places of work, worship and political authority. Collectively, institutions in a locality possess the potential to evaluate the contribution of the non-money economy care in community. Care in the community and care of the natural environment contribute to the welfare of all. Equally, local institutions have the capacity to explore mechanisms to free the community from debt to the global system by re-assessing the relationship between local resources and the money mechanisms which govern their use and distribution.

The greatest barrier to progress is the permeation of the mass media and educational systems by the values of global culture. The very process of evaluation of local resources can itself be subverted to the cause of the perpetuation of the global 'free market'. Nicholas Hildyard noted the increased use of central funding for regional development in Europe under Article 130c of the Maastricht Treaty:

> It is a moot point, however, whether the beneficiaries of regional development funds are Europe's citizens or EEC [European Economic Community] multinationals, because such funding has been used to break open local economies and force local communities into the economic mainstream. In Spain, for example, the EEC's structural funds have been used to introduce intensive, export-oriented agriculture at great cost to local livelihoods, exacerbating regional inequalities and transforming cultural diversity into economic disparity.[34]

The task ahead is formidable. Fundamental assumptions about our relationship with money need to be taken off the shelf, dusted down and examined dispassionately for their accuracy and relevance to the real world situation we are facing. Money collected by a parish in England may help a good cause in Kenya. However, the purchase by members of flowers and vegetables grown as cash crops in Kenya on land seized from subsistence farmers may be contributing directly to the poverty they seek to alleviate. The inconsistency is compounded as the financial investments of churches and charities are implicated in the injustice of Third World debt and the structural adjustment process.

Conclusion

Home economics shares the guild vision of the need to free work from financial slavery, while enabling money to revert to the role of a useful tool in truly free markets. Reform of an unjust and unsustainable economic system involves more than preaching from the sidelines, seeking remedies for individual, perhaps distant, disasters while remaining in the comfort of a secure income derived from work or investment in the exploitative economy. As members of established institutions, be they families, churches, places of work or voluntary organisations, each person has the capacity to avoid participation in the economy of greed and exploitation through the re-creation of local economies. Money is a useful tool, except where it governs our lives. So long as the question, 'Where is the money to come from?' dominates decision making, we remain slaves to a value-system founded on the instincts of greed and competition.

NOTES

1   Quoted in Tanner, Nancy M. (1981) *On Becoming Human* Cambridge University Press.
2   Chossudovsky, Michel (1997) *The Globalisation of Poverty: Impacts of IMF and World Bank Reforms* London and Penang. Zed Books and Third World Network. p27.

3 Berry, Wendell (1987) *Home Economics: Fourteen Essays by Wendell Berry* San Francisco. North Point Press.
4 See Seager, Joni (1993) *Earth Follies: Feminism, Politics and the Environment* London. Earthscan.
5 Personal e-mail correspondence: the question was asked by Richard Douthwaite. The answer came from Gideon Kossoff. Emphasis original.
6 For more details see The Corner House (1997) *Climate and Equity: After Kyoto* Briefing 3. Sturminster Newton. The Corner House.
7 Adams, John (1995) *Risk* London: University College London Press. p171.
8 Quoted in Adams op. cit. p172.
9 Adams op. cit. p173.
10 Beaumont, Tim (1997) *The End of the Yellowbrick Road: Ways and Means to the Sustainable Society* Charlbury. Jon Carpenter. p110.
11 Ibid.
12 See Beder, Sharon (1997) *Global Spin: The Corporate Assault on Environmentalism* Totnes. Green Books.
13 See Rowell, Andrew (1996) *Green Backlash: Global Subversion of the Environment Movement* London and New York. Routledge.
14 Quoted in *Red Pepper* (1997) 'Oily Tactics'. December.
15 Quoted in Doherty, Ann and Hodeman, Olivier, (1994) 'Misshaping Europe: The European Round Table of Industrialists' *The Ecologist* Vol.24. No.4 July/August. p135.
16 Quoted in Doherty and Hodeman op. cit. p136.
17 Quoted in Doherty and Hodeman op. cit. p136.
18 Quoted in Doherty and Hodeman op. cit. p138.
19 See George, Susan and Sabelli, Fabrizio (1994) *Faith and Credit: The World Bank's Secular Empire* London. Penguin.
20 Monbiot, George (1995) 'Mad Scientist Disease' *The Guardian* 5 December.
21 *Organic Gardening News* (1997) 'New Pesticide Bans' December. p5.
22 Mabey, Richard (1972) *Food for Free: A Guide to the Natural Wild Foods of Britain* London: Peerage Books (1986 edn). (Emphasis original).
23 Mabey, op. cit.
24 Quoted in Doherty and Hodeman op. cit. p140.
25 King, Stephen and Bullmore, Jeremy (1971) *Tomorrow's Food* London. J. Walter Thompson. (Emphasis original).
26 Paxton, Angela (1994) *The Food Miles Report* London. SAFE Alliance.
27 Moss, Helga (1994) 'Consumption and Fertility' in Wendy Harcourt (ed) *Feminist Perspectives on Sustainable Development* London. Zed Books. p239.
28 Moss op. cit.
29 Moss op. cit.
30 See Dauncey, Guy (1988) *After the Crash: The Emergence of the Rainbow Economy* Basingstoke. Green Print. Sparkes, Russell (1995) *The Ethical Investor: How to make money work for society as well as for yourself* London. Harper Collins. Lang, Peter (1996) *Ethical Investment: A Saver's Guide* Charlbury. Jon Carpenter.
31 For further examples see Tibbett, Rachael (1997) 'Alternative Currencies: A Challenge to Globalisation?' *New Political Economy* Vol.2. No.1 pp 127-135.
32 See Groh, Trauger M. and McFadden, Steven S. H. (1990) *Farms of Tomorrow: Community Supported Farms: Farm Supported Communities* Kimberton USA. Biodynamic Farming and Gardening Association.
33 Douthwaite, Richard (1996) *Short Circuit: Strengthening Local Economies for Security in an Unstable World* Totnes. Green Books.
34 Hildyard, Nicholas (1993) 'Maastricht — The Protectionism of Free Trade' *The Ecologist* Vol.23. No.2. March/April.

Chapter 10

Coming into focus

I AM NOT an economist.

Anon

If I had £1 for every time I have heard these words said, I would be a great deal richer in money terms than I am today. The conversation stopper indicates a desire to avoid embarking upon a consciousness-raising exercise for fear of where it might lead. Like Frodo Baggins, we would all prefer to live out our days quietly at Bag End, leaving Mordor and the orcs to the experts.

We are all tempted to take our money and run, asking no further questions as we get and spend what we deem to be ours. However, we are also free to determine our economic actions through informed choice. Our role as producer, investor, consumer and taxpayer is an economic one with implications for the poor, mothers and children in the Third World, victims of oppressive regimes, farmers, food producers and the environment of present and future generations. If we remain powerless and ill-informed, that is a result of conscious choice. This short book has raised a series of questions. The next stage is to extend the quest for answers.

It's your money *and* your life

History

The themes explored in this book are not new. They have been developed and debated throughout many countries by people who took the time and trouble to extend their own consciousness and that of the people around them. Guild socialist economics was studied by small farmers, artists, writers, singers, the unemployed, working people, small businesses, churchgoers, volunteer activists, mothers, men and women of all ages. No matter what their educational background, tens of thousands of thoroughly ordinary individuals considered themselves perfectly capable of reading around the subject and holding valid views on economic matters.

Theory

Every day, money to the value of a trillion dollars is moved around the world in the shape of blips on computer screens. Meanwhile restrictive practices in the name of free trade privatise common knowledge and disempower local and national governments. Farmers are enslaved to their investors, their suppliers and their bulk buying customers, the massive food chains. All the while economic theory stands aloof from the reality of global capitalism, maintaining a studied silence on the erosion of economic democracy. The destruction of the real economy by the financial economy of Rational Economic Man rates scarcely a mention in the volumes of texts on economics and econometrics.

Sufficiency

Who is richer: (1) The person who must pay money out to somebody else to fix the lawnmower, or buy another when the model has become obsolete? Or (2) the person who is capable of fixing the lawnmower or digging up the lawn to grow safe organic vegetables for their children? Stocktaking within the household, neighbourhood and locality is a first step to creating a sustainable economy.

Locality

Real resources are rooted in locality. The latter day Frodo has the option to use his intellect to draw on the international fund of ideas, but to base his material demands upon the area in which he lives. In each locality the land and its people are rich in resources. Not only soils, water, energy, vegetation and wildlife, but also schools, colleges, churches, farms, small businesses and a host of voluntary organisations provide a framework for informed collective action against the mindless destruction perpetrated by 'Rational' Economic Man. Knowledge of the local area's history and resources is an indispensable pre-requisite for regaining community control over common resources in the face of individualistic greed and competition.

However, the economics of greed and competition have become entrenched in everyday thought. The daily use of money, including the raising of funds for good causes, now seems as natural as breathing fresh air. Money is demanded from any group of people seeking to meet together in a public place, not only in business premises, libraries and town halls but even in churches. Money values predominate over all other value systems. There are rich resources available to guide the individual or group seeking to free themselves from intellectual dependence upon the so-called experts — if they can find the money to further their knowledge, and locate others willing to embark on the journey.

Christian values versus money values

True Christianity (as opposed to state religion) is compatible with many other religious and non-money-value systems. However, it constitutes a body of thought that is incompatible with prevailing neoliberalism, which would have us put our spiritual values aside when we become economic actors. As a result, global capitalism presents itself as value free and non-judgemental, when it is anything but value neutral.

The conventional view of social justice is that those who have more of their fair share of wealth should give up some of 'their' wealth so that the poor can have more. This is not the Christian view.

> The seventh commandment (you shall not steal) enjoins respect for the integrity of creation. Animals, like plants and inanimate beings, are by nature destined for the common good of past, present and future humanity. Use of the mineral, vegetable and animal resources of the universe cannot be divorced from respect for moral imperatives. Man's dominion over inanimate and other living beings granted by the Creator is not absolute; it is limited by concern for the quality of life of his neighbour, including generations to come; it requires a religious respect for the integrity of creation.[1]

Christian teaching holds that the *potential* to create wealth is held in common. Land, knowledge, skills, energy, all the necessary elements for creation of material, intellectual and cultural wealth are God-given and held in trust. Nothing that is made by individuals can be created without drawing upon the common stock. The teaching of the established Christian churches is crystal clear on the issue of ownership of property and access to common resources. The catechism of the Roman catholic church includes a quote from St. John Chrysostom on the seventh commandment: 'Not to enable the poor to share in our goods is to steal from them and deprive them of life. The goods we possess are not ours, but theirs'.[2]

The realisation that giving to those in need is merely giving to others what by rights belongs to them may come as a shock to many people accustomed to making generous donations to good causes. In this context, the *Catechism of the Catholic Church* calls for reform of 'international economic and financial institutions so that they will better promote equitable relationships with less advanced countries'. It notes that:

> (t)he *right to private property*, acquired by work or received from others by inheritance or gift, does not do away with the original gift of the earth to the whole of mankind. The *universal destination of goods* remains primordial, even if the promotion of the common good requires respect for the right to private property and its exercise.[3]

To the extent that goods can benefit others as well as the owner, the use of goods is not exclusive to the owner. The owner of any property is more properly regarded as a steward, making it fruitful and communicating its benefits to others:

> Goods of production — material or immaterial — such as land, factories, practical or artistic skills, oblige their possessors to employ them in ways that will benefit the greatest number. Those who hold goods for use and consumption should use them with moderation, reserving the better part for guests, for the sick and the poor. ... *Political authority* has the right and duty to regulate the legitimate exercise of the right to ownership for the sake of the common good.[4]

In common with other major religions, Christian teaching lends no support to the argument that a small number of individuals, operating on the basis of greed and competition, should appropriate to themselves the power to determine the communal agenda. While writings like those cited in this book are excluded by the mainstream, merely studied by sociologists for their curiosity value as 'minority' (crank) ideas, the affluent citizen of the 'developed' world remains bereft of meaningful guidelines for beliefs and action. Therefore the well-meaning drop donations into collecting tins, participate in charity fund-raising and trade generously with indigenous craftspeople while on safari holidays in Third World countries. Meanwhile governments cut provision for health, education, culture and the poor and needy on grounds of financial expediency. The problem is not new. Decades ago Massingham observed that fragmented patterns of information eradicate rational thought:

> Modern knowledge is departmentalized while the essence of culture is initiation into wholeness, so that all the divisions of knowledge are considered as the branches of one tree, the Tree of Life whose roots went deep into earth and top was heaven.[5]

Denial of access to basic skills, knowledge and culture confuses the affluent and robs the poor, reducing the capacity for self-help based upon common knowledge and sound judgement.

It's your choice

And so it is business as usual with the multinational corporations. They set the agenda, so they are probably right to claim there is no cause for alarm. Global warming may be inevitable. In any case, it's not proven. Nor does the loss of biodiversity matter much: species are faced with extinction all the time. Every so many millions of years, the whole plant and animal kingdom is wiped out. So why worry? There's nothing you can do about it. In the last resort, we can adapt to change through genetic engineering and other new technologies. Shortages will make the market adapt to financial reality. If you're still doubtful, contact any multinational corporation for their supply of free literature on the help they give to local people to create a greener world. When the literature arrives, note the names of environmental pressure groups whose expertise has been bought by the global corporations.

On the other hand, one might consider the advice of the American environmentalist Donella Meadows:

> There's one solution to the world's problems that I never hear the frenzied activists suggest.
>
> Slowing down.
>
> Slowing down could be the single most effective solution to the particular save-the-world struggle I immerse myself in — the struggle for sustain-

ability, for living harmoniously and well within the limits and laws of the Earth.

Suppose we went at a slow enough pace not only to smell the flowers but to feel our bodies, play with children, look openly without agenda or timetable at the faces of loved ones. Suppose we stopped gulping fast food and started savouring slow food, grown, cooked, served and eaten with care. Suppose we took time each day to sit in silence.[6]

The choice is in our hands. Whatever we decide, we are not alone. Wherever we live, there are others of like mind in our locality. Home can cease to be a resource to be exploited by global capitalism, and become once more a place to love and respect.

That will not happen, however, until we cease to sell our time for money in order to exchange that money for goods and services which 'save time'. So long as we wait for the system to spew enough money in our direction we will continue to find no time to care for the community and the land upon which it exists.

To conclude ...

This book has told the story of money from the earliest times to the present. Money is not a mysterious value-system with god-like power over our lives. It is simply a tool to be used by those who control it. Like any powerful tool or weapon, it can be dangerous in the wrong hands. At present banks and financial institutions are unlikely to release their grip on the community's money-power in response to special pleading. As the history of the social credit movement demonstrates, there are no easy answers.

The Alberta Experiment merits further study as an example of the potential for ordinary people to understand the financial causes of their rejection by society and alienation from the land. Historical evidence indicates that the social credit movement in Alberta, as elsewhere, was something more than the exercise of banner-waving protest in times of economic adversity. However, the bid to secure social credit through the ballot box served to compound the misapprehension that social credit was a demand for top-down monetary reform as a means to alleviate unemployment and stimulate economic growth. The way forward is through some form of cooperation, combining guild socialist theory with LETS, Mondragon[7] and other successful alternatives to global capitalism.

Monetary reform through the ballot box alone is barely distinguishable from Keynesianism, labourism or any other attempt to remove impediments to capitalist economic growth. By contrast social credit, with its guild socialist components, provides the theoretical framework for an ecologically sustainable post-capitalist political economy. Rooted in locality, the new economics recognises finance as one institution among the many essential to secure a viable community and a healthy environment capable of supporting that community over the long run. The economics of social credit is the very antithesis of the short-termist global economics of Bretton Woods.

Social credit seeks to counter economic globalisation by securing control over the institutions of finance by local communities, enabling values other than money values to resurface. It runs counter to the prevalent misapprehension that capitalism in general and its financial institutions in particular, just 'happen': that, like the constellations and planets and the very waves of the sea, some blind force dictates the direction of economic 'progress'; and that any form of agitation against what happens naturally is at best utopian, most likely misguided and always a thorough nuisance to serious authority going about its lawful business.

While reformist parties like the Labour Party have sought adaptation through negotiation, social credit recognised the limitations of reforms based upon fundamental power inequalities. The Alberta Experiment demonstrated the inability of the political process to introduce economic reform. Social credit never 'failed' because it was never tried. The route to social credit lies in some adaptation of the Douglas Credit (Draft Mining) Scheme, locally based, but keyed into a system of state finance. That experiment has yet to take place.

... and finally

For those readers who have flicked to the end of the book to find the solution. Sorry! The solutions are embedded within this text, and within the many referenced works which accompany it. It's the oldest trick in the book to demand a simple proposal from a would-be monetary reformer in order to refute it, discredit it, and strengthen the case for business-as-usual. As the social and ecological crisis gathers momentum, it is in the interests of all that each one of us gathers the time and energy to understand where the money comes from and how it can be controlled.

NOTES

1   Chapman, Geoffrey (1994) *The Catechism of the Catholic Church* London. Cassell (English translation).
2   Ibid.
3   Ibid.
4   Ibid.
5   Massingham, H. J. (1943) *The Tree of Life* London. Chapman and Hall.
6   Meadows, Donella in *Resurgence* 184.
7   For more detailed experimental examples of modern alternatives to wage-slavery see Douthwaite, Richard (1996) *Short Circuit: Strengthening Local Economies for Security in an Unstable World* Totnes. Green Books. Also Lutz, Mark A. and Lux, Kenneth (1988) *Humanistic Economics: The New Challenge* New York. The Bootstrap Press, and Dauncey, Guy (1988) *After the Crash: The Emergence of the Rainbow Economy* Basingstoke. Green Print.

Appendix

The archaeology of economic thought

ECONOMIC THEORY IS an axiomatic system: as long as the basic assumptions hold, the conclusions follow. But when we examine the assumptions closely we find that they do not apply to the real world... The assumption of perfect knowledge proved unsustainable, so it was replaced by an ingenious device. Supply and demand were taken as independently given. This condition was presented as a methodological requirement rather than an assumption. It was argued that economic theory studies the relationship between supply and demand; therefore it must take both of them as given.

George Soros[1]

In September 1992 George Soros made £1.3 billion by leading the speculative attack on the pound on Black Wednesday, forcing Britain out of the Exchange Rate Mechanism (ERM) and demonstrating a mastery of practical economics unrivalled by professional economic theorists. Nevertheless, economic theory is held in great esteem not only by supporters of the *status quo* but also by critics of economic growth. Attempts to create a more socially just and environmentally sustainable economy are therefore labelled 'alternative', 'new', 'heterodox', or even 'heretical'. Using quotes from mainstream economics texts, this chapter explains neoclassical general free market equilibrium theory with a view to assessing its merits as a guide to rational action.

Economics — a belief system, not a science

As Douglas' first writings appeared in print (1918-24) the economics profession was in the final stages of establishing itself as the dominant science of society. By modelling itself upon a natural science, physics, it purported to offer a value-free analysis of the economy as a guide to public and private policy formation. A decade later Hugh Gaitskell could with confidence classify Douglas as an 'economic heretic'. According to Gaitskell, although orthodox economists might differ on specific matters, they held a common world view. Heretics could easily be identified: despite public recognition they were amateurs. 'None of them has ever held an academic appointment in economics'.[2] Throughout the interwar years social credit theory was judged heretical because it did not conform to neoclassical orthodoxy. It is valuable to study the origins and development of this economic orthodoxy, partly because this can help us understand why Douglas's analysis found so little favour amongst economists. But more importantly, such a review sheds light on the proven incapacity of orthodox economics to guide policy formation on social and environmental issues. The issues which Douglas attempted to address have certainly not been tackled effectively in the seventy years since his proposals were so roundly rejected by the establishment of his day.

The economics profession would today describe itself as a broad church embracing many schools of thought, from the right-wing Austrian, through the neoclassicals, the macroeconomics of the Chicago School, orthodox Keynesianism, post-Keynesianism and institutionalism to a collection of Marxian and radical economists. However, the distinguishing feature of a school of economics is that it accords with the neoclassical paradigm. J. M. Gee broadens the religious metaphor in a manner that is quite startling in its implications:

> The neoclassical school is a broad church, offering a methodology and a paradigm embracing many sects. The high-priests of the church are well versed in mathematical technique, which they employ to trace out the consequences of individual behaviour on the assumption that economic agents constantly strive to maximise their economic well-being. These agents may not be, indeed typically are not, regarded as flesh and blood actors; they are mythical creations, designed so that their behaviour is perfectly predictable according to a hypothetico-deductive chain of reasoning.[3]

In other words, this orthodox economist of the neoclassical school maintains that neoclassical theory consists of 'a hypothetico-deductive chain of reasoning' flowing from the assumed actions of a group of 'mythical creations'. Such an evaluation of the actions and motives of human beings is so completely at odds with our actual experience, that it is tempting to leave the matter there; to simply ignore the paradigms and projections of such a blatantly reductionist group of thinkers. However, so deep-rooted are these assumptions and so great is the practical influence of economists over policy formation in matters of production, distribution, exchange and all other concerns relating to the conduct of our daily lives, that it is necessary to look further into neoclassical theory. We must attempt to understand the behaviour of these mythical creatures and their perfectly-predictable, hypothetico-deductive reasoning.

General free market equilibrium theory

Anybody seeking to understand orthodox economics faces an almost insuperable problem. The first step for any student is to suspend disbelief on a number of vital matters, all at the same time. As Gee explains:

For the neoclassicist, an individual is in economic equilibrium when, given the commodity prices he faces, given his ownership of factors of production and their prices, given his initial endowments in general, he cannot increase his utility through altering the mix of products bought or factor services supplied to others.[4]

To consider what the above sentence may mean we consider one phrase at a time, starting with the 'individual in economic equilibrium'.

Mushroom Man

The 'mythical creation' the budding economics student must first come to grips with is the 'agent' or economic actor. Rational Economic Man (REM) is not a real flesh and blood person existing in space and time. *He* (for there is no Rational Economic Woman in neoclassical theory) has no ties, duties or responsibilities save that of operating as an economic agent. He exists to register the pleasures and pains of the various options open to him as he makes his rational choices in the role of consumer. In his exercise of choice he operates purely from rational self-interest.

Julie Nelson quotes Thomas Hobbes, who wrote: 'let us consider men ... as if but even now sprung out of the earth, and suddenly, like mushrooms, come to full maturity, without any kind of engagement to each other'. As Nelson goes on to explain, the mythical 'agent' studied by economists in their abstract models has 'no childhood or old age, no dependence on anyone, no responsibility for anyone but himself'. He appears from nowhere, 'fully active and self-contained', influenced by nothing except his rationality. In an ideal market he has perfect knowledge of prices, which form the only medium for his interaction with society.[5]

> The hedonistic conception of man is that of a lightning calculator of pleasures and pains, who oscillates like a homogenous globule of desire of happiness under the impulse of stimuli that shift him about the area, but leave him intact. He has neither antecedent nor consequent. He is an isolated definitive human datum, in stable equilibrium except for the buffets of the impinging forces that displace him in one direction or another. Self-imposed in elemental space, he spins symmetrically about his own spiritual axis until the parallelogram of forces bears down upon him, whereupon he follows the line of the resultant. When the force of the impact is spent, he comes to rest, a self-contained globule of desire as before.[6]

Although Veblen's early picture of REM remains a classic expression of the limitations of orthodox theory, it has been neatly sidelined by generations of economists as they induct their students into the mysteries of the subject. According to the rules of orthodoxy, the individual undertakes rational calculations at lightning speed in order to remain in equilibrium, that is, at a point where he could not adjust his purchases in such a way that he would be better off. His 'rationality' dictates that purely economic considerations determine his actions. He does not act 'irrationally' by allowing sentimental or ethical considerations to sway his judgement. The data upon which he bases his calculations are commodity prices.

Commodity prices

'Commodity' is the general name given to goods and services, the basic objects of production and exchange. To qualify as a commodity, the good or service must not merely exist: it must exchange on the market. Although fresh air is essential to life, it is not normally exchanged on the market. Therefore, in terms of economic theory, it does not exist. Equally, the desire of the starving for food does not register if the starving person has nothing to offer in exchange for food on the market. To feature in the story of economics, a commodity must be both in demand and supply: economic agents must be prepared to 'demand' it by offering and 'supply' it by accepting something in exchange for it, normally money. Where the forces of supply and demand are equal (in equilibrium), price is determined. In other words, the individual makes rapid calculations which determine price. However, as Gee indicates, the commodity prices the individual faces at the point of purchase are 'given': they are determined by the accumulated costs of the production process. At this point in his or her studies Rational Person (RP) turns to the world of classical fiction or politics, leaving REM to his own devices! For those prepared to believe anything in prospect of earning a good income, the story unfolds as follows. The next phrase indicates that REM's 'ownership of factors of production and their prices' are 'given'.

Ownership of factors of production

If goods are 'demanded' for exchange on the market, the theory suggests they must be supplied, since production for exchange is an essential element of the science of economics. Production occurs in two forms. Nature produces trees, fruits, flowers, crops, minerals and the soil upon which every form of civilisation ultimately depends. Equally, society produces human beings and many services, including mothering, socialisation of the young, care of the physically and mentally exhausted, spiritual guidance, mutual support and other forms of service which may be exchanged, but not *on the market*. Unless or until the products of nature or the services of society become 'commodities', that is, subject to exchange on the market, as far as the economist is concerned they do not exist.[7] Although the formal economy would cease to function if the natural world or human society became incapable of providing the goods and services upon which the real life economy depends, this minor detail is ignored by orthodox economic theory. Hence it is necessary to suspend disbelief on this point also in order to pursue the study of economics.

In terms of orthodox theory, production is production for exchange on the market. Factors of production are, therefore, 'the economy's productive resources — land, labour and capital'. They are defined as follows. Land is natural resource of all kinds: the earth and all that is therein *before* it becomes subject to economic exchange. Labour, often termed 'human resources', is the muscle power and brain power of human beings. Capital is the physical assets generated from past output, including equipment, buildings, tools and other manufactured goods used in production. Although land and capital may be owned by a household, firm or government, economic theory reduces the economic agent to the individual, REM.

To participate in the economy the factor of production must be owned by REM. From its sale he derives an income: if he sells the use of land, he claims rent, if he sells capital he derives profits and if he owns labour he draws wages. In this way he can register as a consumer, able to 'demand' the products he wants the economy to supply. The number of exceptions and objections and the gross simplification involved in elaborating an economic theory from such a narrow starting point are obvious, but again, disbelief must be suspended.

Of particular importance is the fact that these narrow definitions lead to a glaring confusion between profits and interest. In assessing factor incomes paid by firms to households (the incomes paid to consumers in respect of their contribution to the productive process) 'interest' appears in GNP calculations; interest is thus included in the general measure of productivity. However, interest derives from the sale of the use of money, that most mythical of all 'factors of production': it is not even included within economics texts in the standard definition of capital as a factor of production. General equilibrium theory (see below) has nothing to say about the role or origin of money in the economy: its proponents make the mind-boggling assumption that money just 'happens to be present' in the economy. The narrow terms of their original definition then forces them to classify interest payments on this mystical entity, whose origins are not discussed, as the sale of the use of capital. In other words, interest is considered a form of profits accruing not to real capital (machines) but to that mythical entity, 'money capital'. The significance of this confusion becomes apparent when the creation and availability of money is discussed more fully.

To the economic theorist REM's 'ownership' and sale of a factor of production (land, labour or capital) entitles him to an income in the form of rent, wages or profit. As Gee indicates, economists do not consider how or why some people come to own the land or capital which the producer needs in order to produce goods and services, nor why a large number of people own nothing but the 'labour power' which they are forced to accompany as they 'sell' it on the market in the attempt to survive: as far as the study of economics is concerned, ownership of the factors of production is settled by some inexplicable mechanism outside their field of expertise. Equally, in studying equilibrium, the prices of the factors of production, determined by demand and supply, are 'given'.

Initial endowments

Further confusion relates to the practice in economics of classifying labour as a factor of production. The notion that 'labour time' can be sold as a commodity subtly obscures the relationship between the factors of production. No person can sell his or her labour time when they are not present physically within the productive process. The implications of the statement form a major part of this book. Here, it is sufficient to note that in the real world labour, the worker, is a real person, a citizen with rights and responsibilities, who produces goods and services needed by the community. In real life the worker is not merely a factor of production to be bought and sold on the free market, handing over all responsibility and judgement to the employing body: that is wage slavery.

Utility and factor services

The final phrase of Gee's explanation contains words requiring further definition. 'Utility', the benefit or satisfaction that a person obtains from the consumption of a good or service, is a key term in neoclassical theory. It is assumed that REM registers the level of utility of a good or service by selecting it in a certain quantity through exchange on the market. Using their sophisticated mathematical techniques, the high priests of neoclassical theory can measure two types of decisions. They can measure opportunity costs, in the form of goods and services rejected by REM as he makes his lightning calculations (they assume that the economic actor, REM, has perfect knowledge of all possible alternative choices). Also, they can measure the 'disutility' to REM of supplying his land, labour or capital. When REM supplies capital or land for exchange on the market he gives up the present or alternative use of the factor.

However, REM's supply of labour also registers as a disutility, implying that work is a purely unsatisfying activity. In Chapter 5 we see that pure disutility of labour belongs to the slave state. This provides us with a further paradox in view of the stress placed by orthodox economists on their libertarian stance. Moreover, the notion of disutility cannot be applied to finance capital with any degree of accuracy, since the lending of money is done through the agency of banking. As Chapter 6 indicates, the holder of original capital does not give up use of any concrete goods or services. The lending of money is a purely accounting process.

General equilibrium

The freedom of the individual is paramount in neoclassical theory. As Gee further explains, since the economy is made up of a large number of individuals and firms, the general equilibrium theorist raises two questions in relation to the economy as a whole:

1. Is there a theoretical price configuration for all goods and services, from, say, bananas for final consumption, to steel used as an input (a factor of production) in the production process, such that *none* of the economic agents (individuals or firms) could increase their utilities through further

trade, that is, so that supplies equal demands in all markets? Such a state is known as general equilibrium.

2. If there is such a theoretical price configuration, can general equilibrium be attained, that is, are the price adjustments in the market likely to move towards it: and would the general equilibrium state be stable?[8]

Neoclassical economists see their task as pointing the way towards achievement of general equilibrium in order to secure social harmony. As Gee explains: 'If it cannot be shown theoretically that a general equilibrium price configuration will always exist, and that general equilibrium can be attained and maintained, *through free exchange between individuals* under reasonable assumptions, then it can hardly be shown that a spontaneous, harmonious, economic and social order is possible (let alone likely!).' As we have demonstrated, the assumptions postulated by economists are *not* reasonable.

The archaeology of economics

It is very difficult to argue with the logic encapsulated in Gee's statements, since they are the products of generations of theoreticians, each adding their contributions to the body of thought known as neoclassical theory. However, for those who wish to see sane management of natural resources and equitable distribution of access to the necessities of life for all who comprise human society, it is not enough to argue that 'we would not set out from here'. Economic orthodoxy has a firm hold over the minds of producers and consumers and the everyday reality they face. In order to change perceptions of reality it may be useful to retrace our steps in order to discover the primitive origins of Rational Economic Man, to work out 'how we got here'. First, however, it is necessary to pause a while and consider what has happened to the central subject of study, money.

Money

The greatest mystery of all is that, so far, the role of money has not registered. Economics students are informed early in their studies that, contrary to popular perception, money is not a major feature of the study of economics. Supply and demand reach an equilibrium through price, prices are money prices and REM performs his lightning calculations in money. Nevertheless the neoclassical theorist assures his students that money is a matter for mere accountants. Economic theory studies equilibrium between commodities. Money is a commodity like any other. It just *happens* to be used because it is very convenient, and money is just assumed to 'be there'.

Of course, orthodox economics does have a theoretical analysis of money. In the dim and distant past, when money was waiting to be invented, commodities were bartered directly for each other. This was highly inconvenient. A person with a cow to sell and wishing to buy a cabbage had problems too numerous to mention here. The invention of money abolished the necessity to achieve a 'double coincidence of wants'. It offered four benefits. *As a medium of exchange* it guaranteed that people with something to sell would always accept money in exchange for it, while people wishing to buy would always offer money in exchange. *As a unit of account* it offered an agreed measure for stating the prices of goods and services. *As a standard of deferred payments* it enabled contracts to be written for future receipts and payments. And finally, money could be used *as a store of value* for later exchange.

The many and various forms that money can take, and how it is created and supplied to an economy, will be explored in later chapters. What is so striking is that it is actually possible to leave a close analysis of money to a later stage. This underlines the surprisingly minor role of money in neoclassical theory.

Although students are taught that money does exist, but is of little importance, they are asked to perform yet another leap of faith. The study of economics is divided into two levels, micro and macro.

Microeconomics is the study of the determination of relative prices of commodities, relative employment of the factors of production and relative distribution of income through the pricing of the factors of production. Subjects considered at this level include technological change, production and consumption, wages and earnings. Money is a useful tool as people register their choices or 'preferences', but at the micro-level money has no theoretical function: REM operates his lightning calculations on a moneyless barter-system, still mentally comparing cows and cabbages.

Macroeconomics is the study of the aggregated behaviour of the entire national income, price level and employment. The whole system, rather than its individual components, now becomes the subject of study. Macroeconomics looks at what determines unemployment, aggregate income, average prices, inflation and the differences in wealth among nations. At this level it is impossible to ignore the existence of money as a relevant factor. It therefore becomes a specialist branch of the subject (monetary economics). However, money is still regarded as functioning purely as a useful tool enabling the free market to achieve general equilibrium. In orthodox theory, money has no role to play in its own right as a determinant of the subjects of the study of economic theory — production, distribution and exchange.

From tradition to reason

Originally, the study of economics was a quest for a theoretical framework to explain and justify the break from an inegalitarian and unjust feudal tradition. The pre-industrial economy was dominated by a religious world view which placed God at the centre of the universe. The natural world was considered to operate according to God's decree, with higher plants taking precedence over lower ones, animals over plants and humans having dominion over all earthly interests. The human economy operated within this framework, each class within the hierarchical system being assigned appropriate duties and obligations towards other humans. In the medieval world the lending of money and trading for profit were unacceptable: exchange was determined by custom in support of the God-given hierarchy of class. Industrial 'progress' could not be accommodated within this world view.

Therefore it became necessary to create a 'scientific' body of economic theory based upon objective facts and rational thought. In the 'Age of Reason' individuals should be at liberty to follow their own self-interest. If individuals wished to operate according to Christian values they were free to do so. They could not, however, cling to an outdated model of the universe in order to justify their oppression of others.

Adam Smith

The social science of economics was born under the protective shade of the Scientific Revolution. René Descartes, the seventeenth-century philosopher, mathematician and founder of analytic geometry, took the view that mathematics was more reliable than human sense perception. To Descartes, a distinction could be drawn between the incorporeal mind and the physical body with its clockwork attributes. Isaac Newton followed with his picture of an orderly and predictable universe governed by natural, God-given law. It was but a short step to assume that the economy had also been set in motion by the hand of God, so that attempts to improve upon it by policies formed by mere humans would upset the mechanism and disturb its ability to function in an orderly way. As a social science, economics was from the outset framed by its founding father's admiration for Newton's mechanical view of the universe.

In *An Inquiry into the Nature and Causes of the Wealth of Nations* (1776) Adam Smith established the scientific study of the market system, developing the world view that capitalism is necessary for freedom and wealth creation. The 'Invisible Hand' must be left to create order out of chaos. Smith's rational social science rescued commerce and industry from the restraints and regulations imposed by the ruling aristocracies of powerful trading nations. His targets were mercantilism and the physiocrats.

Mercantilism was the first alliance in modern history between government and business, established to increase national wealth and state power. Since power and wealth were equated with gold and silver, the mercantilists believed that output of domestic goods should be stimulated, while domestic consumption by the masses should be limited. Meanwhile imports should be discouraged by tariffs or quantitative restrictions and exports encouraged, in order to create a favourable balance of trade. In this way a country would have a strong economy, with wealth and power flowing to its aristocracy. The role of the church, allied to government or business interests, is outside the scope of this analysis, save to note that church leaders tended to be drawn from the families of the powerful, whether landed aristocracy or the newly emerging bourgeoisie. For this reason the church was attacked *both* as an agent of reaction *and* as condoning new forms of exploitation. Hence the attraction of the rational scientific approach to the study of society. Wealth accumulation was allowed to become the dominant value-system.

However, Smith's rejection of physiocratic theory presents the most intriguing insights into the future development of economics. Based in France, the physiocrats argued that land, the gift of nature, was the form and source of a nation's real wealth. Land, not mercantilist trade, enabled agriculture to produce a positive net product in excess of its production costs. Hence agriculture was the only truly productive enterprise. The physiocrats took issue with government restrictions, mercantilist subsidies and privileges which protected industry and commerce. In their view manufacturing produced no more than it received. It generated no surplus. Their proposals included the elimination of the feudal landholders' tax exemption, relief of peasant farmers from their heavy tax burden and an end to the protected status of manufacturing.

On the eve of the Industrial Revolution in England, Smith's positive view of the role of manufacturing in the creation of wealth had more appeal than the views of mercantilists on the one hand and physiocrats on the other. Reared in urban comfort, Smith identified the peasant lifestyle with material, cultural and spiritual poverty. In his view, *production* created real wealth. Trade restrictions and gold accumulation did not create wealth, neither was land the ultimate source of wealth. Rather, free trade and the creation of machinery and new technology existed in a symbiotic relationship: the expansion of markets would enable the economy to grow, creating wealth for all. Workers and merchants would be free from feudal overlords and state bureaucracy. As machinery replaced the sweat of the brow in rural field and urban factory alike, wealth could be created in abundance so that all could live in urban affluence. Although misguided, this exhilarating dream forms the basis of Western economic thought.

The selfish economist

Smith presented two concepts which have underpinned economic theory throughout its history: *self-interest* and the *division of labour*. The two are closely linked. In a world where people are motivated by pure self-interest, where tasks are divided up in the name of speed and efficiency, both the notion of service to others within the community and the intrinsic satisfaction of labour are rejected. 'It is not from the benevolence of the butcher, the brewer or the baker, that we expect our dinner: but from their regard for their own interest.' In Smith's well-known sentence the theory of the money economy was born.

Smith regarded specialisation as the key to the growth of wealth in a nation. At the level of the individual worker, he argued in his famous example, one worker *could* create a pin unaided, but the process would be very inefficient. If ten men specialised in the ten separate stages they could make 4,800 pins each, 48,000 in total, where one worker on his own would struggle to produce twenty. On the same principle specialisation between trades and countries would improve skills, vastly increasing output and thus expanding economic growth. The question of need — whether there was intrinsic utility in owning more pins or other artifacts of the industrial age — did not enter into the debate. It was assumed that expanding markets were necessary to put food on the workers' tables.

On its own, division of labour merely initiated growth in the industrial process. Growth needed to be maintained through capital accumulation, for somebody had to buy the new machines and pay for the raw materials and the wages (i.e. to buy fixed and circulating capital). Production takes time. When workers enjoyed some access to subsistence from the land, wages might be paid *after* production and sale had been completed. However, the urban landless labourer must be paid in advance from an accumulated pool of wealth, the 'wages fund' which was thought to rise as production expanded. As profits rose, they enabled manufacturers to accumulate plant and machinery — capital — the life-blood of the economy.

Private ownership, private wealth

The accumulation of property gave rise to a further principle of the secular social science of economics that was novel to the Industrial Revolution, the notion of private ownership of property. Following John Locke's natural rights arguments, Smith held that accumulated private property should be protected from state appropriation. Manufacturers needed to accumulate capital in order to acquire the machines, raw materials and labour essential to the expansion of wealth production. The vesting of property in individuals by virtue of their *future* potential to create wealth, unhindered by community rights and obligations, accorded well with the Newtonian vision of a clockwork society. Where the scale of production was small, the numbers of manufacturers capable of entering the market would be large. Hence competition would be the dominant regulatory influence in the 'atomistic' economy of self-interested individuals.

According to Smith, unregulated natural laws operating in the economy enable the market mechanism to work through a process of price adjustment. The money price of a commodity is part of a natural economic balance. Although fluctuations in supply and demand may cause the price of a commodity to deviate from its 'natural price', such deviations will only be temporary. Over the long term the price of every commodity is determined by its costs of production. The forces of competition, he argues, are the vital regulators of the economy. Individual consumers and suppliers are both too small and too numerous to influence the market as a whole. Left to itself, the market is completely self-regulating.

Although the value of wealth created by self-interest and the division of labour could be quantified and measured, a question lingered to trouble Smith's disciples: how was value created? Money was merely a measure, of no intrinsic value. Did all wealth come from the land, as the physiocrats maintained? Could it come from machines, although they were themselves created? Smith advanced the labour theory of value, the notion that the value of a product can in some way be equated with the quantity of labour used in its production. In the atomistic world of economic theory the questions of value creation and of values struck a discordant note. The labour theory of value, further developed by Ricardo, and in turn by Marx, was bypassed by mainstream economic theory.

The classical economists and J. B. Say

Smith's theoretical framework dominated economic thought for the following century. The classical theorists of this period believed in economic, political and religious freedom, that is, freedom from traditional restraints. Government should not interfere save in matters of national military defence and criminal justice, where protection of private property was vital. The maintenance of the unprofitable infrastructure and institutions necessary to promote economic growth were also sanctioned as 'rightful acts of government'. Ricardo, Malthus, James and John Stuart Mill refined and developed Smith's theories. However, it was J. B. Say, the leading French advocate of *laissez faire*, who amplified a crucial aspect of Smith's theorising, the neutrality of the role of money in wealth creation.

Say followed Smith in regarding money as a neutral arbiter of exchange. According to Say, money has no intrinsic value. It follows that supply and demand are inextricably linked. Say's theory of the market rested on the concept that every supply creates a demand. Hence product exchanges for product: every commodity put on the market creates its own demand, and every demand exerted on the market creates its own supply. Therefore in the clockwork economy there can be no *general* glut of commodities, no *general* over-production. Since money has no intrinsic value, savings will be invested in new production, generating new demand and re-establishing the balance. Hence a glut of an individual product is a symptom of a temporary malfunction which should be left to correct itself. The classicals, including Marx, expended considerable mileage on these issues.

However, it is in the theory of *money* that Say consolidated Smith's mechanical principles of economic activity, paving the way for general competitive equilibrium theory. The presumed neutrality of money (Smith), and asserted neutrality (Say), forms a major plank upon which the mechanism of free markets and the free choice of REM are based. Hence the supposed neutrality of money was a principal point of contention by Douglas, which thus sets him apart from the developing orthodoxy of neoclassical theory.

Theories and practicalities

The Scientific Revolution established that natural objects had neither souls nor emotions, being impelled by physical forces alone. Since the science of economics was founded upon the same principles, it followed that economics was the study of individuals impelled by impersonal forces. As practitioners of a positive science, economists sought to ensure that normative values based upon subjective opinions of individuals or groups (i.e. beliefs in any but money values) did not interfere with the free play of market forces and so hamper long-term economic progress.

Many economists struggling to understand the new social science drew attention to the unsustainability of unrestrained economic growth. In 1857 J. S. Mill questioned the value of 'the kind of economical progress which excites the congratulations of ordinary politicians; the mere increase of production and accumulation'. Using thoroughly normative language, Mill expressed the view that an undiluted diet of material satisfactions in overcrowded urban conditions might be limited in value:

> Nor is there much satisfaction in contemplating the world with nothing left to the spontaneous activity of nature; with every rood of land brought into cultivation, which is capable of growing food for human beings; every flowery waste or natural pasture ploughed up, all quadrupeds or birds which are not domesticated for man's use exterminated as his rivals for food, every hedgerow or superfluous tree rooted out, and scarcely a place left where a wild shrub or flower could grow without being eradicated as a weed in the name of improved agriculture. If the earth must lose that great portion of its pleasantness which it owes to things that the unlimited increase of wealth and population would extirpate from it, for the mere purpose of enabling it to support a larger, but not a better or happier population, I sincerely hope, for the sake of posterity, that they will be content to be stationary, long before necessity compels them to it.

> It is scarcely necessary to remark that a stationary condition of capital and population implies no stationary state of human improvement. There would be as much scope as ever for all kinds of mental culture, and moral and social progress; as much room for improving the Art of Living, and much more likelihood of its being improved, when minds cease to be engrossed by the art of getting on. Even the industrial arts might be as earnestly and as successfully cultivated, with this sole difference, that instead of serving no purpose but the increase in wealth, industrial improvements would produce their legitimate effect, that of abridging labour.[10]

Although generally more optimistic about the long-term outcomes of industrial capitalism, Marx also sounded a cautionary note:

> In modern agriculture, as in the urban industries, the increased productiveness and quantity of the labour set in motion are bought at the cost of laying waste and consuming by disease labour-power itself. Moreover, all progress in capitalistic agriculture is a progress in the art, not only of robbing the labourer, but of robbing the soil; all progress in increasing the fertility of the soil for a given time, is a progress towards ruining the lasting sources of that fertility. The more a country starts its development on the foundation of modern industry, like the United States for example, the more

rapid is this process of destruction. Capitalist production, therefore, develops technology, and the combining together of various processes into a social whole, only by sapping the original sources of all wealth — the soil and the labourer.[11]

However, mainstream orthodoxy threw caution to the wind. Economic theorists increasingly rejected the notion that human beings and their actions were rooted in space and time of everyday earthly reality. Hence the science of economics studied a particular version of reality, the material aspects of human activity capable of being isolated from all other dimensions of reality and measured in terms of money. Failure to establish the existence of the ether led in science to the suspension of belief in time and space and the establishment of the relativity principle. Similarly, failure to establish the existence of a value system outside the money economy led to belief in a market economy operating outside time and space.

Divorced from everyday life, economic theory began to merge with the body of ideas known as 'political economy,' as a means to inform and justify political change. In this form it emerges as neither natural nor scientific. Shorn of its traditional community and religious restraints, unbridled self-interest would, left to itself, result in a permanent state of mayhem and destruction. The freedom to starve and the freedom to exploit, or be exploited by, others was enshrined in a legal system which rejected traditional rights and duties in favour of the sanction of physical force.

On the ground, in the real world, the history of 'economic progress' is a catalogue of injustice and brutal suppression. Hanging in chains, the highland clearances, enclosures, transportations, the slave trade, colonialism, and child labour in mines and mills are justified by economic historians as 'adjustments' necessary to smooth the path of economic progress. The seizing of the commons and the creation of the institutional framework of private ownership of land, capital, and intellectual property in its many forms was justified by the theory of market freedom.

Economics became a new secular religion, beautiful in its soaring logic, yet divorced from the land and from traditional social restraints necessary for the long-term survival of the human venture. Whilst Marx, Mill and many others searched for explanations, traditional checks and balances were stripped away in the name of a 'freedom' informed by economics, enshrined in law and consolidated by force. Economic theory became a belief system in which faith had a greater role to play than fact.

From political economy to neoclassical economics

As economists rejected the normative values of political economy in favour of a more 'scientific' body of theory the number of assumptions, stated and unstated, increased. When assumptions conflicted with reality, economists increasingly advocated policies which were undesirable to many people. A common assumption made by economists was that 'factor endowment' (who owns what in the first place) could be taken as 'given', having no bearing on outcomes (who ends up with a massive share of the cake and who ends up with the crumbs). However, the fact that some individuals might own land, others capital and many nothing more than the labour of hand and brain was of considerable significance in relation to income distribution.

The assumed irrelevance of 'factor endowment' to influencing outcomes was further disproved by the vast increases in scale of productive enterprises in the latter part of the nineteenth century. Whereas Smith believed that competition would prevent monopoly, Marx more accurately predicted that the search for profit and higher levels of technology would result in production being concentrated in large enterprises. This 'second industrial revolution' placed enormous power in the hands of private banks and the joint stock companies they financed. Small farmers, businesses and landless workers were powerless to negotiate with vast enterprises, which followed the introduction of the internal combustion engine, transcontinental railways, steel manufacture of precision tools and the oil and electricity industries. Although industrial power was concentrating in fewer hands, economists continued to advocate *laissez-faire* policies, enabling states and industrialists to cooperate in a form of economic development based on state enforced 'freedom'. As economic activity broke the bounds of tradition and ignored the physical restraints of nature, economic theory was invoked to guide policy formation.

Money and value

The definition of wealth or 'value' presented a problem. The mercantilists equated particular commodities — gold, silver and other precious metals — with wealth and power. However, as the industrial revolution progressed one did not require formal training in economics to notice that money did not hold a constant value. When gold was used as money, a gold rush in South Africa or California would exert a discernable economic impact. The creation of money does not create real wealth: it merely facilitates the extension of the money economy into areas hitherto not monetised.

Wealth might, perhaps, derive from land, capital or labour. Neoclassical economists rejected land as the source of all value: it held potential, but it did not create wealth. Coal in the ground, timber in the forest and wool on the sheep possessed potential value, but it did not register within the economy. Perhaps exchange created value? Clearly it did not. If machines were the source of wealth, this might explain and justify the disproportionate share of wealth claimed by the owners of large factories. However Marx, following Smith and Ricardo, argued that labour was the ultimate source of wealth, since machines were the product of past labour. The debate over the relationship between money, wealth and value was neatly sidestepped by the so-called 'marginalist revolution.' Occurring in the

1870s, this theoretical 'revolution' coinciding with the 'second industrial revolution,' enabled economics to evolve into a pure science of society. But this pure economic science was constructed upon a question that was unresolved and eventually deemed irrelevant by default. Despite heated controversies over the instability of money throughout the nineteenth century, the debate over the nature of the medium of exchange and its relation to wealth, value and general economic activity was never pursued, still less resolved.

The evolution of economics into a pure science of society gave the discipline a new status. As in any other science, theoreticians adopted the view that significance rested in measurable and hence countable objective facts. While the *application* of this knowledge might rest upon subjective opinion and the outcome of debate, the role of the theorist was to describe how the system worked. The task of the economist was to observe and measure the mechanisms which made the market tick. The scope for mathematical calculation of market transactions was evident. A crucial question remained; what was being measured?

Utility

Neoclassical economic theory is based upon the ethical principle of hedonism. Hedonism is the doctrine that moral value can be defined in terms of pleasure and that the pursuit of pleasure is the highest good. The doctrine of utilitarianism was enshrined as economic theory's most fundamental assumption through the work of Jeremy Bentham. According to this doctrine, 'right [sic] action consists in the greatest good for the greatest number, that is, in maximizing the total benefit resulting, without regard to the distribution of benefits and burdens' (*Collins English Dictionary*). The implications of accepting this doctrine as the basic assumption underlying the objective science of society are profound, and beyond the scope of this book.[12] It is sufficient to note that students of economics are swiftly marched on to the next point. Accepting that pleasure can be greater or smaller introduces the notion that it can be measured as an objective fact. Rational Economic Man was in business!

Equilibrium

Economists took the concept of equilibrium in Newtonian physics and applied it to the market. Just as the harmony of the spheres indicated that equilibrium in the natural order was God's design, a balance among contending economic forces was normal and natural, a part of the same overall design. Equilibrium can be static or dynamic. In physics an object in dynamic equilibrium moves along a predictable path over time. It is kept on that path by the balance of opposing forces as it moves through free space. Speed, distance and force can be quantified and measured.

Similarly, economists floated the concept of an 'equilibrium' price maintained by the forces of supply and demand. Their argument is traditionally illustrated by appropriate graphs showing two intersecting lines, one rising from left to right labelled 'supply', the other falling from left to right labelled 'demand'. The higher the price[13] of a commodity (guns, apples, anything) the greater the number suppliers will bring on to the market. The lower the price, the greater the number consumers will be willing to buy. As price rises, supply rises and demand falls. The equilibrium price is reached when the forces of supply and demand are in balance at the point where the two lines intersect on the graph. Once this price is established it will persist, so that the market maintains its equilibrium.

Although Alfred Marshall is hailed in Britain as the high priest of neoclassical economics, Leon Walras was the pure theorist whose fascination with mechanical systems encapsulates the world view of the late industrial revolution. Walras' complex mathematical general equilibrium theory was published in the 1870s. The concept of two commodities (one of which may be money) exchanging at an equilibrium rate was extended to embrace all commodities and factor markets simultaneously. Walras' economic universe operated like a machine. As prices moved up and down, they functioned like levers and pulleys in a mechanical system.

Building upon the work of economists like Say, Walras regarded the economy as a closed system in which markets cleared at each stage of operations, resulting in multi-market stability. Hence if all markets except the wheat market and at least one other are in equilibrium, adjustment must automatically occur. If, at the present price of wheat, the amount of wheat demanded is greater than the amount supplied, the price of wheat must be raised to eliminate excess demand.

However, all markets are interdependent. Since all equilibria were defined with reference to the initial price of wheat, this price increase must upset the equilibria in other markets. To accommodate the change from the 'wrong' to the 'right' price, further adjustments in all other markets must be made, and then again in the wheat market, continuing until the whole system moves relentlessly towards multi-market equilibrium.

As within the Newtonian model, economists used the calculus to aid their interpretation of data presented by their observations. Whether applied to the natural world or to human economic agents, it proved possible to study the effect on a function of an infinitesimal change in an independent variable which tends to zero. 'Marginalist' theory has dominated economic theory ever since: more on this below.

As economists constructed their mechanical model universe, several practical problems arose. Ignorance of alternatives, for example, could hamper the smooth working of the system of pulleys and levers and act as a impediment to the blind forces of the market. Therefore such ignorance had to be eliminated as a possibility. If simultaneous equilibria were to be achieved, market agents needed to know about all quantities and all prices. In this way fine adjustments could be made smoothly. Walras conceptualised the 'auctioneer', a hypothetical mechanism which allowed buyers to reduce their price offers when there is excess supply and increase them when demand is in excess. In this way both buyers and sellers discover the true equilibrium price before any actual exchange takes place.

Hence price is *not* after all determined in actual markets through the working of supply and demand at disequilibrium prices over time. It pre-exists as an etherial force. Prices of the factors of production, including wage rates, are determined within the mechanical system in such a way that there is no 'involuntary unemployment' or poverty. Excess of any type will register and be corrected by market forces. Perfect knowledge ensures that no unfair advantage exists. Hence the profit rate is always and everywhere equal, and no costs are involved in transferring factors of production across physical space. Monopoly cannot exist.

Marginalism

Economists needed data to feed into their models. While Smith and the early classicals focused upon output, the supply of wealth, the marginalists focused on demand, adopting Bentham's hedonistic view of human nature. The good of the community as a whole was determined by the interest of the individual in increasing his total sum of pleasure and diminishing his total sum of pain. The marginalists' calculus of pleasure and pain sought to establish that perfect competition maximises pleasure while minimising pain.

The point of change in pleasure or pain is called the 'margin'. Hence 'marginal pleasure' is an extremely small increase in pleasure over some arbitrary unit of time, capable of expression in terms of Newton's calculus. In a world of perfect competition people acted, at the margin, as rational balancers of pleasure and pain, creating a mathematically elegant equilibrium. In this mystical world Rational Economic Man, the economic agent, was entirely rational, never acting on impulse. Marginalists focused upon the point of change between variables, extending the marginal principle to all economic decisions made by producers and consumers. Motives, inclinations and desires were conscious and consistent. There was no room for emotion.

Value, in marginalist theory, is based upon psychological satisfaction. A product is therefore defined as any object or service which can give pleasure or avoid pain. This subjective value system is illustrated by the 'law of diminishing marginal utility'. Taking a range of products, different levels of satisfaction will accrue from consuming more and more units of each good or service. It is possible to indicate the amount of extra satisfaction associated with each unit, or 'marginal' increase in quantity. The diminishing 'want-satisfying power' to an individual of consuming additional units of the same good or service can be represented in terms of declining numerical values. In pure theory, these subjective values would be represented in terms of other commodities. In practice, prices are quantified in terms of money, considered a more 'scientific' measuring device.

Marginalism and distribution

The mechanical economic universe of the marginalists consists of two types of agents, producers and consumers, operating in their different markets. Consumers register their demands, according to their diminishing marginal utilities and preference orderings, while producers supply goods and services on the commodity markets. Meanwhile, the factor markets combine the factors of production — that is, land, labour and capital (machines and plant) — to maximum advantage in the production of wealth. That wealth constitutes the income of society and is distributed according to a law which gives every agent of production the amount of wealth created by the agent. Factors are rewarded according to their 'productivity', which is itself determined by observable laws. According the 'law of diminishing returns', a firm using constant amounts of capital and land but employing additional workers will find that the output of each additional worker will eventually and successively decline. The same is true for the other factors of production. Left to itself, the system assigns to all people the value of what they have specifically produced. The allocation of total income from production in the form of wages, interest and profits is fair and equitable because each individual is paid according to their worth. In this world of suspended animation, technology never changes and so cannot disrupt the fair and equitable distribution of wealth.

The theoretical flaws in the 'science' of economics

Early neoclassical economists and social Darwinists shared the view that people neither can nor should change society through collective action. In the late nineteenth century, and ever since, powerful business leaders concurred with the view that survival of the fittest was a law of nature, so that human regulations constitute an unnecessary hindrance to the struggle for survival. As neoclassical theory asserted that economic progress could only be hampered by government regulation and interference, massive industrial combines concentrated monopolistic control over the production of coal, oil, iron, steel and cotton.

Although practice and theory have seen adaptation and modification over the past century, the basic paradigm of Newtonian general free market equilibrium (sometimes termed simultaneist) economics holds sway. In the world of equilibrium economics time is suspended and money has no role to play save that of a facilitating tool. In the real economy, goods exchange for money, at money prices. If price was inflexible, and determined before exchange took place, there would be nothing for economists to study. 'Any analysis of a real market economy has to explain trade at disequilibrium prices because they are the only prices anyone actually uses. To start by assuming they do not exist is like studying a centipede by nailing it to the floor'.[14] Exchange at a point in time establishes price at a point in time. Nevertheless, generations of students have suspended their disbelief in order to study economic theory, learning to dismiss the economics of so-called alternatives economists like Douglas and Marx as unsound and heretical.

The fact that money plays a proactive role in the real economy demolishes the entire edifice of equilibrium economics. According to Freeman, 'if a simultaneist allows money into his or her system as anything other than a numeraire, s/he confronts an insuperable problem. If agents are allowed to accumulate money in exchange, then *any* set of price ratios are compatible with *any* required distribution of products. If I have a sweet and you have a biscuit and we want to strike a deal, then under barter we can only exchange at the rate of one sweet to one biscuit. But if money can change hands, you can sell me the biscuit for £2, buy the sweet for £1, and end up £1 the richer. That's all there is to it. The determinacy of a simultaneous system is wrecked by this simple calculation'.[15]

Conclusion

The Douglas analysis questioned certain basic assumptions of neoclassial theory. While Walras regarded the economy as a closed system in which markets cleared at each stage of operations, resulting in multi-market stability, Douglas challenged the ability of markets to clear. According to general equilibrium theory, prices are infinitely flexible. However, as Douglas pointed out, prices cannot fall below total costs. Orthodoxy holds that a depression, gluts and unsold goods and involuntary unemployment cannot happen where markets and prices are infinitely adjustable. Douglas pointed out that maybe these things should not happen, but they were occurring nonetheless. Douglas' analysis was bound up with a deep criticism of the nature of money: yet equilibrium theory is silent on this topic.

Douglas re-opened the debate about money, value and wealth. In most economic analysis, money is just assumed to 'be there'. Its origins, its method of creation and its point of entry into the economy are not considered particularly relevant either to broad economic theory or specific economic problems. Yet, for Douglas, the matter of how money was being created, and the macro and micro economic effects this had, was pivotal. Douglas rejected the basic theoretical assumptions of orthodoxy in favour of an analysis which could be applied in the real world.

If prices are determined mechanically by the exchanges they are set to effect, money cannot perform as a store of value or in any other operational role. Neoclassical theory is an elegant belief system which enshrines money and money value as the hidden motive-power of a clockwork economy where flesh and blood, soil and sea, sun and sky, indeed life itself have neither relevance nor meaning. In the real economy money has more significance than as a mere facilitator of exchange, and cooperation is essential to the survival of all, even the fittest. It has been the purpose of this book explore the role of money in relation to the real world of production, distribution and exchange.

NOTES

1 Soros, George (1997) 'Capital Crimes' *The Guardian / The Week* January 18 pp1-4.
2 Gaitskell, Hugh T. N. (1933) 'Four Monetary Heretics' in G. D. H.Cole (ed) *What Everybody Wants to Know About Money* London. Gollancz.
3 Gee, J. M. Alec (1991) 'The Neoclassical School' in Douglas Mair and Anne G. Miller (eds) *A Modern Guide to Economic Thought: An Introduction to Comparative Schools of Thought in Economics* Aldershot and Brookfield. Edward Elgar. p71.
4 Gee, op. cit. p83.
5 Nelson, Julie (1993) 'Gender and Economic Ideologies' in *Review of Social Economy* Vol.LI, No.3. pp287-301.
6 Veblen, Thorstein (1915) 'Why is Economics not an Evolutionary Science?' in *The Place of Science in Modern Civilisation and Other Essays* New York. Russell & Russell. (1946 edn). p73-4.
7 For example, if two people clean their own homes, as far as the economy is concerned they are not contributing wealth to the economy. However, if they each agree to clean the other's house in return for a money wage, they are now contributing to society's economic welfare. Their work registers as a rise in Gross Domestic Product (GDP). To orthodox economists this is merely an amusing aberration. However, it has profound implications, not only in terms of measuring wealth but also in the distribution of incomes.
8 Gee, op. cit. p83, emphasis original.
9 Gee, op. cit. p84, emphasis and parenthesis original.
10 Mill, John Stuart (1857) *Principles of Political Economy* Vol.II, New York. D. Appleton & Co. (1901 edn). p339-40.
11 Marx, Karl (1867/1887) *Capital* Vol. I. Moscow. Progress Publishers (1974 edn). pp474-5.
12 See Lutz, Mark A. and Lux, Kenneth (1988) *Humanistic Economics* New York. Bootstrap Press.
13 Note that the price of a commodity must be expressed in terms of some other commodity for which it is exchanged. That can be anything. Normally it is money, which economists regard as just another (but very useful) commodity.
14 Freeman, Alan (1995) 'Marx without Equilibrium' in *Capital and Class* 56 (Spring) pp49-89).
15 Freeman, Alan and Carchedi, Gugliemo (eds) (1996) *Marx and Non-Equilibrium Economics* Cheltenham and Brookfield. Edward Elgar. p21.

Glossary

Capital In conventional economics, capital is defined as all manufactured resources, including buildings, machines, equipment and improvements to land. In common usage, the term 'capital' is often used to denote finance, i.e. blips on a computer screen.

Dialectical materialism A useful term for aspiring academics.

Factor markets In conventional economics, households are the sellers in the factor market. They sell resources such as labour, land, entrepreneurial ability and capital. Businesses are the buyers. Business expenditures represent incomes for households.

Function A term used by guild socialists to denote rights deriving from the usefulness to the community as a whole of the 'function' performed by the individual.

Labour In conventional terms, labour is classed as human resources of hand, eye and brain.

Land In conventional economics, land is defined as the natural resources available without effort on the part of labour. It includes the original fertility of the soil, mineral deposits, topograph, climate, water and natural vegetation.

Macroeconomics The study of economy-wide phenomena, such as unemployment and inflation. The study of the economy as a whole, rather than of individual choices.

Markets clear: no commodities are left unsold and there is no involuntary unemployment. J. B. Say implied that in barter, a seller must also be a buyer, and if a good is sold, someone must have bought it. It followed that there could be no underutilisation of resources on the free market because supply creates its own demand.

Microeconomics The study of the economic behaviour of individual households and firms, and of how prices of goods and services are determined.

Numeraire Measure or numbering system.

Utility The benefit or satisfaction that a person obtains from the consumption of a good or service.

Bibliography

Achebe, Chinua (1964) *Arrow of God* London, Ibadan, Nairobi, Lusaka. Heinemann (1977 edn).

Adams, John (1995) *Risk* London. University College London Press.

Beaumont, Tim (1997) *The End of the Yellowbrick Road: Ways and Means to the Sustainable Society* Charlbury. Jon Carpenter.

Bailey, Robert (1989) 'The Efe: Archers of the African Rain Forest' *National Geographic* Vol. 176. No.5 Nov: 664-686.

Balikci, Asen (1968) 'The Netsilki Eskimos' *in* Richard B. Lee and Irven DeVore (eds) *Man the Hunter* Chicago. Aldine (1975 edn).

Baumann, Miges, Bell, Janet, Koechlin, Florianne and Pimbert, Michel (eds) (1996) *The Life Industry: Biodiversity, people and profits* London. Intermediate Technology Publications.

Becker, Gary, (1976) *The Economic Approach to Human Behaviour* Chicago. University of Chicago Press.

Beder, Sharon (1997) *Global Spin: The Corporate Assault on Environmentalism* Totnes. Green Books.

Bender, Barbara (1975) *Farming in Prehistory: From hunter-gatherer to food producer* London. John Baker.

Berry, Wendell (1981) *Gift of Good Land* North Point Press.

Bettelheim, Bruno (1955) *Symbolic Wounds: Puberty Rites and the Envious Male* London. Thames and Hudson.

Bramwell, Anna (1989) *Ecology in the 20th Century* London. Yale University Press.

Bromley, Daniel W. (1991) *Environment and Economy: Property Rights and Public Policy* Oxford. Blackwell.

Bull, Angela (1980) *The Machine Breakers: The Story of the Luddites* London. Collins.

Carpenter, Niles (1922) *Guild Socialism: An Historical and Critical Analysis* New York and London. D. Appleton.

Carson, Rachel *Silent Spring* (1962) Greenwich, Connecticut. Fawcett Publications.

Chapman, Geoffrey (1994) *The Catechism of the Catholic Church* London. Cassell (English translation).

Chossudovsky, Michel (1997) *The Globalisation of Poverty: Impacts of IMF and World Bank Reforms* Zed Books/Third World Network. London.

Chossudovsky, Michel (1997) 'Global Financial Crisis' Unpublished e-mail memo.

Clastres, Pierre (1972) 'The Guakai' *in* M. G. Bicchieri (ed) *Hunters and Gatherers Today* Holt, Rinehart and Winston.

Cobbett, William, (1835) *Rural Rides* London. J. M. Dent & Sons (1948 edn) (See also *The Political Register*).

Colbourne, Maurice (1933) *The Meaning of Social Credit* (Revised edition of *Economic Nationalism*. London and Canada: Social Credit Board.

Cole, G. D. H. (ed) (1933) *What Everybody Wants to Know About Money* London. Gollancz.

The Corner House (1997) *Climate and Equity: After Kyoto* Briefing No.3. Available from The Corner House, Box 3137, Sturminster Newton, Dorset DT10 1YJ, England.

Cousens, Hilderic (1921) *A New Policy for Labour: an Essay on the Relevance of Credit Control* London. Cecil Palmer.

Crowther, Geoffrey (1940) *An Outline of Money* London and New York. Thomas Nelson.

Dauncey, Guy (1988) *After the Crash: The Emergence of the Rainbow Economy* Basingstoke. Green Print.

Davies, Glyn (1994) *A History of Money from Ancient Times to the Present Day* Cardiff. University of Wales Press. (1996 pbk. edn.)

Dewhirst, Ian (1974) *A History of Keighley* Keighley Corporation.

Dinnerstein, Dorothy (1987) *The Rocking of the Cradle and the Ruling of the World* London. The Women's Press.

Doherty, Ann and Hodeman, Olivier (1994) 'Misshaping Europe: The European Round Table of Industrialists' *The Ecologist* Vol.24. No.4 July/August.

Dominguez, Joe and Robin, Vicki (1992) *Your Money or Your Life: Transforming Your Relationship with Money and Achieving Financial Independence.* Harmondsworth. Penguin.

Douglas, Clifford H. (1920) *Credit-Power and Democracy* London. Cecil Palmer. (1921 edn).

Douglas, Clifford H. (1922) *The Control and Distribution of Production* London. Stanley Nott. (1934 edn).

Douglas, Clifford H. (1923) *The Breakdown of the Employment System* The Manchester Economic Research Association (Pamphlet).

Douglas, Clifford H. (1919) *Economic Democracy* Sudbury. Bloomfield (1974 edn).

Douglas, Clifford H. (1924) *Social Credit* Vancouver. Institute of Economic Democracy (1974 edn).

Douglas, Clifford H. (1931) *The Monopoly of Credit* London. Chapman and Hall.

Douglas, Mary (1992) *Risk and Blame: Essays in Cultural Theory* London and New York. Routledge (1994 edn).

Douthwaite, Richard (1992) *The Growth Illusion* Dublin. The Lilliput Press.

Douthwaite, Richard (1996) *Short Circuit: Strengthening Local Economies for Security in an Unstable World* Totnes. Green Books.

The Ecologist (1996) 'CGIAR (Consultative Group on International Agricultural Research) Agricultural Research for Whom?' Vol.26. No.6. Nov/Dec pp259-270.

Freeman, Alan (1995) 'Marx without Equilibrium' in *Capital and Class* 56 (Spring) pp49-89.

Freeman, Alan & Carchedi, Gugliemo (eds) (1996) *Marx and Non-Equilibrium Economics* Cheltenham. Edward Elgar.

Gaitskell, Hugh T. N. (1933) 'Four Monetary Heretics' *in* G. D. H. Cole (ed) *What Everybody Wants to Know About Money* London. Gollancz.

Galbraith, John K. (1975) *Money: Whence it came, where it went* Harmondsworth. Penguin.

Gee, J. M. Alec (1991) 'The Neoclassical School' *in* Mair, Douglas, and Miller, Anne G. (eds) *A Modern Guide to Economic Thought: An Introduction to Comparative Schools of Thought in Economics* Aldershot. Edward Elgar.

George, Susan and Sabelli, Fabrizio (1994) *Faith and Credit: The World Bank's Secular Empire* Harmondsworth. Penguin.

Goering, Peter, Norberg-Hodge, Helena and Page, John (1993) *From the Ground Up:*

Rethinking Industrial Agriculture London and New Jersey. Zed Books and International Society for Ecology and Culture.

Goldsmith, Zac (1997) 'Virtual Future' *The Ecologist* Vol.27, No.4. July/August. pp162-3.

Gregg, Pauline (1976) *Black Death to Industrial Revolution* London. Harrap.

Groh, Trauger M. and McFadden, Steven S. H. (1990) *Farms of Tomorrow: Community Supported Farms: Farm Supported Communities* Kimberton USA. Biodynamic Farming and Gardening Association.

Hamilton, Clive (1994) *The Mystic Economist* Fyshwick, Australia. Willow Park Press. (Distributed in the UK by Jon Carpenter).

Hammond, J. L. and Hammond, Barbara (1913) *The Village Labourer 1760-1832* New York. Kelley (1976 edn).

Hargrave, John (1945) *Social Credit Clearly Explained: 101 Questions Answered* London. SCP Publishing (pamphlet).

Henderson, Hazel (1997) *Building a Win-Win World* San Francisco. Berrett-Koehler. (Distributed in Europe by McGraw Hill.)

Henderson, Hazel (1995) *Paradigms in Progress* San Francisco. Berrett-Koehler. (Distributed in Europe by McGraw Hill.)

Hildyard, Nicholas (1993) 'Maastricht — The Protectionism of Free Trade' *The Ecologist* Vol.23. No.2. March/April.

Hobson, S. G. (1914) *National Guilds: An Inquiry into the Wage System and the Way Out* London. Bell (1919 edn.).

Hobson, S. G. (1920) *National Guilds and the State* London. Bell.

Hunt, C. J. (1970) *The Leadmines of the Northern Pennines in the Eighteenth and Nineteenth Centuries* Manchester University Press.

Hutchinson, Andrew and Hutchinson, Frances (1997) *Environmental Business Management: Sustainable Development in the New Millennium* Maidenhead. McGraw-Hill.

Hutchinson, Frances 'A Heretical View of Economic Growth and Income Distribution' *in* Kuiper, Edith and Sap, Yolande (eds) *Out of the Margin: Feminist Perspectives on Economics* London & New York. Routledge.

Hutchinson, Frances and Burkitt, Brian (1997) *The Political Economy of Social Credit and Guild Socialism* London and New York. Routledge.

Jameson, Storm (1935) *The Soul of Man in the Age of Leisure* London. Stanley Nott.

King, John E. (1988) *Economic Exiles* London. Macmillan.

King, Stephen and Bullmore, Jeremy (1971) *Tomorrow's Food* London. J. Walter Thompson.

Lang, Peter (1996) *Ethical Investment: A Saver's Guide* Charlbury. Jon Carpenter.

Leakey, Richard (1981) *The Making of Mankind* London. Michael Joseph.

Lee, Keekok, (1989) *Social Philosophy and Ecological Scarcity*. London and New York. Routledge.

Lee, Richard B. (1968) 'What Hunters Do for a Living' *in* Lee, Richard B. and DeVore, Ivan (eds) *Man the Hunter* Chicago. Aldine. (1975 edn).

Lee, Richard (1979) *The !Kung San. Men, Women and Work in a Foraging Society* Cambridge University Press.

Luke, T. W. (1995) 'Reproducing Planet Earth?' *The Ecologist* 25. (4) pp157-62.

Lutz, Mark A. and Lux, Kenneth (1988) *Humanistic Economics* New York. Bootstrap Press.

Mabey, Richard (1972) *Food for Free: A Guide to the Natural Wild Foods of Britain* London.

Peerage Books (1986 edn).

Maishe, Shravan (1997) 'City of Dreams' *New Internationalist* 290. May.

Marx, Karl (1867/1887) *Capital* Vol.I Moscow. Progress Publishers (1974 edn).

Massingham, H. J. (1941) *Remembrance: An Autobiography* London. Batsford.

Massingham, H. J. (1942) *The English Countryman: A Study of the English Tradition* London. Batsford.

Massingham, H. J. (1943) *The Tree of Life* London. Chapman and Hall.

Massingham, H. J. (1945) *The Wisdom of the Fields* Collins. London.

Mill, John Stuart (1857) *Principles of Political Economy* Vol.II. New York. D. Appleton & Co. (1901 edn).

Meade, James E. (1993) *Liberty, Equality and Efficiency: Apologia pro Agathotopia mea* London. Macmillan.

Mellanby, Kenneth (1975) *Can Britain Feed Itself?* London. Merlin Press.

Monbiot, George (1995) 'Mad Scientist Disease' *The Guardian* 5 December.

Moss, Helga (1994) 'Consumption and Fertility' *in* Wendy Harcourt (ed) *Feminist Perspectives on Sustainable Development* London. Zed Books.

Myers, Norman (1985) *The Gaia Atlas of Planet Management* London. Gaia Books.

Needham, Angela (1996) 'Hawks and Doves' *Squall* No.13. Summer. pp34-5.

Nelson, Julie (1993) 'Gender and Economic Ideologies' *Review of Social Economy* Vol.LI, No.3. pp287-301.

Norberg-Hodge, Helena (1992) *Ancient Futures: Learning from Ladakh* London. Century Hutchinson.

Orage, A. R. (1926) 'An Editor's Progress' *The Commonweal* February.

Organic Gardening News (1997) 'New Pesticide Bans' December. p5.

Orr, David (1994) *Earth in Mind: On Education, Environment, and the Human Prospect.* Washington DC. Island Press.

Paxton, Angela (1994) *The Food Miles Report: The dangers of long distance food transport* London. SAFE Alliance.

Penty, Arthur, J. (1921) *Guilds, Trade and Agriculture* London. George Allen and Unwin.

Purdy, David (1992) 'Mad Cows and Warble Flies: A link between BSE and Organophosphates?' *The Ecologist* Vol.22. No.2. March/April pp52-57.

Reckitt, Maurice B. and Bechhofer, C. E. (1918) *The Meaning of National Guilds* London. Cecil Palmer (1920 edn).

Red Pepper (1997) 'Oily Tactics' December.

Richards, Paul (1985) *Indigenous Agricultural Revolution: Ecology and Food Production in West Africa* London. Hutchinson.

Rowbotham, Michael (1998) *The Grip of Death: A Study of Modern Money, Debt Slavery and Destructive Economics* Charlbury. Jon Carpenter.

Rowell, Andrew (1996) *Green Backlash: Global Subversion of the Environment Movement* London and New York. Routledge.

Sahlins, Marshall (1974) *Stone Age Economics* London. Tavistock.

Schor, Juliet (1991) *The Overworked American* New York. Basic Books.

Seabrook, Jeremy (1996) 'Revolutionary Craftsman' *Red Pepper* September. pp28-9.

Seabrook, Jeremy (1997) 'A Curious Mysticism' *New Internationalist* 295 October. pp12-14.

Seager, Joni (1993) *Earth Follies: Feminism, Politics and the Environment* London. Earthscan.

Shiva, Vandana (1996) 'The Losers' Perspective' *in* Migues Bauman, Janet Bell, Florianne

Koechlin and Michel Pimbert (eds) *The Life Industry: Biodiversity, People and Profits* London. Intermediate Technology Publications.

Smith, Henry (1962) *The Economics of Socialism Reconsidered.* London and New York. Oxford University Press.

Soros, George (1997) 'Capital Crimes' *The Guardian / The Week* January 18. pp1-4.

Sparkes, Russell (1995) *The Ethical Investor: How to make money work for society as well as for yourself* London. HarperCollins.

Tannahill, Reah (1980) *Sex in History* London. Hamish Hamilton.

Tanner, Nancy M. (1981) *On Becoming Human* London, New York, Sydney. Cambridge University Press.

Tibbett, Rachael (1997) 'Alternative Currencies: A Challenge to Globalisation?' *New Political Economy* Vol.2 No.1 pp127-135.

Thompson, Edward P., (1991) *Customs in Common* London. The Merlin Press.

Veblen, Thorstein (1899) *The Theory of the Leisure Class* New York. Mentor Books (1953 edn).

Veblen, Thorstein (1915) 'Why is Economics not an Evolutionary Science?' in *The Place of Science in Modern Civilisation and Other Essays* New York. Russell & Russell. (1946 edn).

Veblen, Thorstein (1921) *The Engineers and the Price System* New York. Burlinghame (1965 edn).

Veblen, Thorstein (1923) *Absentee Ownership and Business Enterprise in Recent Times* London. Allen and Unwin.

Waring, Marilyn (1989) *If Women Counted* London. Macmillan.

Wilkinson, Richard D. (1973) *Poverty and Progress* London. Methuen.

Wright, Lesley and Smye, Marti (1997) *Corporate Abuse* London. Simon and Schuster.

Young, W. A. (1921) *Dividends for All: Being an Explanation of the Douglas Scheme* London. Cecil Palmer.

Zaslavsky, Claudia (1973) *Africa Counts: Number and Pattern in African Culture* Connecticut. Lawrence Hill (1979 edn).

Resources

Organisations

Christian Council for Monetary Justice General secretary: Mike Rowbotham, Brett's Cottage, Chapel Road, Thurgarton, Norwich NR11 7NP, UK.

Citizen's Income Research Group Citizen's Income Study Centre, St. Philips Building, Sheffield Street, London, WC2A 2EX, UK.

The Corner House PO Box 3137, Station Road, Sturminster Newton, Dorset, DT10 1YJ, UK.

The International Society for Ecology and Culture (ISEC) Apple Barn, Week, Totnes, Devon, TQ9 6JP, UK., and PO Box 9475, Berkeley, CA 94709, USA.

The Lifestyle Movement General Secretary Denise Moll, 21 Fleetwood Court., West Byfleet, Surrey, KT14 6BE, UK.

New Economics Foundation 1st Floor, Vine Court, 112-116 Whitechapel Road, London E1 1JE, UK.

The Soil Association 86 Colston Street, Bristol, BS1 5BB, UK. E-mail: <soilassoc@gn.apc.org>

Biodynamic Farming and Gardening Association Cadmus Corporation, PO Box 333, Wilton, NH 03086, USA. Community supported agriculture.

SAFE Alliance (Sustainable Agriculture, Food and Environment) 21 Tower Street, London WC2H 9NS, UK.

Periodicals

The Aisling Quarterly The Aisling Magazine, An Charraig, Mainistir, Inis Mor, Aran Islands, County Galway, Eire.

The Ecologist is available from *The Ecologist*, c/o Cissbury House, Furze View, Five Oaks Road, Slinfold, West Sussex, RH13 7RH, UK.

Living Earth is the magazine of the Soil Association, campaigning for sustainable food, farming and forestry. Available from The Soil Association (see above).

Organic Gardening is available from *Organic Gardening*, Editorial and Subscriptions Offices, PO Box 4, Wiveliscombe, Taunton, Somerset, TA4 2QY, UK

Positive News and *Living Lightly* available from *Positive News*, The Six Bells, Bishops Castle, Shropshire, SY9 5AA, UK.

Resurgence available from: Jeanette Gill, *Resurgence*, Rocksea Farmhouse, St. Mabyn, Bodmin, Cornwall, PL30 3BR.

Additional resources

The Food Programme (Derek Cooper) BBC Radio 4.

Richard Douthwaite's *Short Circuit: Strengthening Local Economies for Security in an Unstable World* contains a wealth of information on groups and resources.

Course in Christian Rural Studies: Faith and the Future of the Rural Environment (in association with Keele University Adult Education). Details from Dr Ken Wilkinson, Christian Rural Concern, 2 Curborough Road, Lichfield, Staffs, WS13 7NG, UK

Our Money System in Cartoons, available from Community SHCJ, 35 Hampden Retreat, Birmingham, B12 9TB, UK.

Bloomfield Books, 26 Meadow Lane, Sudbury, Suffolk CO10 6DT have a catalogue of books on social credit, including many works by C. H. Douglas.

Index

Also published by Jon Carpenter

The Grip of Death

A study of modern money, debt slavery and destructive economics

Michael Rowbotham

This lucid and original account of where our money comes from explains why most people and businesses are so heavily in debt. It explodes more myths than any other book this century, covering subjects very close to home: mortgages, building societies and banks, food and farming, transport, worldwide poverty, what's on the supermarket shelf, and lots more.

It explains —

• why virtually all the money in the world economy has been created as a debt; why only 3% of UK money exists as 'legal tender'; and why in a world reliant upon money created as debt, we are kept perpetually short of money.

• how and why mortgages are responsible for almost two-thirds of the total money stock in the UK, and 80% in the US.

• why consumers can't get quality products.

• why business debt is at its highest level ever.

• why debts mean that a small farm can be productively very efficient, but financially not 'viable'.

• why national debts can never be paid off — without monetary reform.

• how debt fuels the 'need to grow', revolutionising national and global transport strategies, destroying local markets and producers and increasing waste, pollution and resource consumption.

• how 'Third World debt' is a mechanism used by the developed nations to inject ever-increasing amounts of money into their own economies, and why debtor nations can never repay the debts.

• why politicians who rely on banks to create money can't fund public services.

• why 'debt-money' is undemocratic and a threat to human rights.

The author proposes a new mechanism for the supply of money, creating a supportive financial environment and a decreasing reliance on debt.

£15 pbk 352pp 1 897766 40

Our books may be ordered from bookshops or (post free) from
Jon Carpenter Publishing, 2 The Spendlove Centre, Charlbury, England OX7 3PQ
Please send for our free catalogue
Credit card orders should be phoned or faxed to 01689 870437 or 01608 811969

Our US distributor is Paul and Company, PO Box 442, Concord, MA 01742
(phone 978 369 3049, fax 978 369 2385).